Latin American Studies Series

Series Editors   Michael C. Meyer   John D. Martz   Miguel León-Portilla

Examining the politics and social implications of food, this collection of ten original essays addresses a largely unexplored but vital element in the dynamics of Latin America's history and contemporary life. The authors emphasize the importance of politics in determining patterns of food production and distribution, and ultimately in reinforcing or transforming social structures by affecting levels of food consumption and nutrition. Ranging chronologically from the Conquest to the present and geographically from Cuba and Mexico to the Southern Cone, the essays bring to bear perspectives from history, political science, anthropology, rural sociology, and agricultural economics.

University of Nebraska Press   Lincoln and London

Food, Politics,

and Society in

Latin America

Edited by John C. Super and Thomas C. Wright

Library of Congress
Cataloging in Publication Data

Main entry under title:
Food, politics, and society
in Latin America.

(Latin American studies series)

Bibliography: p.
Includes index.
1. Food supply – Latin America –
Addresses, essays, lectures.
2. Food consumption – Latin America –
Addresses, essays, lectures.
3. Food supply – Government policy –
Latin America – Addresses, essays,
lectures.   4. Latin America – Social
conditions – Addresses, essays,
lectures.   I. Super, John C., 1944-
II. Wright, Thomas C.   III. Series.
HD9014.L32F66   1985
363.8ʺ098   84-15313
ISBN 0-8032-4137-2 (alk. paper)

Material in "Latin
American Food Production and
Population in the
Era of Land Reform since the
1950s," by James W.
Wilkie and Manuel Moreno-
Ibáñez, has previously
appeared in James W. Wilkie and
Manuel Moreno Ibáñez,
"New Research on Food
Production in Latin
America since 1952," in James
W. Wilkie and Adam
Perkal, eds., *Statistical Abstract
of Latin America,*
vol. 23 (Los Angeles: UCLA
Latin American Center
Publications, 1984), pp. 735-82.

The paper in this book meets
the guidelines for
permanence and durability
of the Committee on
Production Guidelines for
Book Longevity of the
Council on Library Resources.

Contents

Preface

This study of food was conceived, appropriately enough, over *tapas* and *fino* sherry in Seville. We met in 1980 while working on separate projects at the Archivo General de Indias and discovered a mutual interest in the history of food. Thomas Wright's interest stemmed from his work on the struggle between pressure groups representing food producers and consumers in early twentieth-century Chile. John Super's study of food at the opposite chronological and geographic extreme of Latin America—early Mexico— had convinced him of the importance of food in the dynamics of Latin American history.

Lengthy discussions led us to the conclusion that food as an object of study in Latin America, past and present, had been sadly, almost irresponsibly neglected. By the time several tapa hours had stretched through late-night Seville *comidas*, we had determined that the complexity of the subject and the paucity of published research precluded any attempt at synthesis. The best alternative, we felt, was a collection of original essays on different aspects of food in Latin America.

In several ways, these essays reflect the current concerns of the scholarly community on the subject of food. More attention is given to matters of modern production and distribution than to the broader question of the relationship between food and the historical processes that shaped today's Latin America. Yet our historians' biases show through, especially in the opening essays where we attempt to present a broad chronological and spatial view for evaluating recent developments such as those examined in several of the essays that follow.

Many of the ideas expressed in the introduction are the result of work we have done separately on narrower aspects of the food question. For support of previous research on food in Latin America and the new findings presented in this volume, Super wishes to thank the American Philosophical

Society, the American Council of Learned Societies, the John Carter Brown Library, and West Virginia University. Wright acknowledges the University of Nevada, Las Vegas, for a sabbatical leave and the Barrick Fund of the same institution for additional research support. Thanks also to Olga Lyles for editorial assistance.

Finally, we have appreciated the enriching experience of working with the fine group of Latin Americanists whose essays appear in the volume. We hope that our collective effort on food will foster a renewed appreciation of the usefulness of dialogue between the past and the present and among the many disciplines that address Latin America.

Introduction:
Perspectives on Food in Latin America

The history of food in Latin America is the familiar story of continuity and change. Today, contrasts and extremes in food production, distribution, and consumption are found throughout Latin America. John Deere tractors turn the soil for some cultivators, while others employ the *coa*, an ancient digging stick; Indians sacrifice maize to increase harvests, while scientists work in sophisticated laboratories to produce "miracle" strains of wheat and corn; *tianguis,* or Indian markets, sell alongside modern *supermercados;* ambulatory vendors of *tamales,* a pre-Columbian favorite, compete with McDonald's for the fast-food trade; Argentines, who consume 100 grams of protein and 3,235 calories per capita a day, are among the world's best-fed people, whereas Haitians, who survive on only 39 grams of protein and 1,750 calories per day, are among the world's worst nourished.

Today's contrasts are the result of the interplay between environment and history. The sixteenth century and the period since 1850 have experienced particularly intense changes in established food patterns. Introducing a cornucopia of alien plants and animals, the European conquest worked a revolution in New World dietary tastes and customs. The conquest also triggered a drastic decline in the Indian population that affected the food supply in both positive and negative ways. The last century and a quarter have brought dramatic change in technology and patterns of world trade, along with a population explosion that has multiplied the demand for food. Cultural changes and contests for political power have been particularly significant forces through the centuries, shaping the production and distribution of foods and molding the lives of Latin Americans in an immediate way.

Food is a complex, multifaceted phenomenon with different properties and meanings, affecting everyone in at least four discernible ways. Most fundamentally, food is a nutrient essential to the survival and well-being of the species. The quality of nutrition is influenced by diverse biological and human factors that have interacted to produce the basic Latin American diet: soil and climate, population levels, and social organization. Cultural practices, themselves undergoing continual change, also influence the diet.

Food is also an economic phenomenon, the end result of systems with varied divisions of resources and labor, ranging from the subsistence plots that still feed much of Latin America's population to the sophisticated agribusinesses of the food-exporting regions. Not only landowners and agricultural laborers, but also muleteers and truckers, bakers, workers in fish canneries, supermarket clerks, vendors in village market stalls, cooks in homes and restaurants, waiters, and dishwashers—all make their living from food. For the rest of the Latin American population, and for most of the above-named groups as well, food involves expenditure; among the poor, it accounts for half or more of the family budget.

Food is also a cultural and social matter, part of ritual and belief systems and patterns of social interaction. Some foods and combinations of foods are considered curative, aphrodisiac, or dangerous. Others are associated with religious practices: Indians still bring food for the departed when visiting cemeteries on All Souls' Day, and *limeños* consume *turrón de doña Pepa* during the Lord of Miracles celebration each October. The social meaning of food pervades Latin American culture. Hosting lavish banquets brings status to cosmopolitan elites and humble villagers alike, and the prestige of airy white bread (*pan* Bimbo) over the more nutritious tortilla is based on the racial and class connotations of the pre-Columbian staple. While modernization has blurred somewhat the cultural and social meanings of food, both persist as integral aspects of the phenomenon.

Finally, because of its centrality to human needs and desires, food is an object of dispute and therefore has an important political dimension. The essays presented here, while dealing with other aspects of the subject, emphasize the politics of food in its various manifestations. The thesis that underpins this volume is that the political process, operating upon the total agricultural and food resources of a society, determines the distribution of food. While it is trite to point out that we are what we eat, it is nonetheless necessary to emphasize that nutrition is the single most important element in physical well-being. Power relations within a society determine how income is distributed; and income distribution is the primary factor in controlling which groups will be well nourished and thus biologically favored and which will suffer dietary and biological deprivation. Before the days of modern nutritional knowledge, and for many today who remain ignorant or unconcerned, the primary political question is who will have full bellies, who will not. Nutrition and the satisfaction of hunger, while separate questions, are difficult to distinguish in the politics of food.

Beyond these fundamental considerations, politics determines access to luxury foods and to those desirable for gastronomic, social, or ritual reasons. This level of food politics appears in various guises. The Aztec nobility, for example, claimed the right to eat human flesh—with limited exceptions—as a sign of prestige and authority. Today, the wealthy reserve the finer cuts of beef and imported liquors and pâtés for themselves by rationing money. Access to foods beyond the staples necessary for nutrition and satisfaction of hunger is an integral aspect of the struggle for improved standards of living that underlies much of Latin American politics.

Finally, politics determines the use of a country's agricultural resources. Traditionally, landowners' political power allowed them to use their land for any product, food or nonfood, or not to use their land for productive purposes at all. In the twentieth century, urbanization and the extension of political participation have created a potent force speaking for the urban consumer; the result may be the dictation that more land be used to produce food for domestic consumption. The power of urban consumers, however, competes with the power of multinational corporations, governments, domestic landowners, and other forces that can counteract the attempt to acquire a better diet.

Levels of nutrition, degree of hunger, and access to nonessential foods, then, are not determined primarily by a country's total food production, its food production potential, or its ability to import food in exchange for other products. Rather, nutrition levels and access to food within any society are results of the political process that directs the distribution of a country's food resources, whether those resources are scarce or abundant. The essential message of Frances Moore Lappé and Joseph Collins' popular *Food First: Beyond the Myth of Scarcity* is that food distribution is more important to human welfare than is the total amount of food produced, once a minimum safe level of production has been achieved.[1] Amartya Sen's *Poverty and Famines: An Essay on Entitlement and Deprivation*, which examines the selectivity of death and debilitating malnutrition in four famines on the Indian subcontinent, offers the same conclusion in starker terms. Sen's work illustrates that famine is not necessarily caused by declines in food production and that its effects are predictably uneven, affecting the propertyless poor most severely.[2]

Latin American food politics, fortunately, has unfolded in a less grim setting than that described by Sen. While the issue of food for survival has been an important one, it has never dominated Latin American life to the extent that it has in other regions of the world. Colonial period evidence speaks of times of surplus more often than of scarcity; even the crises of subsistence that periodically swept through some regions were less frequent and generally less severe than those in contemporaneous Europe. Periods of "semi-starvation," when stores were depleted and early plantings had not yet been harvested, did not punctuate each year. Instead, the environment, along with a demographic decline and supportive social and political institutions, ensured reasonably adequate food supplies.

As the population recovered from early disasters and then increased quickly with the lowering of the death rate in the nineteenth and twentieth centuries, the pressure on food resources for subsistence increased. Concurrent with the population rise was the extension and elaboration of an agricultural export sector. In essence, a flowering of economic seeds planted in the sixteenth century began to threaten the food resources of parts of Latin America. These trends contributed to growing popular unrest and helped define food more sharply as a social and political issue. The working classes in most of Latin America today, while reasonably secure from famine and even extreme hunger, do not have the luxury that their North American and European counterparts enjoy of choosing between beefsteak three nights a week and a new automobile. For the workers of Latin America, the politics of food is very serious business because food looms so large in their economic lives.

Reflecting Latin America's historical condition as a region of reasonably adequate food production but sharp class divisions, food has often been the focal point of social conflict. This has been violent on occasion, as in colonial *tumultos* or the anti-inflation movement in turn-of-the-century Chile. Class conflict over food is generally much less spectacular, taking the form of wage bargaining or the setting of staple prices, conducted out of the public eye. Beyond the confrontation over access to food, much of the substance of food politics in Latin America is a struggle for profit from food. In the eighteenth century, small shopkeepers in Mexico struggled to wrest control of bread distribution from the bakers. In the twentieth century, rice growers engage wheat producers in a struggle for vital government investments and price supports. Recent reactions to attempts to raise restaurant prices in Cuba or limit Argentine consumption of beef illustrate the point that food politics in Latin America goes far beyond the struggle between haves and have-nots.

The foregoing themes and issues are explored in far greater detail in the essays in this volume. The methods and perspectives of scholars from several disciplines—history, anthropology, political science, rural sociology, and agricultural economics—are brought to bear on food in Latin American life. Some essays deal directly with the politics and social implications of food production, distribution, and consumption; others are less explicitly political and social in their analysis but still offer information and interpretations essential to the study of food as a primary determinant in Latin American politics and social relations.

John C. Super opens the volume with a wide-ranging essay on food during the era of Iberian control. He explores the many influences that shaped diets as Old World foods, tastes, and technologies clashed and then blended with those of the New World. This essay not only conveys current knowledge of food in the colonial period but also delineates questions for future research in that field of Latin American history.

Thomas C. Wright offers an overview of the politics of supplying Latin America's cities with food, from the colonial period to the 1950s. Drawing on a broad range of data, he explores the conflict between the urban poor and the producers and distributors of food staples. This frequently volatile aspect of Latin American politics has been a major element in the development of political consciousness and organization among the urban poor and an often-overlooked factor in twentieth-century political change.

Vincent Peloso next assesses one of the least-known periods of Latin American food history: the century after independence. Exploring class and regional aspects of diet in Peru, he suggests ways in which changing access to food may have created important social fissures that contributed to political conflict in the twentieth century. Peloso's essay thus offers a new interpretive focus for exploring Peru's modern history.

James W. Wilkie and Manuel Moreno-Ibáñez describe recent changes in nutritional regimes in Latin America over the last quarter century. They organize and interpret an enormous amount of statistical data, providing a valuable perspective for studying food and population problems in individual countries as well as throughout the hemisphere. Their chapter is both an important reference source for statistical data and a pioneering attempt at comparative analysis of trends in food production.

Roland Bergman assesses the nature and importance of subsistence regimes in Latin America. Concentrating on three distinct geographic zones, he reveals what peasants have known all along but politicians and bureaucrats have had difficulty understanding: that subsistence agriculture under normal conditions is an efficient system that can sustain large populations in modest well-being. This argument has far-reaching policy implications for the planning of economic development in much of Latin America.

Lana L. Hall analyzes Public Law 480, the United States "Food for Peace" program, which has been a major international influence on food supply and politics in recent Latin America. In a comparative study, she finds that the domestic grain sector in Colombia suffered from competition with cheap United States surpluses, while in Brazil domestic production was not adversely affected. National politics in both cases played a crucial role in determining the long-range consequences of food aid.

The next three essays examine agricultural and food policy in the context of reform or revolution. Eleanor Witte Wright investigates the efforts of reformist governments to remedy dependency on imported food and widespread malnutrition in Venezuela between 1958 and 1974. This case study illustrates the difficulties of transforming the food sector in the face of international political and economic pressures and a cautious approach to reform. Wright concludes that more vigorous measures will be required to meet the challenge of increasing staple food production and improving Venezuelan nutritional standards.

Howard Handelman and Nancy Forster then analyze the food and agricultural policies of revolutionary Cuba, which contrast sharply with those adopted in Venezuela during the same period. They argue that despite important failures in agricultural policy, the revolution has succeeded in improving the diet of most Cubans. The essay is particularly instructive in examining how a regime committed to nutritional improvement can use rationing to enhance the diets of its citizens, even in the context of generalized economic problems.

Rose Spalding offers a look at agricultural and food policy in another setting of rapid political change: contemporary Nicaragua. Her essay assesses the Somoza legacy and evaluates the policies, achievements, and problems of the first three years of Sandinista control. She concludes with projections about the future directions of Nicaragua's food and agricultural policies and the prospects for their success.

In the final chapter, Ivan Sergio Freire de Sousa, Edward Gerald Singer, and William L. Flinn use the "Green Revolution" to examine problems of decision making and creativity in agricultural programs. They explicitly address the social and political assumptions underlying research on food production, pointing out the need for reorienting the inquiry into the determinants of "appropriate" technology. The outcome of the expected "Second Green Revolution" will hinge largely on the answers to questions raised in this provocative article.

Together, these essays strive to present some of the keys to understanding the role of food in Latin America's development by emphasizing the variety of international and domestic conditions affecting the supply and distribution of food. Beginning in the late fifteenth century and continuing until today, external developments have been agents of change. The essays thus highlight the introduction of new plants and animals, changing patterns of world trade, international conflicts, foreign assistance programs, and the creation of new technologies. These imported forces, however, have always unfolded in a domestic context. The continuation and evolution of subsistence economies, the rise of export agriculture, the appearance of labor and consumer groups as powerful food bargaining agents, and the reallocation of resources through revolution and reform receive extensive coverage in the chapters which follow.

Through this deliberately broad range of essays, the editors hope to contribute to an awareness of the importance of food, and particularly of food politics and its social implications, in Latin America. Throughout Latin America's historical experience, the politics of food has generally been quiet, often implicit, and only occasionally violent. Yet it has been a very real element in the constant power struggle that is life, and the results—differentiation in health, stature, and mental capacity along class lines—bear mute but vivid testimony to the primacy of food politics in Latin American history.

Notes

1. Frances Moore Lappé and Joseph Collins, *Food First: Beyond the Myth of Scarcity* (Boston: Houghton Mifflin, 1977).

2. Amartya Kumar Sen, *Poverty and Famines: An Essay on Entitlement and Deprivation* (New York: Oxford University Press, 1981).

Food, Politics,
and Society in
Latin America

John C. Super

The Formation of Nutritional Regimes in Colonial Latin America

The arrival of Europeans in the New World unleashed a series of changes that altered the history of food. Changes in dietary habits initiated by the discovery of the Americas eventually swept through the world. The most immediate changes were experienced in Latin America. There Indians, Europeans, and Africans had to resolve the fundamental problems of food production and distribution under new and often strange circumstances. They clung to old habits when they could but at the same time adjusted to changing historical and biological realities. The gradual, selective introduction of new foods in other parts of the world was compressed into a few decades in Latin America, a period of intense experimentation that had far-reaching consequences.

The conquest and concurrent introduction of new foods make the history of food in Latin America particularly exciting. The obvious political and social importance of food in all societies became exaggerated in early Latin America as distinct food traditions clashed and then meshed to offer solutions to the problems of providing nutrients necessary for survival and growth.

Geographic and cultural diversity make it particularly difficult to explain the history of food in pan-Latin American terms. It is possible to study the region as a whole, however, by concentrating on the formation of new nutritional regimes. Maximilien Sorre, one of the foremost students of man and biology, described nutritional regimes as the "combination of foods, produced locally or brought in by exchange, which assures [the group's] daily existence by satisfying its tastes and which assures its persistence in a given way of life."[1] Focusing on the forces that influenced these regimes, rather than on the regimes themselves, permits a discussion in broad terms of the colonial period in the political and social history of food. Such an approach requires generalizations and hypotheses, whose appropriateness for every region of Latin America has not yet been tested.

Nutritional regimes are usually dominated by one food, so essential to community survival that it has a "quasidivine status."[2] Examples include rice in China, taro in the Pacific, maize in Mexico, and cassava in the Caribbean. One or two foods dominated nutritional regimes of early Latin America, but a simple description of these foods and their relationship to life would fall short of an adequate introduction to the history of food. Nutritional regimes were dynamic, fluid arrangements, the result of complex historical processes that went beyond local man-land relationships. Any attempt to grasp the significance of the history of food must be attentive to changes and the reasons for them.

Change and Continuity in Nutritional Regimes

It is appropriate to begin with Columbus and the sixteenth-century voyages. Ships moving with the tide down the Guadalquivir River carried foods basic to the Iberian diet. Except for fresh fruits and vegetables, ships' fare was a nutritional microcosm of the diet of southern Spain. The foods that sailors ate fed colonists, Indians, and Africans in succeeding centuries. High on the list of the score or so foods that nourished sailors were hardtack made from wheat, broad beans, chick-peas, salted fish, dried meat, cheese, vinegar, olive oil, and wine. The missing fruits and vegetables started to arrive on Columbus' second voyage, and within fifty years flourished in the new land.[3]

These foods constituted the first links in a nutritional chain that held the old and the new together. Expansion within Latin America always depended on previously established food reserves. Residents of San Juan, Puerto Rico, waited impatiently for seven years until a fleet arrived from Spain carrying flour, oil, and wine, the Mediterranean triology that brought gustatory contentment to Spaniards. Wine drinkers in Mexico held empty goblets while the casks were unloaded at the port of Veracruz.[4] Some regions continued to rely on Spain into the nineteenth century, but for most of Latin America, interregional self-sufficiency developed soon after the conquest. The Atlantic lifeline was replaced by hundreds of threads tying agriculturally rich regions with those poor in foods. The Indians of Quito went to impoverished Zaruma to establish farms to feed miners; Anzerma received all of its foods from Cali; Zacatecas supplied maize and stock for missions in the north; the temperate valleys of Mexico became major suppliers of grain for the Caribbean.[5] The whole epic of Latin America depended on food surpluses, first in Spain and then in the New World, that freed men and resources from agriculture. Each step in the settlement of Latin America was possible because of a positive balance in food supplies.

The presence of granaries in Spain and Latin America did not always prevent hunger. Breakdowns in the lifeline forced Spaniards to turn to local resources. Foraging, fishing, and hunting turned up tropical fruits, turtle eggs, and crocodile and monkey flesh that complemented the foods obtained by bartering with Indians. Spaniards gave hawks' bells, beads, and cut glass in exchange for maize and cassava cakes, venison, and fish. When Indians balked at the exchange, food raids on villages helped procure the provisions necessary for staying alive. Temporary methods of provisioning, satisfactory for small, mobile populations, gave way to direct control over Indians and the establishment of farms as the number of Europeans grew.[6]

The Spanish lifeline and Indian production brought the foods from the two worlds together. It is difficult to say whether Indians or Europeans were more astonished at the richness and diversity of the other's diet. We have some idea of the pleasure or disgust of Europeans as they first tasted cassava, *chuño* (freeze-dried potatoes), tortillas, and iguana,[7] but the reaction of Indians to their first bites of wheat bread fresh from the oven, goat slowly turned over the spit, and Spanish spirits is seldom recorded.

Old World foods forever altered New World dietary patterns. European cereals, meats, fruits, and vegetables soon fed Indians and blacks. Of the cereals, wheat, rice, and barley had the greatest impact on early nutritional regimes. Very little rye, an important staple north of the Pyrenees, grew in Latin America. All the barnyard quadrupeds and fowl of Spain found the New World to their liking. Economically, the most important have always been cattle, first for hides and tallow, then increasingly for meat. Nutritionally, cattle might have been second to pigs and chickens, familiar residents of the houses of the Latin American poor. Animal flesh, milk, cheese, and eggs offered the heavily vegetarian diet of the Indians a welcome source of protein and fat. A veritable cornucopia of Old World plant foods—sugarcane, grapes, figs, peaches, apples, quinces, pears, pomegranates, oranges, limes, lemons, melons, cabbages, lettuces, radishes, onions, garlic, turnips, borrages, cucumbers, and pulses—embellished tables from the sixteenth century onward. The Old World contribution found almost its match in the profusion of New World fruits and vegetables: tomatoes, peppers, chayotes, avocados, pineapples, cocoa, guava, chirimoyas, and squashes, to name only a few.[8]

The combination of New and Old World vegetables, full of minerals and vitamins, self-propagating or easily grown, provided a rich, abundant element in the emerging nutritional regimes.[9] These foods figure so prominently in the descriptive literature that they cannot be ignored. Settlers in Brazil survived on the bounty of nature, while those in Peru did not even need wheat to have a good diet, or at least so contemporaries thought.[10] Unfortunately, a detailed understanding of the place of these foods in the overall Latin American diet is elusive, since they seldom figure in account books, tax records, or trade documents. Perhaps their abundance simply reduced the need for commercial distribution. This was true, for example, of bananas, introduced in the first part of the sixteenth century and soon cultivated from the Caribbean islands to Andean valleys. Eaten raw, boiled, roasted, turned into flour, or fermented as a beverage, they were staples everywhere in tropical and subtropical America.[11] Yet they usually did not appear in the records as a commodity.

Despite their importance, fruits and vegetables did not stamp the character of nutritional regimes as did the staples of maize, manioc, potatoes, squash, and beans. Maize was the most venerable staple, at times even referred to as "sacred maize." The Indians of central Mexico were exceptionally imaginative users of maize, inventing many types of tortillas and atoles (gruels) for different occasions. The Incas, less creative in their use of maize, usually ate it toasted or boiled. When they made bread from maize, it was for ceremonial feasts. Unlike the Aztecs, however, the Incas did use maize to make an alcoholic beverage. In addition to being versatile, maize contributed to a reasonably nutritious diet when complemented with pulses, thus reducing the chances for outbreaks of pellagra similar to those that occurred in the United States and the Mediterranean region.[12]

Manioc, a tuber widespread in the Caribbean and tropical America, followed maize in importance as a staple. Sweet manioc, common to the mainland before the arrival of Europeans, was eaten roasted or boiled. Not so the bitter manioc, or yuca brava of the Caribbean, which contained potentially fatal amounts of hydrocyanic acid. Before it could be eaten, the poisonous liquids had to be expressed, the pulp grated, heated, slapped into cakes, and fried or baked. Manioc, like maize, was prepared plain and fancy to satisfy different tastes. The food has been so central to Brazilian history that the Portuguese word for flour (farinha) refers to manioc meal. For four centuries manioc has provided nutritional stability during the cyclical movements of sugar, gold, rubber, and coffee in the Brazilian economy.[13]

More confined geographically were potatoes, the food of the highland Indians of the Andes. At altitudes where maize succumbed to frost, potatoes served as a staple, supplemented by the hardy grain quinoa, used for breads and gruels. Potatoes, like maize and manioc, were easy to cultivate, offered good yields, and when combined with other local foods provided essential nutrients. All three of the New World staples outstripped the major European competitors of wheat, barley, and rice in productivity per unit of land.[14]

Europeans did not hesitate to eat Indian staples during the first years of colonization. Manioc became a food of enduring importance for Spanish sailors and Portuguese settlers. Portuguese princes and paupers in Bahia developed such a fondness for manioc that they seldom complained of the lack of wheat bread.[15] Settlers in the temperate zones did not have to rely permanently on Indian foods. After an initial period of scarcity, wheat production soon surpassed local needs, pushing down the price of early postconquest days. When locally milled wheat bread was first sold in Lima in 1540, it cost one *real* per pound; three years later it cost one real for three and one-half pounds.[16] Highland basins close to Quito produced so much wheat that only one-tenth was consumed locally, prompting entrepreneurs to seek markets for flour in the Caribbean.[17] By the seventeenth century, most Spanish colonists easily satisfied their cultural predilection for wheat bread.[18] Only in the outback, far from any permanent settlement, did they experience difficulty finding European grains, fruits, and vegetables.[19]

Scarcity and traditional resistance to a new staple limited Indian consumption of wheat in the sixteenth century. As wheat acreage increased and farmers faced problems of abundance, prices dropped and wheat bread became available for more people. By the eighteenth century, the many different types of wheat bread and their association with special cultural and social groups suggest that wheat had very widespread nutritional importance.[20] Indians became accomplished millers and bakers, competing with Spaniards for the right to supply towns.[21] The main difference between the Spanish and Indian attitudes toward wheat bread might have been the Indians' flexibility, the ease with which they shifted from wheat to maize depending on supply and price.[22]

Spanish livestock spread more rapidly than grains and had a more pronounced impact on diet. Sheep did not thrive in the tropical wetlands, nor cattle in the Andean highlands, but everywhere else livestock multiplied so rapidly that many communities viewed them as a nuisance. All commentators on livestock abundance seemed to rely on hyperbole: over sixty thousand cattle killed a year by wild dogs on Hispañola and Curaçao; carcasses littering the ground for two miles outside Montevideo; cattle so cheap that meat was free for the taking.[23] Or is it hyperbole? Comments on the rapid depletion of the great herds of the Caribbean and Central Mexico suggest that observers were just as willing to describe decline as expansion. Livestock-land imbalances, indiscriminate slaughtering, the insatiable demand for hides, and the increasing number of rustlers led to the disappearance of herds.[24]

The role of livestock in nutritional regimes varied in time and space. Overgrazing contributed to the decline in the Caribbean, while the demand for plant food led to the gradual displacement of sheep and cattle estates in central Mexico. In the Bajío, the vast flocks grazing in 1600 had given way to haciendas producing wheat, maize, and beans by 1700.[25] But new areas entered periods of livestock expansion while old ones declined. In South America, three great cattle regions emerged after the sixteenth century. In seventeenth-century Brazil, cattle so dominated life along the São Francisco River that João Capistrano de Abreu described it as "the era of leather."[26] Cattle supplied materials for everything from water jugs to furniture for colonial Brazil. A little later, the pampas of Argentina and the llanos of Venezuela entered similar phases. During "the era of leather" people ate beef three times a day, often little else. Beef was so plentiful that corral fence posts served as hanging racks, where the hungry cut away the spoiled parts to get at good meat. The more discriminating ate only tongue, loin, or the tender flesh of unborn calves. Even in the cities beef was abundant. Caracas, for example, consumed half as much beef as Paris, even though it had only one-tenth the population. This was not succulent English roast beef, but it provided the protein necessary for health and strength.[27]

Indians quickly developed a taste for Old World meats, consuming large quantities of beef, pork, and mutton, not to mention chickens and goats. Charles Gibson concludes that by the end of the sixteenth century "the Indian taste for meat had become fixed and unalterable."[28] Indian, black, and mestizo cowboys had the most confirmed love of meat, but even Indians living in more traditional associations enjoyed regular diets of meat. As urban centers grew and supplies dwindled or became more expensive, Indians, or more precisely those with little income, gave up beef for bull and ox meat, viewed by the wealthy as less nutritious and less palatable.[29]

It is evident that Fernand Braudel's observation, "History shows two opposing species of humanity: the rare meat-eaters and the innumerable people who feed on bread, gruel, and roots and cooked tubers,"[30] does not apply to Latin America during the colonial period. Meat, a scarce commodity before the conquest, became commonplace in the nutritional regimes of Spaniards and Indians by the middle of the sixteenth century.

The Indians welcomed new foods such as meat and wheat while continuing to eat traditional ones. Andean people relished potatoes, maize, quinoa, and oca, and added meat, pork, fowl, lettuce, onions, and radishes to their diets. Mexicans continued to depend on maize, beans, chiles, tomatoes, and squash but also readily took to European meats, fruits, and vegetables.[31] The acceptance and widespread use of European foods after the conquest forever altered the nutritional regimes of Indians.

Changes in the use of traditional pre-Columbian foods also contributed to the overall shifts in nutritional regimes. This assertion of change counters the views of some anthropologists, who see Indian diets today as basically the same as before the conquest.[32] Even if today's Indian diets resemble those of the preconquest era, the continuity implied in this interpretation is not borne out by the little evidence available on colonial diets. Indeed, the use of traditional New World foods during the colonial period differed in many important ways from their use before the conquest.

Alcohol use is a good example. Before the conquest, alcohol among the Aztecs and Incas was a controlled drink, restricted to ceremonial occasions. A major reason for the limitation of alcohol consumption might have been ecological: as the population rose in the two empires during the fifteenth century, all possible agricultural production had to be oriented toward basic food production. Thus in the Andes the use of maize to make *chicha* was limited, and in central Mexico the cultivation of maize and beans took precedence over the growing of the agave plant, the major source of *pulque*. These ecologically based restrictions were shored up by legal and social sanctions. The Aztecs took excessive drinking so seriously that they punished public drunkenness by death. Pulque was "the root and origin of all evil and of all perdition," according to an Aztec emperor.[33] The Incas did not take such a strict view of chicha but still limited its use.[34] Success in curtailing alcohol abuse among the Aztecs and Incas is difficult to determine, but the incidence of excessive consumption was probably less than after the conquest if for no other reason than the relationship between alcohol availability and food supplies.

Food needs declined after the conquest, and so did the sanctions against alcohol abuse. Beverages previously limited to ceremonies became foods of everyday consumption, providing nutrients but also causing widespread concern about social decay. Hipólito Unanue, the sage of Lima, wrote, "The strength and obesity of Indians who eat little but drink much chicha is proof that chicha is very nutritive."[35] It is possible to advance a nutritional argument for the use of alcohol, pointing out that chicha and pulque provided needed nutrients during shortages of traditional foods and that they provided an escape from hunger. The sociopsychological defense also has its appeal, viewing Indian drunkenness as a response to cultural trauma.[36] What these views neglect is the matter of taste. Simply stated, it is possible

that Indians drank more after the conquest because of the increased availability of an enjoyable and valued food.

Interpretations of the widespread use of capsicums (*chile* in Mexico, *ají* in
Peru), fall prey to a similar type of unnecessary complexity. A nutritional
explanation for the importance of capsicums emphasizes that they help
secrete saliva, which in turn stimulates appetite. Hot peppers thus motivate
a listless, poorly nourished population to eat. This explanation overlooks
the general lack of spices in the New World and the bland taste of maize,
potatoes, and manioc.[37] A more straightforward interpretation is that hot
peppers were widely used, not because they stimulated hunger, but because
they were a readily available, inexpensive food that made eating more enjoyable. They tasted good and became a habit. That is why they are still eaten
today.

Forces of Change

The evidence presented up to this point demonstrates that nutritional regimes
abruptly began a period of transition in the sixteenth century as New and Old
World foods found their place in the diet. The transition followed different
tempos in different regions, responding to the interaction of people and environment. The second part of this study attempts to describe some of the
forces that regulated the intensity and scope of these changes.

Population size was a critical dynamic influencing food patterns. The first
demographic trend after the conquest was a decline so precipitous in a few
regions that the implications are staggering. Some demographers estimate
that the central Andes before Pizarro had 32,000,000 inhabitants, a number
that dropped to 3,030,000 by 1650 and to 1,076,122 by 1800. Based on these
figures, it took until the 1970s for the combined populations of Peru, Bolivia,
and Ecuador to equal the pre-Columbian Andean population. For Mexico,
the decline may have been just as sharp, falling from 25,000,000 in 1519 to
less than 1,000,000 in the 1620s, followed by a gradual recovery until the
1519 population level was reached again in the 1940s.[38]

Though much less important than disease, hunger is another possible
explanation for the decline. The evidence for this interpretation, however, is
far from compelling. Causal relationships between food availability and
demographic trends in the past are difficult to substantiate except in a general sense. An example of consensus among demographers is the connec-
tion between food and population in China and Europe, where the New
World foods of maize and potatoes lifted the ceiling on the production of
nutrients that had limited population growth.[39] Nonetheless, few historical

studies have attempted to gauge the exact relationship between diet, disease, and population that many nutritionists and anthropologists suggest exist.[40] If the history of London from the 1550s to 1750s can serve as an example, the epidemics of plague, smallpox, typhus, and influenza did their deadly work despite adequate food supplies.[41] About the best that can be said of the relationship between diet and disease in early Latin America is that poor diets (when they existed) contributed to the destructive force of epidemics, while disease itself contributed to poor diets by disrupting normal patterns of production and distribution.[42]

More important for the history of food than the relationship between nutrition and disease were the lasting consequences of the population decline. It is appropriate that Woodrow Borah, the dean of New World demographers, inaugurated the discussion of the complex connections between food production and population loss in Latin America. Borah summarizes the situation nicely, pointing to the land newly available for the expansion of wild animals and plants (foraging and hunting remained important ways of procuring food) and the increased yields from tilled lands. The result was an increase in production, and "with it per capita consumption."[43] What took place in Latin America was broadly analogous to fourteenth-century Europe after the Black Death, when increased yields and higher wages dramatically augmented the diet of the average European.[44]

Larger food supplies did more than improve the nutritional regimes of subsistence farmers. They supported complex economic institutions linking country to city and colony to metropolis. Plantations growing tropical products covered the Caribbean, stretched along the coast of Brazil, and spread through the tropical basins of Mexico and Peru. Haciendas produced wheat, cattle, and sheep for local and regional markets. Factories turned out cotton and woolen cloth for those who could not afford imported silks and taffetas. Silver and gold mines enriched many and helped stimulate trade. Just what these new institutions and relationships meant for nutritional regimes cannot be reduced to encompassing interpretations. Production for a commercial economy may have limited foods available for consumption, but it did not necessarily lead to impoverished nutritional regimes. Polemical writings and hasty judgments based on inferences are no substitute for hard evidence here.[45]

The evidence shows that Spanish and Portuguese economic institutions hastened the formation of new nutritional regimes. As Indians and Africans became a part of European society through forced or voluntary participation their habits often shifted. Rations, so unimportant today, exerted a powerful influence on nutritional regimes in the past. Slaves working mines in the

Caribbean and Indians laboring in Mexican textile mills supposedly ate meat as a part of their regular rations; Indian laborers in the Andes usually ate maize, barley, mutton, beef, soups, peppers; workers on Mexican haciendas enjoyed mutton, maize, beans, fish, hams, turkeys, sugar, lard, salt, and a little tobacco. Slaves on sugar plantations in Brazil had a similar diet, with prominent roles for manioc and fish. The effervescent Concolorcorvo summed up the situation for Andean textile workers: "It is likely that in Europe and even in Lima it will not be believed what I am going to tell in respect to food for forced and voluntary workers. All receive, at least twice each week, a good ration of fat and tender mutton." [46]

Ration records, as suspect as other types of evidence, do not always prove whether workers ate well or poorly. They do, though, document the foods available for consumption, illustrating that nutritional regimes embraced old and new commodities. Rations, or food regularly supplied by contract or other obligation, guided the life of many besides those working for the new economic institutions. The provisioning of specific amounts of food as service, charity, or obligation influenced rich and poor, Indian and European. School teachers lived from their rations of maize, beans, and meat; parents sought guardians who could feed their children well; apprentices received a guaranteed food supply from their masters; nuns in convents ate because of specific provisions in their dowries; charitable organizations distributed foods to the poor; breads confiscated from bakers fed those in prison. [47] Legal contracts and traditions of charity committed individuals and groups to supply regular amounts of nutrients, insuring continuity in diets and social relationships. Viewed from this perspective, Latin American society was a complex of relationships designed to maintain adequate nutritional regimes.

Ration records are good evidence of consumption patterns, but they do not explain the overall nature of nutritional regimes because only a small proportion of the population lived from rations. Food was first of all a commodity in the marketplace, and most people obtained food through exchanging something of value for it. A vigorous trade in food was the ultimate arbiter of what and how much people ate. It is unfortunate that the scholarly attention given to export economies has obscured the trade in subsistence foods, a trade with immediacy for all. [48] For every cart headed toward ports with dyes, cocoa, and sugar, another rumbled through the provinces with hams, cheeses, chuños, maize, fruits, and vegetables; for every ship setting sail for Europe with silver, another carried dried beef and grain along the coast.

Food on the table was the end of a complex of transactions that ranged from the Atlantic trade to the local store. Actually, the Atlantic trade was the least important after the sixteenth century, reduced for the most part to supplying high value foods and spices, especially wine, saffron, cloves, and cinnamon.[49] The volume of overseas imports was far less than that of regional trade in Latin America. The Andean region, for example, with its extremes of altitudes and climates, supported a flourishing trade that linked complementary agricultural zones. Root crops from higher elevations were exchanged for grains and vegetables from the valleys, which were then traded for fish, sugar, and imported goods on the coast.[50] The string of basins between Popayán, Quito, Cajamarca, Cuzco, La Paz, and Potosí, with important threads running down to the ports of Buenaventura, Guayaquil, Paita, and Callao, constituted an elaborate network of food exchange. Quito had such an abundance of beef and grain that it was profitable to supply cities as far away as Lima. Merchant adventurers in Quito profited from a more local trade too, buying wheat and hardtack, transporting them to the coast, buying fish, and returning with it to the highlands.[51] Farther south, in the highlands around Puno, traders shipped potatoes, quinoa, barley, and fish to La Paz and Arequipa in exchange for brandy, wine, shrimp, sugar, honey, beans, ají, and coca.

The growth of the great urban centers of Mexico City, Lima, and Potosí testifies to the success of the trade in comestibles. Within several miles of Potosí nothing grew, not even grass. Despite the lack of local foods, the markets were well stocked, even with wheat, which eighteen thousand Indians brought from the province of Cochabamba. Lima was so well supplied with meats, fruits, vegetables, and grains that Bernabé Cobo gave the title "The Abundance of Foods" to the chapter of his book describing this city. Mexico City, the island capital, continued to live as it had in the past, through a procession of food into the city. In the early seventeenth century, one thousand canoes and three thousand mules daily brought the city bread, meat, fish, game, maize, sugar, and other foods.[52]

Once in the city, foods moved to the consumer through *tianguis* (Indian markets) and *pulperías* (small general stores selling foods and dry goods). Pulperías assumed increasing importance as settlements grew, and by the late eighteenth century they characterized a food economy far more complex than the food trade still existing in some parts of Europe.[53] The number of pulperías helps document the extent of the commercialization of food. By 1600, Potosí already had 80 pulperías; Mexico City in the 1770s had 470, while the much smaller northern city of Querétaro had over 200; Buenos

Aires in the early nineteenth century might have had 700.[54] Pulperías, probably more than any other Spanish institution, influenced the quality and quantity of food available.

The consumer, the one with the least control in the food trade, was the only one to view food as a nutrient, vital for life. The astute Pedro Vicente Cañete y Domínguez recognized the problem when discussing the grain trade in Potosí. Hacendados saw grain as the end of their labors, a combination of capital and energy to be disposed of arbitrarily. Merchants thought of grain as a commodity, to be bought and sold for profit. Only the public viewed grain as food. To reconcile the views and insure production and fair distribution, the government acted on its commitment to "maintain in harmony the classes that divide society."[55]

Spain had an arsenal of food regulations that it used to maintain social harmony in America. Custom and law called for the establishment of *pósitos* (public granaries) and *alhóndigas* (public markets) to regulate the supply and prices of grain; the *abastos de carne* (meat supply system) did the same for meat. *Aranceles* and *posturas,* official declarations of wholesale and retail prices, applied to most items of consumption. Posturas, for example, regulated the price of grain bought at the alhóndiga, while the arancel governed the prices that bakers could charge for bread. The *fiel ejecutoría,* a municipal office, struggled to see that the regulatory system worked properly. Toward the end of the colonial period, the crown became more comprehensive in its food supply efforts and actually tried to measure the production of basic staples throughout Spanish America by requiring semiannual reports from all provinces. The result for nutritional regimes was that government regulation tempered the excesses of a purely commercial food distribution system. Public policy clashed with the desire for profit in much of Latin America, precipitating struggles that made the distribution and price of food a central political issue.[56]

When it actually came to selecting foods, taste, custom, and accepted medical wisdom interacted with supply and price to determine what people ate. A bewildering variety of cultural determinants, many of them conflicting, influenced the consumption of foods. One example is medicine, or more precisely, nutritional beliefs. Hippocratic and Galenic thought, equating health with the proper balance of foods, wielded influence into the nineteenth century. Unanue drew on Hippocratic principles in advising that red meats were more nutritious than light ones and that only those with strong stomachs should eat fruit before meals. Physicians with experience in Mexico disagreed. As disciples of the new advances in chemistry they believed that the nutritive quality of flesh depended little on the type of animal, though taste and palatability did. They argued that mutton, the most revered of Spanish meats, was no better than other meats for the health of soldiers.[57] Indian beliefs about the hot and cold qualities of food, supposedly so critical in dietary patterns, were as inconsistent as European beliefs about food.[58]

One cultural influence had the potential for affecting diets in all Latin America. The Catholic Church, replete with its dietary regulations, did not take lightly its role of enforcing fasting. It was especially concerned with violations of the prohibition of meat and meat by-products during Lent. The custom began when colonists who lacked olive oil dressed their food with *grasa de vaca* and *manteca de cerdo* (grease from cattle and pigs). Special dispensation from the church permitted the practice for thirty years beginning in 1562, but instead of developing acceptable alternatives, settlers aggravated the problem by the increasing use of *lacticinios*—eggs, milk, cheese, and butter—on fast days. More annoying still was the socially accepted practice of eating meat on Fridays and during Lent. A late eighteenth-century discussion of the problem throughout the empire revealed the food supply network underlying these practices. From San Luis Potosí, Mexico, to Concepción, Chile, residents bemoaned the lack of Lenten foods, especially olive oil, which they reserved for church lamps, salad dressing, or a "few precious drops on fish and soups." In addition, beef was often much less expensive than grains or fish, leaving the poor the easy decision of whether to eat meat or fast. By the late colonial period, nutritional regimes that relied on meat and lacticinios had become so entrenched that the church could not hope to eradicate them.[59] It is paradoxical that the church, the one Iberian institution with specific interests in diet, exerted less influence on nutritional regimes than did many other institutions.

Abundance and Scarcity

The recurring crises of epidemics and bad weather had a more dramatic influence on nutritional regimes than did trade, customs, and laws. The hideous movement of measles and smallpox from village to village became a march of death. Early frosts sent a shiver of panic through communities hurrying to bring in the harvests. Disease and weather could quickly change what people ate. The fortunate times were those when an element of choice remained. In 1589, the viceroy of Peru responded to the measles and smallpox epidemic by enumerating the foods for the healthy and the sick. To give strength to the healthy he recommended foods of "good substance," mutton, fowl, and goat; those already burning from fever had to settle for concoctions of barley, quinoa, amaranth, sugar, and raisins, dressed with vinegar and oil.[60]

Crop failures often denied people the luxury of choosing from different foods. Frosts, floods, droughts, plant diseases, the nemeses of farmers everywhere, took their toll from the fertile valleys of the Bajío in Mexico to the harsh altiplano of Bolivia. When shortages were particularly severe, every agency of authority responded with vigor and commitment. Evidence from the Mexican crisis of 1785–86 depicts a comprehensive effort to ward off starvation: taxes were cut, private and public donations increased, new lands sown, and new techniques of planting introduced. At the local level, the clergy used the pulpit to direct the attack against hunger.[61] Just as important was the individual response to the crisis of subsistence. Previously disregarded foods such as wild grasses and fruits become staples, and ingenious methods of expanding scarce foods become commonplace; in other words, ideas and the imagination led to substitutes for traditional nutritional regimes.[62]

The severity of some of the crises might encourage an overestimation of their impact on Latin American life. The past was not a succession of frantic searches for food in the face of disease and drought. These were short-term, intermittent disruptions in normal patterns with little lasting effect on nutritional regimes. It appears that Latin America enjoyed a more privileged and abundant food history than Europe from 1500 to 1800. Much of the evidence presented in this essay supports the contention of adequate, at times plentiful, food supplies in Latin America. It is appropriate to conclude with a further word on the evidence supporting the interpretation. The intent is not to answer the question "Did the peasants really starve?" as Peter Laslett attempted to do for England, but to mention some additional aspects of Latin America's history that influenced nutritional regimes.[63]

One of the reasons why Latin America escaped chronic starvation was the widespread use of food preservation techniques. This vital subject has not yet been explored in any meaningful way. Before the advent of canning, food preservation techniques included drying, salting, pickling, smoking, freezing, and cooling. All were used in Latin America, often in enterprises involving large numbers of people. The preparation of chuños and cured meats became important local industries that shipped food to distant populations. Fish preservation, whether by salting, smoking, or making a ground meal, permitted most inland cities to eat fish. Preservation of grain reached the stage of a domestic art with wheat and manioc. Wheat as *bizcocho* (hardtack) and manioc as *pão da guerra* (military bread) lasted for over a year. Simpler techniques were also effective. Manioc was cut at the stalk and kept in the ground for months, maize was left on the cob and hung over a smoking fire, wheat was buried, and granaries were fumigated.[64] Preservation of staples facilitated their transportation and storage, alleviating some of the shortages during times of crisis.

The availability of foods for preservation means that the basic requirements of the nutritional regime have been satisfied. A surplus, however limited, had to exist before preservation was considered. Contemporaries singled out the frequency of the planting and harvesting cycle as an important explanation for surpluses. Land and climate encouraged two and at times three harvests a year for maize in the humid wetlands and irrigated areas, an agricultural marvel that awed observers. Just as impressive was the diversity of agricultural production within limited distances, because of the extremes of climate and soil that accompanied sharp changes in elevation. What a delight to have sugar, coffee, maize, potatoes, wheat, bananas, pineapples, and dozens of other foods growing within a few miles of each other.[65] In Europe, a much more rigid schedule of planting and harvesting dominated life. The single autumn harvest was followed by the long winter months when only preserved foods and thoughts of spring kept people alive. Whereas failure of the harvest portended an especially miserable winter in Europe, in Latin America, one crop failure had less significance because of the diversity of foods and frequency of harvests.[66]

The abundance of the land and the many opportunities for hunting and gathering impressed observers almost as much as the productivity of agriculture. Even in the late eighteenth century in the Valley of Mexico, the most densely populated region in Latin America, the migration of water fowl provided so much food that there was a noticeable periodic decline in the butchering of livestock.[67] With the rise of truly large cities in the late nineteenth and twentieth century, urban people could no longer rely on wild foods, but rural people could and did.[68]

Some testimonials on eating habits describe a profusion of food. In Mexico City, people ate much more than in Madrid, often consuming three pounds a day at four sittings. The abundance of food led to "vulgar, repetitive, wasteful" eating habits unheard of in Madrid. Residents of Lima, "one of the best provisioned of all cities," had so much food that they ate anything at any time with no thought to health.[69] Exactly how many people enjoyed such abundance is not known. It is certain, however, that Latin America's voracious indulgence in foods was so commonly observed that it elicited explanatory theories. Some theorized that Latin Americans had to eat more than Europeans because the foods were not as wholesome as those in Europe, a view that convinced very few by the end of the eighteenth century.[70]

The evidence on scarcity does not necessarily invalidate the preceding observations. Comments on the spare eating habits of Indians, for example, often mention extensive reliance on alcohol or coca, not a shortage of food, as the reason for decreased food consumption.[71] Scarcities occurred in coastal towns and newly established mining communities, but staple supply networks ensured the nutrients necessary for survival.[72] As seen, disease and crop failure disrupted food supply, but their permanent effect on nutritional regimes is not adequately understood. These examples do not prove a history plagued by hunger. Nor does the more dramatic evidence of food shortages contributing to riots, as in Mexico City in 1624 and 1692. Use of such evidence as proof of continuous hunger is tantamount to categorizing the recent history of the United States as one of hunger because of food riots in the 1890s and 1930s.

Conclusion

Further research may definitively show whether the peasants starved in early Latin America. New evidence and more sophisticated methods can yield quantitative information on the diet. When enough examples from different occupation groups and regions are available, conclusions can be drawn. But these conclusions have to be placed in the perspective of biological and social forces for the history of food. Iberian and Indian commercial activities, imperial and local food policies, demographic swings and labor needs, and rations and cultural habits interacted with the environment to determine nutritional regimes. Food was continually reacting to and promoting changes in colonial society.

The rapid dispersal of Old World plants and animals, in some cases complementing and in other cases displacing traditional Indian foods, had important political dimensions. Decisions on which foods to grow and how to distribute them were especially important as Indians and Europeans competed for lands and markets. The European presence became the dominant one, though Indian concerns were never entirely neglected. Indian nutritional needs were met, even as mercantilist institutions increased production for external markets. This was possible because of the high yields of many Old and New World foods and the light demand for subsistence crops. Protein and carbohydrates from Old World animals and plants (especially bananas) ensured an improved diet for many people. With the abundance of food, the rapid expansion of Spain and Portugal in the New World was bound to succeed.

Iberian political and social institutions contributed to the maintenance of adequate nutritional regimes. Without them, surpluses would have shrunk much faster as neglect, hoarding, and speculation ran their course. The food bureaucracy was extensive and often effective in providing food for cities and towns. The social commitment of the church and of individuals to feeding the poor helped the state in its efforts. Only toward the end of the colonial period, as the size of cities outstripped the abilities of regulatory agencies, did weaknesses in the social and political support for provisioning lead to severe problems.

Changes in nutritional regimes always hinged on social and environmental changes, making food use much more than an expression of cultural preferences. Instead of being simply carryovers from earlier periods, nutritional regimes were an expression of the changing historical reality of Latin America. While the regimes reacted to the changes, they simultaneously contributed to change, especially in agricultural and economic activities. In this way, food was both cause and effect of the early development of Latin America.

Notes

Abbreviations

AGI: Archivo General de Indias, Seville
AGN: Archivo General de la Nación, Mexico City
ANH: Archivo Nacional de Historia, Quito
MNAH: Museo Nacional de Antropología e Historia, Mexico City

1. *Maximilien Sorre, Les fondements biologiques de la géographie humaine: Essai d'une ecologie de l'homme* (Paris: A. Collins, 1971), p. 249.

2. Derrick B. Jelliffe and E. F. Patricia Jelliffe, "Field Assessment of Dietary Intake and Nutritional Status," in *Malnutrition, Learning, and Behavior,* eds. Nevin S. Scrimshaw and John E. Gordon (Cambridge, Mass: MIT Press, 1968), p. 398.

3. For an example of sailor's fare see AGI, Contaduría, 487, no. 4, 6 July 1575.

4. Licenses for wine shipments help illustrate the importance of wine in the diet, despite the widespread availability of local drinks. See AGN, General de Parte, vol. 5, exp. *43, 23 March 1599,* f 9; Berta Rodríguez de Cabanillas, *El puertorriqueño y su alimentación a través de su historia (siglos XVI al XIX)* (San Juan, P.R.: Instituto de Cultura Puertorriqueña, *1973), pp. 107, 132.*

5. AGN, Alhóndigas y Pósitos, vol. 14, exp. 2, 23 Oct. 1684, ff 24–55; "Relación del distrito del cerro de Zaruma . . . ," in Marcos Jiménez de la Espada, *Relaciones geográficas de Indias: Perú,* 3 vols. (Madrid: Ediciones Atlas, vols. 183–85 of Biblioteca de Autores Españoles, 1965), 2:315; Juan López de Velasco, *Geografía y descrip-*

ción universal de las Indias (Madrid: Ediciones Atlas, vol. 248 of Biblioteca de Autores Españoles, 1971), p. 211.

6. The basic elements of the story of early food supply in the Caribbean can be reconstructed from Gonzalo Fernández de Oviedo, *Sumario de la natural historia de las Indias* (Mexico City: Fondo de Cultura Económica, 1950); Bartolomé de las Casas, *Historia de las Indias,* 3 vols. (Mexico City: Fondo de Cultura Económica, 1951); and Richard Hakluyt, *The Principal Navigations, Voyages, Traffiques, and Discoveries of the English Nation . . . ,* 10 vols. (London: J. M. Dent, 1927–28).

7. For contemporaries, taste was important but usually did not overshadow concerns about health. For example, Oviedo thought pineapples delicious and an appetite stimulant; coconut milk was better than cow's milk and did not cause indigestion; many wild fruits tasted good but caused urine to turn red (Oviedo, *Sumario,* pp. 208, 236, 240).

8. Sugar is one of the most controversial foods in the new Latin American diet. It was a cheap substitute for honey, the traditional sweetener in the nutritional regime, and by the end of the sixteenth century it was consumed in enormous quantities. Certainly sugar influenced health and behavior in early Latin America, contributing to obesity, hypoglycemia, and dental caries; but perhaps it did not do so to the extent argued by Carlos Malpica Silva Santisteban, who sees it as causing everything from increased diabetes to severe social and psychological disorientation. See his *Crónica del hambre en el Perú* (Lima: Moncloa Campodónico Ediciones, 1970), pp. 72–74.

9. It is illusory to give specific estimates on nutrients when data are so sparse, but it is just as misleading to minimize the importance of fruits and vegetables in the diet. For an example of the problems that result from a recognition of the importance of fruits and vegetables but a failure to include them in an evaluation of the diet see Luis Lisanti, "Sur la nourriture des 'Paulistes' entre XVIIIe et XIXe siècles," *Annales: Economies, Sociétés, et Civilisations* 18, no. 3 (May–June 1963): 531–40.

10. Bernabé Cobo, *Obras,* 2 vols. (Madrid: Ediciones Atlas, vols. 91–92 of Biblioteca de Autores Españoles, 1956), 2:317; Pero Magalhães de Gandavo, "History of the Province of Santa Cruz," in *The Histories of Brazil,* trans. John B. Stetson, Jr., 2 vols. (New York: Cortes Society, 1922), 2:48.

11. Alexander von Humboldt noted that an acre of bananas produced twenty times as much food as an acre of corn (*Personal Narrative of Travels to the Equinoctial Regions of America during the Years 1799–1804,* trans. Thomasina Ross, 3 vols. [London: Henry G. Bohn, 1852–53], 1:205).

12. Francisco Hernández, *Cuatro libros de la naturaleza . . .* (Mexico City: Oficina Tip. de la Secretaría de Fomento, 1888), pp. 213–21; Garcilaso de la Vega, *Royal Commentaries of the Incas . . . ,* trans. Harold V. Livermore, 2 vols. (Austin: University of Texas Press, 1966), 2:498–99; Cobo, *Obras,* 1:164–65.

13. Luis Amaral, *Historia geral da agricultura brasileira . . . ,* 3 vols. (São Paulo: Cia. Editora Nacional, 1939–40), 2:39.

14. Average figures are helpful. Manioc produces 9.9 million calories per hectare, potatoes 7.5, and maize 7.3; for Old World crops, rice produces 7.3, barley 5.1, and

wheat 4.2 (Alfred W. Crosby, Jr., *The Columbian Exchange* [Westport, Conn.: Greenwood, 1972], p. 175).

15. AGI, Contaduría, 487, passim; Thales de Azevedo, *Povoamento da cidade do Salvador* (Bahia: Tipografía Beneditina, 1949), p. 232. Azevedo does not fail to note (and here he disagrees with Gilberto Freyre) that Bahia also consumed enough wheat to make nutritional regimes similar to those in Portugal, p. 327.

16. Cobo, *Obras*, 1:407.

17. AGI, Quito, 201, 6 April 1588, f 68.

18. A comprehensive reference to areas rich in wheat is Antonio Vázquez de Espinosa, *Compendium and Description of the West Indies*, trans. Charles Upson Clark (Washington, D.C.: Smithsonian Institution, 1942).

19. Humboldt, *Travels*, 2:519. A Spaniard who lived far from any large settlement in Venezuela commented to Humboldt that he knew he would never see a Spanish official "because they can only eat wheaten bread" (Ibid., p. 159).

20. In Mexico City in the late eighteenth century, Indians ate *pan baso*, made from poor grains with most of the bran remaining; those of modest means ate *pan común*, a hearty, popular bread that might have improved in quality in the late eighteenth century; the wealthy ate *pan florado* or *francés*, made from finely milled, expensive grains (AGN, Alhóndigas y Pósitos, vol. 4, exp. 1, 26 March 1793, ff 139–44; vol. 4, exp. 1, 28 April 1795, ff 130–44; Historia, vol. 135, exp. 7, f 82).

21. AGN, Industria, vol. 1, exp. 16, 20 May 1796, ff 423–37; vol. 19, 5 Nov. 1790, ff 21–26.

22. Definite changes in consumption patterns followed shifts in the price of grains (Manuel de Flon, "Noticias estadísticas de la intendencia de Puebla (1804)," in *Descripciones económicas regionales de Nueva España: Provincias del Centro Sureste y Sur, 1766-1827*, comps. Enrique Florescano and Isabel Gil Sánchez [Mexico City: Instituto Nacional de Antropología e Historia, 1976], pp. 162–63).

23. "The Voyage made by M. John Hawkings . . . 1564," in Hakluyt, *Navigations*, 7:29–30; John Mawe, *Viagens ao interior do Brasil*, trans. Solena Benevides Viana (Rio de Janeiro: Zelio Valverde, 1944), p. 27.

24. Felix de Azara, *Memoria sobre el estado rural del Río de la Plata y otros informes* (Buenos Aires: Editorial Bajel, 1943), p. 12; Alonso de la Mota y Escobar, *Descripción geográfica de los reinos de Nueva Galicia, Nueva Vizcaya y Nuevo León* (Mexico City: P. Robredo, 1940), p. 53.

25. For a discussion of the Bajío see my *La vida en Querétaro durante la colonia* (Mexico City: Fondo de Cultura Económica, 1982), pp. 39–56; for the Caribbean see Cabanillas de Rodríguez, *Puertorriqueño*, p. 169.

26. João Capistrano de Abreu, *Capítulos de historia colonial, 1500-1800* (Rio de Janeiro: Sociedade Capistrano de Abreu, 1954), p. 217.

27. Mawe, *Viagens*, p. 36; Azara, *Memoria*, p. 12; Humboldt, *Travels*, 3:138.

28. Charles Gibson, *The Aztecs under Spanish Rule* (Stanford: Stanford University Press, 1964), p. 567, note 87.

29. AGI, Mexico, 2770, "Testimonio . . . 1759"; Francesco Carletti, *My Voyage*

around the World, trans. Herbert Weinstock (New York: Random House, 1964), p. 66; François Amédée Frézier, *Relación del viaje por el mar del Sur ...*, trans. Nicolás Peña M. (Santiago, Chile: Mejía, 1902), p. 35.

30. Fernand Braudel, *Capitalism and Material Life, 1400–1800,* trans. Miriam Kochan (New York: Harper and Row, 1973), p. 68. Crosby notes in his *Columbian Exchange* that colonists probably ate "more meat per man than any other large group of non-nomadic people in the world" (p. 108).

31. "La descripción que se hizo en la Provincia de Xauxa . . . ," in Jiménez de Espada, *Relaciones,* 1:170; Angel Palerm, "Agricultural Systems and Food Patterns," in *Handbook of Middle American Indians,* vol. 6, eds. Robert Wauchope and Manning Nash (Austin: University of Texas Press, 1967), p. 44.

32. Richard N. Adams, "Food Habits in Latin America: A Preliminary Historical Survey," in *Human Nutrition: Historic and Scientific,* ed. Iago Goldston (New York: International Universities Press, 1960), p. 7.

33. Jacques Soustelle, *Daily Life of the Aztecs on the Eve of the Spanish Conquest* (Stanford: Stanford University Press, 1970), pp. 156–57. The most impressive historical study of Indian drinking patterns in Mexico is William B. Taylor's *Drinking, Homicide & Rebellion in Colonial Mexican Villages* (Stanford: Stanford University Press, 1979), which concludes that drinking increased after the conquest but often within a ritual context (pp. 40, 42, 72).

34. As with pulque, the increased consumption of chicha still had a ritual importance. George Kubler, "The Quechua in the Colonial World," in *Handbook of South American Indians,* ed. Julian H. Steward, 7 vols. (Washington, D.C.: Smithsonian Institution Bureau of American Ethnology, 1946–59), 2:392; John Howland Rowe, "Inca Culture at the Time of the Spanish Conquest," in the same volume, p. 292.

35. Pedro Vicente Cañete y Domínguez, *Guía histórica ... de Potosí, 1787* (Potosí: Editorial Potosí, 1952), p. 412; José Hipólito Unanue, *Observaciones sobre el clima de Lima . . .* (Lima: Imp. "Lux," 1940), p. 78.

36. Gibson, *Aztecs,* p. 150; Taylor, *Drinking,* p. 30.

37. Azevedo, *Povoamento,* p. 306.

38. Nicolás Sánchez-Albornoz, *The Population of Latin America: A History,* trans. W. A. R. Richardson (Berkeley and Los Angeles: University of California Press, 1974), p. 86; Henry F. Dobyns and Paul L. Doughty, *Peru: A Cultural History* (New York: Oxford University Press, 1976), p. 298; Michael C. Meyer and William L. Sherman, *The Course of Mexican History* (New York: Oxford University Press, 1979), p. 212.

39. Sánchez-Albornoz, *Population,* p. 60; Crosby, *Columbian Exchange,* pp. 165–207; W. L. Langer, "American Foods and Europe's Population Growth, 1750–1850," *Journal of Social History* 8 (Winter 1975): 51–66; Jonathan Spence, "Ch'ing," in *Food in Chinese Culture,* ed. K. C. Chang (New Haven: Yale University Press, 1977), p. 263.

40. Nevin S. Scrimshaw, C. E. Taylor, and J. E. Gordon, "Interactions of Nutrition and Infection," *American Journal of Medical Science* 237, no. 3 (March 1959): 367–

403. Georgeda Buchbinder, "Nutritional Stress and Postcontact Population Decline among the Maring of New Guinea," in *Malnutrition, Behavior, and Social Organization*, ed. Lawrence S. Greene (New York: Academic Press, 1977), p. 136.

41. Andrew B. Appleby. "Nutrition and Disease: The Case of London, 1550–1756," *Journal of Interdisciplinary History* 6, no. 1 (Summer 1975): 1–22.

42. Azevedo, *Povoamento*, p. 175; M. E. Bustamante, "Aspectos históricos y epidemiológicos del hambre en México," *Gaceta Médica de México* 109, no. 1 (Jan. 1975): 23–43.

43. Sherburne F. Cook and Woodrow Borah, *Essays in Population History*, vol. 3, *Mexico and California* (Berkeley and Los Angeles: University of California Press, 1979), pp. 168, 172–74.

44. Lynn White, Jr., "Food and History," in *Food, Man, and Society*, eds. Dwain N. Walcher, Norman Kretchmer, and Henry L. Barnett (New York: Plenum Press, 1976), pp. 13–21. In talking about the period after the Black Death, Braudel says, "real salaries have never been as high as they were then" (*Capitalism*, p. 129).

45. For examples of what I consider unsubstantiated conclusions on the impact of colonialism on nutritional regimes, see Silva Santisteban, *Crónica*, pp. 63–70, and F. A. Monalto, *Panorama de la realidad histórica del Paraguay* (Asunción: Editorial El Gráfico, 1967), pp. 128–33; for a more theoretical argument consult René Dumont and Nicholas Cohen, *The Growth of Hunger: A New Politics of Agriculture* (London and Boston: M. Boyars, 1980).

46. Concolorcorvo's statement implies that forced workers ate very well, a belief that some Brazilianists have advocated in comparing the diets of slaves and colonists (Azevedo, *Povoamento*, pp. 311–12). Contrast this with the rigid distribution of nutrients according to social rank in Europe (A. Wyczanski, "The Social Structure of Nutrition, a Case," *Acta Poloniae Historica* 18 [1968]: 63–74). References to rations are from AGN, Tierras, vol. 1463, exp. 3, 12 Oct. 1745–1 Nov. 1748; ANH, Obrajes, box 32, "Libro de Socorros," 1777; MNAH, Fondo Franciscano, "Quentas," 1625, 1626, vol. 92; Luìs de Câmara Cascudo, *História da alimentação no Brasil*, 2 vols. (São Paulo: Companhia Editora Nacional, 1967), 1:213–16; Alonzo Carrió de la Vandera (Concolorcorvo), *El lazarillo de ciegos caminantes* (Barcelona: Editorial Labor, 1973), pp. 353–54; Cabanillas de Rodríquez, *Puertorriqueño*, p. 222; Ward Barrett, "The Meat Supply of Colonial Cuernavaca," *Annals of the Association of American Geographers* 64, no. 4 (Dec. 1974): 530.

47. AGN, General de Parte, vol. 2, exp. 941, 12 Aug. 1580, f 22; AGN, Hospitales, vol. 77, exp. 1, Feb. 1816, ff 64–65; MNAH, Fondo Franciscano, "Quentas," 1625, 1626, vol. 92; MNAH, Querétaro series, microfilm room, Nicolás de Robles, 23 Feb. 1606, 25 Feb. 1606, roll 5; AGN, Historia, vol. 501, exp. 3, 9 March 1809, f 35; AGI, Mexico, 1681, 1759.

48. The inventory of provincial stores is good evidence here (MNAH, Querétaro series, microfilm room, roll. 22).

49. Items such as wheat and flour were as much a part of local as international trade. Havana, Campeche, Guayaquil, and other tropical coastal cities depended on

wheat imports; even Buenos Aires, traditionally a wheat exporter, had to rely on imports in the early nineteenth century (AGI, Mexico, 2486, 3 May 1798; AGN, Alhóndigas y Pósitos, vol. 3; Goodbine Parish to George Canning, July 30, 1824, in R. A. Humphreys, *British Consular Reports on the Trade and Politics of Latin America, 1824-1826* [London: Offices of the Reports of the Royal Historical Society, 1940], p. 45).

50. For the example of Puno and many others see AGI, Indiferente General, 1559.

51. ANH, Protocolos, 23 Feb. 1597 (volume numbered Diego Bravo, 1593–1597) and 11 Aug. 1606 (volume numbered Alonso Dorado de Vergara, 1606); "La cibdad de Sant Francisco del Quito 1573," in Jiménez de la Espada, *Relaciones,* 2:211–22.

52. "Descripción de la villa y minas de Potosí, año de 1603," in Jiménez de la Espada, *Relaciones,* 1:577; Cobo, *Obras,* 2:315; Vásquez de Espinosa, *Compendium,* pp. 156, 632.

53. H. J. Teuteberg, "Some Aspects of Nutrition as Influenced by Socio-Economic Changes in the XIX Century in Germany," *Proceedings of the Seventh International Congress of Nutrition* (Oxford: Pergamon Press, 1967), 4:77–86. See also Thomas C. Wright's essay in this volume.

54. For a discussion of food distribution in two Mexican cities with special reference to bread and pulperías see John C. Super, "Pan, alimentación y política en Querétaro en la última decada del siglo XVIII," *Historia Mexicana* 30, no. 2 (Oct.–Dec. 1980): 247–72; and John C. Super, "Bread and the Provisioning of Mexico City in the Late Eighteenth Century," *Jahrbuch für Geschichte von Staat, Wirtschaft und Gesellschaft Lateinamerikas* 19 (1982): 159–82; see also Jay Kinsbruner, "The Pulperos of Caracas and San Juan during the First Half of the Nineteenth Century," *Latin American Research Review* 13, no. 1 (1978): 65–86. The number for Buenos Aires is from Mawe, *Viagens,* p. 52; for Potosí, "Descripción," in Jiménez de Espada, *Relaciones,* 1:380.

55. Cañete y Domínguez, *Guía,* p. 496.

56. As far as I know, there is no single source that describes the different agencies and relationships that governed the production and distribution of food. The best analysis of the alhóndiga, the most important agency, is in Enrique Florescano, *Precios del maíz y crisis agrícolas en México (1708-1810)* (Mexico City: Colegio de México, 1969).

57. AGN, Hospitales, vol. 9, exp. 5, 2 Jan. 1810, f 92; Unanue, *Observaciones,* pp. 73, 75–76, 98.

58. Different attitudes about flavor and nutritional value are found among Indians today. See Oscar Lewis, *Life in a Mexican Village: Tepoztlán Restudied* (Urbana: University of Illinois Press, 1963), p. 200; Kathleen M. Dewalt and Gretel H. Pelto, "Food Use and Household Ecology in a Mexican Community," in *Nutrition and Anthropology in Action,* ed. Thomas K. Fitzgerald (Assen: Van Gorcum, 1977), pp. 85–86.

59. The 100-folio review of the problem in AGN, Reales Cédulas (Originales), 99:166–269, almost constitutes a description of late colonial eating practices.

60. Lilly Library, Indiana University, Latin American MS, Peru, Box 1581–1589, March 23, 1589. I want to thank Nicholas Cushner for providing me with a copy of this document.

61. AGN, Alhóndigas y Pósitos, vol. 15, exp. 1, 1786, ff 1–166.

62. Ibid.; José Antonio Alzate y Ramírez, *Consejos útiles para socorrer a la necesidad en tiempo que escasean los comestibles* (Mexico City: Felipe de Zúñiga y Ontiveros, 1786), pp. 7–8.

63. Peter Laslett, *The World We Have Lost* (New York: Charles Scribner's Sons, 1965), pp. 107–27.

64. Francisco Millau, *Descripción de la provincia del Río de la Plata (1772)* (Buenos Aires: Editora Espasa-Calpe, 1947), pp. 48–49; Magalhães de Gandavo, *Histories of Brazil*, 2:44–45; "La cibdad de Sant Francisco del Quito, 1572," in Jiménez de la Espada, *Relaciones*, 2:212–13, are examples of the evidence available.

65. Alejandro de Humboldt, *Ensayo político sobre el reino de la Nueva España*, ed. Vito Alessio Robles, 5 vols. (Mexico City: Editorial Pedro Robredo, 1941), vol. 3:39. Jiménez de la Espada's *Relaciones geográficas* are the best sixteenth-century source for diversity and productivity; somewhat comparable for the eighteenth century are the "Relaciones sobre el tiempo y cosechas de frutos que se hacen en los reinos de Indias," AGI, Indiferent General, 1793.

66. Sorre goes as far to say that "semi-scarcity was an annual" condition in Europe (*Fondements*, p. 278). In comparing the famines of Europe with the abundance of the Caribbean, the eighteenth-century writer Thomas Jeffreys exclaimed, "But in this part of the New World there are six species of vegetables, all as good as bread, which never fail, but multiply in a surprising manner" (*The Natural and Civil History of the French Dominions in North and South America* [London: Charing Cross, 1760], p. 10).

67. Alzate y Ramírez, *Consejos*, p. 11.

68. Richmond K. Anderson, José Calvo, Gloria Serrano, and George C. Payne, "A Study of the Nutritional Status and Food Habits of Otomí Indians in the Mesquital Valley of Mexico," *American Journal of Public Health and the Nation's Health* 36, no. 8 (Aug. 1946): 886–87.

69. AGN, Historia, vol. 74, exp. 1, 14 March 1791, ff 40, 136–37; Unanue, *Observaciones*, p. 72.

70. AGN, Historia, vol. 74, exp. 1, 14 March 1791, f 18; Enrico Martínez, *Reportorio de los tiempos e historia natural de Nueva España* (Mexico City: Secretaría de Educación Pública, 1948), p. 174.

71. Cañete y Domínguez, *Guía*, p. 412.

72. Even towns far from the mines might experience shortages. After the discovery of gold in Minas Gerais, the price of beans in São Paulo jumped 220 percent, sugar 300 percent, vinegar and wine 500 percent, and maize 1300 percent (Roberto C. Simonsen, *Historia economica do Brasil, 1500–1820*, 2 vols. [São Paulo: Companhia Editora Nacional, 1937], 2:100).

Thomas C. Wright

The Politics of Urban
Provisioning in
Latin American History

The feeding of cities has always been a political as well as an economic problem. Urban provisioning generates latent or overt political conflict among four primary groups and many secondary ones, too numerous and amorphous to cite. The primary groups include producers, processors, distributors, and consumers. To the first three food is a commodity and a source of profit, and to the last it is a necessity of life and a potential source of pleasure. For a majority of urban dwellers in Latin America and much of the world, food purchases constitute by far the largest family expenditure.[1] These people, classed here as the urban poor regardless of income or occupational status, are especially sensitive to the cost of food and are active or passive participants in the politics of urban provisioning.[2]

Whether enfranchised or politically marginal, the urban poor from the Roman Empire through the French Revolution to the recent crisis in Poland have expressed themselves sporadically but forcefully about the price of food.[3] Likewise, the Latin American urban poor have expressed their concern about the cost of food staples in a variety of ways. Their early response to shortages and high prices, the colonial *tumulto,* was dreaded by the authorities but ameliorated the food supply problem only temporarily. Later responses, whether rioting, protesting, striking, or voting, have been an important element in determining the political course of Latin American societies.

The politics of urban provisioning in Latin America can be divided into two distinct stages. The first extended from the establishment of Spanish and Portuguese cities to the 1870s and, while complex, took place in a relatively narrow spatial and political context. Most cities were supplied from local or regional sources, and the weather, crop or animal diseases, official policy, and manipulation by producers and middlemen determined the conditions of the urban food supply. During this period, the urban poor were disenfranchised and limited to playing a role in the politics of food only through the implicit threat of disorderly behavior, or tumulto, which erupted occasionally.

From the 1870s onward, the determinants of the politics of urban provisioning became more complex. Latin America became enmeshed in a new world economy in which food, along with other commodities, was an object of global exchange. From the beginning of this period the urban poor took an increasingly active political role, achieving direct influence over food policy in the twentieth century. In response, many Latin American governments assumed broad powers over their countries' food economies by the 1950s.

This essay focuses on the transition in the politics of urban provisioning from the phase of local economy and passive participation of the urban poor to the later stage, characterized by the active participation of the urban poor within a global economy of food. It examines the reasons for the emergence of urban food policy as a central issue in Latin American politics and traces, in general terms, the stages through which government intervention in the food economy evolved.[4]

Urban Provisioning in the Era of Local Supply

The small colonial cities of Latin America were usually located near dependable sources of supply. As a result they were adequately if not abundantly stocked with the staples that constituted the diet of the urban poor. Municipal commons and other open spaces provided some opportunity for the poor to avoid complete dependence on the market for their alimentary needs, while the church offered food to the destitute. Those cities located in difficult or remote terrain, such as Potosí or Cartagena, required special arrangements to assure their provisioning, as did the coastal towns in Brazil, where the sugar fazendas' dominance of the best lands constantly strained the urban food supply.[5] The urban poor, fragmented along racial and occupational lines, lacked the organizational strength to challenge the political systems that excluded them from active participation. They had no alternative to accepting the food supply and price regime established by more powerful elements in society until, provoked on occasion by extremes of shortage and high prices, they engaged in short-lived but destructive tumultos.

During the era of Iberian dominance the politics of food was closely directed in the public interest. Regulation was based on the concept of a moral economy in which food, as a necessity of life, was not considered an object for lucre or speculation; in the words of a royal official in Mexico, "although anyone may do as he likes with his own property, in the things necessary for the sustenance of life sellers should not be at liberty to set and raise prices freely."[6] Extensive regulatory powers enabled municipalities to buy, sell, and store grain, requisition it from growers, and set its price. Local officials also controlled the meat supply and enforced the accuracy of weights and measures. Municipal regulatory powers grew in scope as urban provisioning became more complex.

Despite the many laws and agencies regulating distribution, free market exchange was never entirely eliminated. Indeed, under normal circumstances the price of bread was pegged to the free price of grain. In addition, fraud *was commonplace: Hacendados' influence in local government* often led to abuses of meat supply contracts, and the constant complaints about price gouging and adulteration suggest that protection of the consumer was difficult to achieve when crown policy clashed with local economic interests. As it evolved in America, then, serving the common good came to mean supplying the cities in sufficient quantity to prevent starvation or social disturbances such as the great Mexico City tumultos of 1624 and 1692. This modest objective was normally met, whether owing to government regulation or despite it, sparing America the worst of the intermittent food shortages and riots plaguing contemporary Europe.[7]

The fifty years following independence from Spain and Portugal witnessed radical change in the philosophy and institutions of urban provisioning. Under the banner of liberalism, the ruling elites rejected government intervention and embraced laissez faire as the means for achieving the common good. The municipal codes of the Spanish American republics and imperial Brazil authorized local governments to regulate sanitation and the accuracy of weights and measures in markets but conspicuously omitted the broader colonial powers such as buying grains and fixing prices. The urban poor under liberalism were given full responsibility for their own well-being but no means to defend it.[8]

Attenuating the potential impact of these abrupt changes was a fundamental continuity in the factors affecting the food supply to Latin America's cities. After the destructive wars of independence, agriculture, unlike mining and artisanry, faced no long-term obstacles to revival. The demand for commercially distributed foodstuffs appears to have grown fairly slowly during the half century following independence. While several port cities burgeoned under the impetus of expanded trade, most cities grew slowly; and the decline of mining activity reduced significantly the demand for commercial food in some areas, partially offsetting the growth of urban needs. Urban and suburban open spaces continued to exist, and the new *juntas de beneficencia* supplemented or replaced the church as dispensers of food charity. The scanty research on urban markets and food prices between independence and 1870 supports the hypothesis that the economics and politics of urban provisioning were largely unaffected by the ideological and institutional changes accompanying independence.[9]

The Impact of the Export Economies

After approximately half a century of independence, a number of developments converged to focus attention on the provisioning of Latin America's cities. All were related to the accelerated pace of modernization, which resulted in turn from the development of export economies and greater integration into the world market. Urbanization and the growth of population in food-dependent export enclaves in Latin America increased the demand for commercial foodstuffs. Concurrently, entry into the world economy opened new markets for Latin American agricultural products, creating opportunities for land use that threatened the production of comestibles for domestic consumption in some areas. Imported staples became readily available at the same time, but currency relationships often made these more expensive than locally produced staples. These strains in the food supply contributed to a noticeable inflation of food prices, leading the urban poor to assume a more active role in the politics of urban provisioning.

The primary factor increasing the demand for commercial food was the rapid pace of urbanization. As Latin America's total population grew from 30 to 104 million between 1850 and 1930, the urban population increased much faster. European immigrants, often recruited for agricultural labor, were lured to the cities by opportunities in commerce, industry, and skilled trades. Internal migration contributed to the growth of provincial towns as well as capitals and ports. Mexico City doubled and Santiago tripled their populations between roughly 1870 and 1914. Meanwhile, São Paulo grew nineteenfold (to 579,000), Rio quadrupled (to 1,158,000), and Buenos Aires grew some 800 percent (to 1,576,000). In these expanding metropolises the crowding of poor families into cramped slums and tenements reduced the practice of urban farming; in the case of internal migrants, however, continued ties with their rural roots allowed them to avoid total dependence on urban markets.[10]

The rise of the export economies further increased the demand for commercial food within Latin America. The growth of internal demand, outside the cities, was most visible in the mineral-exporting countries that experienced major population shifts. The revival of mining in Mexico, Peru, and

Bolivia stimulated a substantial migration to colonial and new mineral districts in arid and high altitude zones incapable of provisioning from nearby sources. Heavy migration to the dry nitrate- and copper-producing Norte Grande of Chile created a competitive demand for food between 1875 and 1920.[11] The same occurred with the Amazonian rubber boom, the development of sheep ranching in Patagonia, and the rise of banana culture along the Caribbean coast of Central America. In other cases, such as Cuba and Yucatán, export agriculture contributed to the growth of domestic demand for commercial food by converting land use from food to export production, turning the peasantry into a proletariat dependent on purchased food staples.[12] Overall, urbanization and the rise of export economies greatly expanded the demand for commercial foodstuffs within Latin America.

The new external demand for food also had a substantial impact on domestic food supply. The price of sugar in New York or coffee in Hamburg, the weather in India or Kansas, the development of new industrial needs or taste trends in England or Italy—all impinged heavily on urban provisioning. Latin American agriculture offered the world food staples such as wheat and meat, luxury foods such as coffee and sugar, and nonfood products such as cotton, tobacco, henequen, and wool.[13] In the era of laissez faire, landowners were free, within the limits of their financial and technological means, to develop their land in the most profitable way possible. Food production for national consumption became merely one option for land use, and the urban poor of Latin America found themselves competing in a global market for agricultural products.

Latin American agriculture responded to the growing domestic demand for food and the new international market for a greater variety of its products with vastly increased output between 1870 and World War I. Landowners and governments drew on both local and foreign resources to meet the increased demand for agricultural products. In most of Latin America in 1870, unused arable or grazeable land was not only available, but extremely abundant. These were not necessarily prime lands, but given the variety of products in demand in the world market, they were potentially useful. Haciendas and Indian communities commonly possessed vacant or underutilized land susceptible to production. Many countries also held uninhabited, underexploited, or Indian-occupied territory capable of commercial agricultural production. The final occupation of Araucania in Chile, the "conquest of the desert" in Argentina, and the subjugation of the Yaqui in Mexico coincided with rising demand for productive land connected with urbanization and export economies.[14]

Labor was also available, despite the universal landowner lament about the *escasez de brazos*. After the abolition of the slave trade and of slavery itself, and of compulsory Indian service and tribute, labor was difficult to attract in many areas and through various periods. However, as demand rose, landowners proved quite adept at finding workers. Local populations were recruited by wage advances, land use opportunities, or as in the case of Guatemala, by outright legal compulsion. Contract workers were brought from as far as eastern and southern Asia. When the great exodus from eastern and southern Europe began, Brazilian and Platine landowners were able to lure a large labor force, including the longest seasonal migration in agricultural history, which transported Italians to Argentina for the grain harvest.[15]

The availability of foreign capital and imported technology further increased the possibilities of agricultural expansion. To transport bulky commodities at reasonable cost, a sine qua non for the export economies, foreign and domestic capital invested in railroads, docks, storage facilities, and improved sailing vessels and steamships. Modern methods of husbandry and horticulture, irrigation, labor-saving machinery, steel plows, fertilizers, and sophisticated processing techniques increased productivity and permitted exploitation of previously unusable land. Argentina and Uruguay offered the most dramatic examples of agricultural modernization, but change affected all parts of Latin America that became part of the new international order.[16]

The impact of export agriculture varied by country according to world market demand for its products, its own resources, and its ability to acquire foreign capital and technology. In most nations that developed export agriculture there was a certain amount of encroachment on lands supplying food for Latin American cities, pushing staple food production onto inferior or remoter soils. Banana culture, centered on sparsely inhabited Caribbean coasts, caused the least disruption of any agricultural export crop. On the other extreme, the world's voracious appetite for sugar created insurmountable competitive demands for land use in Cuba, where cane occupied virtually all the island's fertile flat land, pushing food farming onto poorer soils and greatly reducing production.[17] Coffee culture had diverse effects. In Colombia, coffee spread primarily in previously uncultivated highlands. Despite creating a competitive demand for labor and capital, it did not divert much land use away from subsistence and commercial food production. The pattern in Brazil was similar, at least until the rapid growth of São Paulo and Rio de Janeiro placed greater demands on food production. In Central

America coffee displaced food crops and grazing on the best soils, pushing small farmers onto land capable of producing smaller quantities of marketable surplus. [18]

On the Peruvian coast, cotton and sugar stimulated the extension of irrigation but also drove food staples off prime soils. [19] In Mexico, exports such as henequen and sugar cut into land used for subsistence or commercial food production; others, such as cattle and fruits and vegetables from the newly irrigated northwest, were developed on underutilized soils. The availability of land, labor, and capital allowed Mexico to increase food production for the domestic market but without satisfying the national demand for staples. [20] In contrast to the general pattern, the extension of livestock grazing and grain cultivation on the pampas of Argentina and Uruguay greatly increased the per capita availability of food staples, although urban food prices were tied to world market demand and did not consistently benefit the poor consumer. [21]

While the general contours of the extension of export agriculture are visible, it is more difficult to determine how much this affected food production for the domestic market except in the most obvious cases, such as Cuba and Argentina. [22] The quantity and quality of new lands brought into production for the home market, their distance from urban centers, and the amounts of capital and modern technology applied to these soils are among the variables that impinged on urban provisioning. In those countries where staple production failed to keep pace with the growth of domestic demand, Latin America's integration into the world market acted as a safety valve. The same ships and rail lines that carried exports also delivered staples from the United States, Canada, Argentina, and other surplus-producing countries to make up the deficits. Thus, during the heyday of the export economies, urban Mexicans, Cubans, and Peruvians generally suffered no shortage of staples.

Importing staples, however, had its own effects on urban provisioning. The common situation of importation through a single port of entry facilitated oligopoly in processing and distribution. Beyond that, the price of imported food reflected world market prices and the relative values of currencies. Several currencies, including the Chilean, Argentine, Mexican, and Brazilian, began to decline in international markets by the turn of the century, making imports dearer and stimulating exports, thus reducing domestic supplies. This pressure, combined with domestic production shortfalls in some countries, contributed to the rising food prices characteristic of the turn-of-the-century period. The available evidence on prices and wages indicates, moreover, that food prices rose faster than did urban wages.[23]

The Era of Mass Politics

The inflation of urban food prices coincided with and contributed to the development of working-class organization and militance. Denied effective participation in elite-dominated political systems, the urban working classes and other poor began to make their voices heard by protesting the cost of living and other conditions of their existence. There were colonial-style corn riots, as at Durango in 1878.[24] Strikes for wage adjustments in several countries aimed fundamentally at compensating for inflation. In Brazil, Chile, and Peru the high cost of living became a volatile political issue.[25]

Alarmed at the growth of discontent among the expanding urban poor, the elites urged their governments to adopt measures to prevent crises of urban provisioning. The municipality of Lima offered prizes in 1870 and 1873 for the best essay addressing the high cost of food.[26] In 1893, the *Diario Popular* of São Paulo warned, "It is necessary, even urgent, that São Paulo start now to plan its future food supply, or else it will soon find itself (if such is not already the case) at grips with scarcity, high prices, and hunger."[27] In Mexico by the 1890s, the common government response to unanticipated shortages was to suspend import and internal duties, lower rail rates, and provide staples at cost to the local juntas de beneficencia.[28] In Chile, farmers' markets were established and railroad rates cut to fight inflation.[29] Similar expedients were required in other countries from time to time.

Despite makeshift efforts to combat high urban food costs, upward pressures continued until inflation generated political movements that far surpassed the colonial tumulto in long-term impact. Food prices became an explicit political issue in Chile by the 1880s, when the rising cost of living sparked strikes for wage increases and became a primary issue of the new working-class Democratic Party. When food prices rose sharply in 1905 the stage was set for the confrontation known as the Red Week. The unions and Democrats organized a committee to repeal the "cattle tax," a tariff on imported cattle that they blamed for food price inflation. A crowd of fifty thousand protesters in Santiago went out of control and began rioting and looting. With the capital's army garrison away on maneuvers, the aristocratic Club de la Unión formed a "guard of order" to contain the mobs. The ensuing face-to-face class warfare, which left about three hundred dead and a thousand injured, served as a grim warning that unmitigated food price inflation undermined social tranquility and political stability.[30]

In Mexico, a crisis of urban provisioning preceded and contributed to the Revolution of 1910. Prices rose gradually through the nineteenth century, accelerating as the dual pressures of urbanization and export agriculture strained the supply of food staples. The acute problem began in 1907, when successive crop failures created shortages and, despite emergency measures, drove prices sharply higher. This stress was an important factor in generating the movement to overthrow the regime of Porfirio Díaz.[31]

Despite the numerous warning signs pointing to the growth of tension over urban provisioning, Latin American governments did not begin to modify the nineteenth-century approach until compelled by new political and economic conditions. While urbanization and external demand continued to strain the food supply, the most important change affecting urban provisioning was the extension of political participation to the urban lower and middle classes. The rise of populism had both cause and effect relationships to changes in urban provisioning. As a cause of political change, urban provisioning has been largely overlooked in favor of other factors. However, as both colonial tumultos and contemporary food riots show, provisioning crises were unfailing mobilizing agents. Through the 1900s, the "long live the king, death to bad government" jacqueries did not bring structural change, since their participants reverted to political marginality after expressing themselves. In the twentieth century, however, when the urban poor had acquired more sophistication, skilled leadership, and greater expectations, provisioning crises contributed to substantive political change by fostering class and political consciousness, enhancing the appeal of radical organizations and labor unions, and mobilizing the population to riot or to vote for change.[32]

Surveys of family income and expenditures reveal why the urban poor react energetically to food price inflation. These surveys, from a 1902 pioneering investigation to the most recent, graphically illustrate the predominance of food in the economic life of the urban poor. At least until very recent years, the findings indicate that the working-class family dedicated at least half its total income to food purchases (cases of 70–80 percent were not uncommon) and still failed to obtain adequate nutrition.[33] Fifteen urban surveys from seven Latin American countries done between 1933 and 1939 revealed that the food share of total family expenditures ranged from 49.5 percent in Caracas to 71.7 percent in Santiago, while United States and Canadian workers spent 33.5 and 31.5 percent, respectively.[34] Many families in the middle sectors faced similar budgetary strains. For the large underemployed and nonworking segments of urban society, which most surveys ignored, the situation was infinitely worse. A slight rise in food prices in Latin American cities meant the tightening of already constricting belts; an inflationary spiral meant disaster for the urban poor, who, unlike their rural counterparts, had no alternative to the market other than charity or crime for obtaining food.

The role of food prices in fostering political action is well illustrated by Chile in the early twentieth century. The previously mentioned 1905 Red Week had been the culmination of a widespread mobilization against rising food costs, and it in turn furthered the development of working-class political consciousness and militancy. The next major provisioning crisis, at the time of World War I, was an important but generally overlooked element in the "revolt of the electorate" that brought populist Arturo Alessandri to power. Claiming that "the products of the soil belong . . . to the citizens of the country," the left and the labor unions formed a Workers' Assembly of National Alimentation to organize support for relief from spiraling food costs. Within months, its program, proclaimed in massive demonstrations throughout the country, broadened to include general social and political reform. Factors such as high unemployment, the efforts of leftist organizers, the Mexican and Russian revolutions, and the government's ineptitude contributed to the 1918–20 mobilization; but the provisioning crisis that galvanized the popular ire must be counted as crucial. Similar problems of urban provisioning contributed to political change throughout Latin America at the time of World War I and afterward.[35]

After the working and middle classes achieved a share of political power, as in Uruguay, Argentina, Chile, and Mexico at this time, or became capable of exerting some influence on political decision making, as in most other countries, the politics of urban provisioning entered an entirely new phase.[36] Now the urban poor were represented through unions and parties or offered their electoral or physical support to populist leaders in exchange for promises of "pan, techo, y abrigo" or "pan y libertad," in that order.[37] This meant that in varying degrees and within limits, the urban poor for the first time could command government intervention in defense of their interests. Recognizing the political sensitivity of food and the new power of the urban masses, governments in the era of World War I began a close, month-to-month monitoring of the cost of living in order to anticipate and control violent reactions to inflation.[38]

As they achieved a greater political role, the urban poor increasingly recognized that their rising expectations of material progress and improved living standards would remain illusory so long as an inordinate share of their income went for nourishment. As a result, demands for affordable food, under various guises, became an ongoing and explicit issue in Latin American politics. Organized labor addressed the food issue by pursuing wage increases directly through industrial bargaining as well as minimum wage, cost-of-living, pension, and related legislation.[39] Organized or unorganized workers in large enterprises could partially satisfy their demands through company-subsidized food outlets, such as the Despensa system set up in Monterrey in the 1920s or the Industrial Social Service (SESI) and Commercial Social Service (SESC) programs established in 1946 in Brazil.[40] For unorganized workers, much of the middle class, and people working in small enterprises, these kinds of solutions were difficult to achieve, and for the underemployed and the nonworking poor they would have been meaningless. For these last groups, constituting the majority of the urban poor, the only way to ameliorate the high cost of living was to gain direct or indirect controls over the price of food. Farmers' markets, subsidized popular soup kitchens, free food distribution to especially needy and vulnerable groups, subsidized food outlets, export controls, direct ceiling prices on staples—these and related approaches were the only remedy for the politically less influential poor. For organized labor they were an important complement to the drive for increased income.[41]

The ideological underpinning of nineteenth-century provisioning policy came under attack in the 1920s and 1930s. Populist reformers desired government intervention to attain their goals, while conservatives came to embrace varieties of corporatism, with its emphasis on state activism, as an antidote to structural reform.[42] While tenacious defenders of liberalism survived, the general rejection of laissez faire meant that the nineteenth-century ideology of urban provisioning lost vigor, allowing the concept of a moral economy of food to gain favor.

Populist reform and the rise of state activism were accompanied by the development of nutrition consciousness and the "nutrition lobby." The activities and publications of the League of Nations' Commission on Hygiene in postwar Europe inspired the study of mass nutrition in Latin America and elsewhere. With the League of Nations supplying technical aid and staff, many Latin American countries had embarked on systematic studies of popular nutrition by the late 1920s and early 1930s. Most surveys combined nutritional with economic inquiry, and they revealed a stark truth about food in Latin America: The poorer classes were undernourished, some gravely, and nutritional status was a function of income. This was not only a social and humanitarian problem but also a matter of nationalism; to borrow from the Chilean lexicon, the "decadence of the race" resulting from nutritional deficiencies threatened the entire national well-being and security.[43]

The development of consciousness and knowledge of nutritional deficiencies led to the creation of diverse public and private entities that constituted a loosely defined nutrition lobby. By the 1930s Chilean nutrition had been scrutinized in at least a dozen surveys, and a National Council on Nutrition, a nutrition section in the Ministry of Health and Social Welfare, and a highly specialized *Revista de Medicina y Alimentación* had been created to further the investigation and propose remedies. The government of Uruguay established a Council of Proper Nutrition in 1928. Bolivia and Venezuela formed official nutrition agencies in the 1940s. By that time almost no country lacked public and private agencies concerned with popular nutrition, while UNESCO and the Food and Agriculture Organization of the United Nations provided international support for nutritional improvement. The cumulative output of these bodies—studies, statistics, educational material, policy recommendations—constituted a subtle but powerful force favoring government intervention in the food economy to remedy deficiencies attributable to poverty. The approaches and impacts of these agencies varied by country and by time. At a minimum they advocated nutritional education to make inadequate family budgets more nutrition-effective; at a maximum, they called for comprehensive national provisioning policies involving government control over the entire food economy.[44]

New Economic Pressures and the Institutionalization of Controls

New economic trends between World War I and 1960 added to the pressures for state intervention in the food economies of Latin America and led to the institutionalization of controls. World War I affected Latin American countries in different ways according to the kinds of commodities they exported and the degree of their dependence on food imports. In general, the greatest crises occurred near or after the war's conclusion, when merchant shipping became more available and Europe was in desperate need of foodstuffs; but the effects on food supply began during the war. Cuba gained tremendous export income from the wartime and postwar demand for sugar but as a heavy food importer had to compete on the world market for scarce staples. In Peru, the demand for cotton and sugar stimulated a shift of land use away from food. In the Platine countries, Chile, and Brazil, heightened wartime and postwar demand for staples stimulated exportation, causing shortages and higher prices at home, while in Chile the collapse of wartime demand for nitrates added massive unemployment to high prices.[45]

The war-induced crises in urban provisioning spawned potent political reactions as lower- and middle-class consumers mobilized to secure their sustenance. The case of Chile has been described earlier. In Peru, agitation and strikes against the high cost of living went on through 1922, contributing to the imposition of price controls, radicalization of the urban populace, election of the populist Augusto B. Leguía, and the founding of the APRA (Alianza Popular Revolucionaria Americana). In Buenos Aires, the Semana Trágica of 1919 occurred at a time of spiraling domestic food prices caused by competition with greatly inflated European demand. In Brazil, where ad hoc leagues to fight high food costs predated the war, rising wartime prices motivated São Paulo authorities to set up soup kitchens and farmers' markets and to remove workers from the city. The agitation culminated in the São Paulo general strike of 1917, when workers not only demanded wage adjustments but attacked the high cost of staples directly by looting food warehouses.[46]

A second externally generated economic crisis, the Great Depression, furthered the trend toward intervention. After two to seven years of price deflation, Latin America experienced food price and general inflation while still suffering large-scale unemployment.[47] To forestall unmanageable political conflict, several governments enacted price control measures. Control boards authorized to set wholesale and retail prices of food staples were set up in 1931 in every Colombian departmental capital. In 1932, Chile established the Comisariato Nacional de Subsistencias y Precios with vast powers over food and other essentials at all stages from production to consumption. The Mexican government established the forerunner of today's CONASUPO in 1937 to stabilize the rising price of maize and wheat. In Brazil, Venezuela, Chile, and elsewhere, farmers' markets and subsidized public restaurants were adopted in the 1930s. In September 1939, Brazil established the Supply Commission in the Ministry of Agriculture, with wide powers to regulate stocks and prices of foodstuffs and other essentials.[48]

Against the backdrop of uncontrolled inflation at the time of World War I and the move toward state controls in the thirties, Latin American governments did not hesitate to establish stringent supply and price controls over food and other essentials at the outbreak of World War II. With the aid of the United States Office of Price Stabilization and the Institute of Inter-American Affairs, many countries quickly set up agencies modeled upon those of the United States.[49] While the United States abolished most controls at the war's end, many Latin American governments, mindful of the post-World War I experience, extended the mandates of their price control agencies. The director of the program in Cuba, for example, reported to Congress in 1947 that controls might have to be prolonged indefinitely to cope with the post-war adjustment. In Colombia the same situation pertained, while in Brazil the government extended its program of closely monitoring food stocks and operating an extensive network of subsidized restaurants and food outlets.[50]

Latin American governments awaiting the return of "normal" conditions to abolish their wartime controls and return to laissez faire urban provisioning were disillusioned by new developments of the 1950s. Rather than disappearing, the machinery of provisioning controls became more widespread and firmly entrenched in this decade because of the onset of generalized inflation. Ranging from modest rates to bursts of over 100 percent annually in several countries, the rise in prices hit the urban poor hardest in their food budgets. Not only were the diets of the poor threatened but the working and middle classes, accustomed in several countries to a rising standard of living, also felt their gains threatened by inflation.[51] Most countries were forced in the interest of political stability to maintain or expand their machinery to curb food prices within the context of broader anti-inflation programs.

Another kind of economic pressure for controlling urban food prices emerged in the 1950s. Having embraced industrialization as the key to development in the aftermath of the Great Depression, the Latin American countries caught in the inflation of the 1950s faced the threat that high urban food prices would undermine their development goals. Two industry-related objectives were served by controlling urban food prices: Factory wages could be restrained, allowing the production of affordable consumer goods; and consumption of manufactured goods would be promoted by reducing the high food share of working class budgets. Therefore, governments and industrial lobbies worked together to foster low food prices in the cities.[52]

Specific responses to the growing pressures for food price controls varied from country to country. Most availed themselves of cheap United States surplus grains offered under P.L.480; while effective in countering high food prices, P.L.480 grains often had negative effects on domestic agricultural production.[53] Some of the Central American governments limited their actions essentially to monitoring stocks and regulating prices by controlling the supply of foodstuffs. Many governments employed a mix of import-export and currency controls, tax policy, subsidies, and direct price controls. Chile, with the longest and most constant history of food price inflation, developed Latin America's most complex system of controls over the food economy.[54]

By the end of the 1950s, if not earlier, regardless of ideology or form of

government, most Latin American countries had adopted urban provisioning controls. Some governments, including the Bustamante administration
in Peru and the Perón regime in Argentina, proclaimed a return to the
colonial concept of a moral economy of food.[55] Most adopted provisioning
policies as a matter of pragmatic necessity. In the era of mass politics and a
global economy of food, no government, whether electoral democracy or
military dictatorship, could afford the political and economic consequences
of unrestrained food price inflation. Whether actually serving the nutritional and economic welfare of the urban poor or simply preventing social
disturbances and political instability, the policies of urban provisioning had
become a central concern of governments and governed alike and a standard
feature of Latin American life.

Notes

1. International Labor Office, *Household Income and Expenditure Statistics (vol. 1,
1950–1964)* (Geneva, 1967). The food share of total household budgets is increasingly
seen as a prime indicator of standards of living: "The share of food in total expenditure
can be regarded as an [inverse] indicator of welfare; . . . it may be capable of acting as a
better indicator of welfare than measures based on income or expenditure alone"
(Angus Deaton, "Three Essays on a Sri Lanka Household Survey," *Living Standards
Measurement Study*, Working Paper no. 11 [Washington, D.C.: World Bank, 1981],
p. 1). The food share of household expenditure in less developed countries is typically
between 50 and 80 percent today (Ibid., p. 2). For an extensive bibliography of recent
Latin American household budget studies see Philip Musgrove, "The ICIEL Study of
Household Income and Consumption in Urban Latin America: An Analytical His-
tory," *Living Standards Measurement Study*, Working Paper no. 12 (Washington,
D.C.: World Bank, 1982), pp. 67–72.

2. This definition of poverty is necessarily vague. Current attempts to define it are
complicated by both empirical and theoretical problems; historical poverty is of
course even more elusive to define. The use of food share in defining poverty is a
newly rediscovered and much refined approach that goes back to Friedrich Engels.
For Latin America, a recent definition of poverty is household income less than two
times the cost of a "food basket" of adequate nutrition for household members; i.e.,
food share of over 50 percent indicates poverty. By this measure, it is estimated that in
1970 the proportion of poor urban households ranged from a low of 5 percent in
Argentina to a high of 40 percent in Honduras, with an average of 26 percent for urban
Latin America. By a more elastic definition, one which would include a larger proportion of households in which the food share is the primary expenditure, the estimated
range of "relative" poverty is from 25 percent of urban households in Uruguay to 52
percent in Brazil. The presumption of declining food share as a product of modernization suggests that at least one-third, and up to two-thirds, of urban households in the

early twentieth century in Latin America were poor by the food share-based definition of absolute poverty, and even more were poor by the definition of relative poverty. From the standpoint of the politics of urban provisioning, it would not be adventuresome to suggest that the entire group classified as relatively poor would be susceptible to mobilization in the event of food supply and price crises. See Oscar Altimir and Juan Sourrouille, "Measuring Standards of Living in Latin America: An Overview of Main Problems," *Living Standards Measurement Study,* Working Paper no. 3 (Washington, D.C.: World Bank, 1980), esp. pp. 30–45. I wish to thank William P. McGreevey for introducing me to the Living Standards Measurement Study working papers.

3. Geoffrey Rickman, *The Corn Supply of Ancient Rome* (Oxford: Clarendon Press, 1980); George Rudé, *The Crowd in the French Revolution* (Oxford: Clarendon Press, 1959); Richard C. Cobb, *The Police and the People: French Popular Protest, 1789–1920* (Oxford: Clarendon Press, 1970), pp. 215–324. For samples of news coverage of Poland, see *Time* 118, no. 6 (Aug. 10, 1981): 36; and *Time* 118, no. 13 (Sept. 28, 1981): 37.

4. The effectiveness of efforts to protect the poor urban consumer is a question lying beyond the scope of this essay.

5. For a methodological and bibliographic introduction, see Francisco de Solano, "An Introduction to the Study of Provisioning in the Colonial City," in *Urbanization in the Americas from its Beginnings to the Present,* eds. Richard P. Schaedel, Jorge E. Hardoy, and Nora Scott Kinzer (The Hague: Mouton, 1978), pp. 99–129; an excellent overview is Constantino Bayle, "Capítulo de abastos en la historia americana," *Razón y Fe: Revista Mensual Hispanoamericana* 49, no. 622 (1949): 294–311; 50, no. 632–33 (1950): 274–85; and 50, no. 639 (1951): 388–403 (title varies slightly); on Brazil, Caio Prado Júnior, *Historia económica do Brasil,* 12th ed. (São Paulo: Editôra Brasilense, 1970), pp. 41–46; and Charles R. Boxer, *Portuguese Society in the Tropics: The Municipal Councils of Goa, Macao, Bahia, and Luanda, 1510-1800* (Madison: University of Wisconsin Press, 1965), pp. 103–107.

6. Quoted in Eric Van Young, *Hacienda and Market in Eighteenth-Century Mexico: The Rural Economy of the Guadalajara Region, 1675-1820* (Berkeley: University of California Press, 1981), p. 43.

7. On the provisioning function of the municipality, see: Constantino Bayle, *Los cabildos seculares en la América española* (Madrid: Sapientia, 1952), pp. 453–500; and Francisco Domínguez y Compañy, "Funciones económicas del cabildo colonial hispanoamericano," in *Contribuciones a la historia municipal de América* by Rafael Altamira y Crevea, et al. (Mexico City: Instituto Panamericano de Geografía e Historia, 1951), pp. 137–78. Recent studies of eighteenth-century Mexico suggest that, at least in that time and place, the moral economy of food was more theoretical than real. See Enrique Florescano, *Precios del maíz y crisis agrícolas en México (1708-1810)* (Mexico City: Colegio de México, 1969); Van Young, *Hacienda and Market,* pp. 43–71; John C. Super, "Bread and the Provisioning of Mexico City in the Late Eighteenth Century," *Jahrbuch für Geschichte von Staat, Wirtschaft, und Gesellschaft Lateinamerikas* 19 (1982): 159–82; and John C. Super, "Pan, alimentación, y política en

Querétaro en la última decada del siglo XVIII," *Historia Mexicana* 30, no. 2 (Oct.–Dec. 1980): 247–72.

8. A summary of Liberal philosophy is found in William Rex Crawford, *A Century of Latin-American Thought,* rev. ed. (Cambridge: Harvard University Press, 1961). For samples of municipal law see: Buenos Aires, Oficina de Información Municipal, *Recopilación de los debates de leyes orgánicas municipales y sus textos definitivos,* vol. 1: *1824–1876* (Buenos Aires: H. Consejo Deliberante de la Ciudad, 1938): 60–65; João Baptista Cortines Laxe, *Regimento das câmaras municipales* (Rio de Janeiro: Eduardo e Henrique Laemmert, Editores, 1868); Uruguay, *Código municipal* (Montevideo: Tipografía Goyena, 1893); and Juan José Calle, *Diccionario de la legislación municipal del Perú* (Lima: Imprenta Torres Aguirre, 1906–11), 1: 6–7.

9. Tulio Halperín Donghi, *The Aftermath of Revolution in Latin America,* trans. Josephine de Bunsen (New York: Harper and Row, 1973), pp. 60–70; Charles C. Griffin, *Los temas sociales y económicos en la época de la independencia* (Caracas: Fundación John Boulton and Fundación Eugenio Mendoza, 1962), pp. 31–52; and William P. Glade, *The Latin American Economies: A Study of Their Institutional Evolution* (New York: Van Nostrand, Reinhold, 1969), pp. 175–210. See also the essay by Vincent Peloso in this volume.

10. Nicolás Sánchez-Albornoz, *The Population of Latin America: A History,* trans. W. A. R. Richardson (Berkeley: University of California Press, 1974), p. 192; and Richard M. Morse, ed., *The Urban Development of Latin America, 1750–1920* (Stanford: Center for Latin American Studies, Stanford University, 1971), pp. 23, 37, 54, 95. Close ties between recent migrants and their rural places of origin are suggested in Robert Oppenheimer, "Rural-Urban Migration and the Role of the Railroads in the Chilean Central Valley in the Nineteenth Century," in *Population Growth and Urbanization in Latin America,* eds. John Hunter et al. (Cambridge, Mass.: Schenkman, 1983), pp. 57–75.

11. For the Chilean case of market expansion, see Thomas C. Wright, "Agriculture and Protectionism in Chile, 1880–1930," *Journal of Latin American Studies* 7 (1975): 48–49.

12. For example, see Ramiro Guerra y Sánchez, *Sugar and Society in the Caribbean: An Economic History of Cuban Agriculture,* trans. Marjory M. Urquidi (New Haven: Yale University Press, 1964), pp. 29–99; and Allen Wells, "Henequen and Yucatan: An Analysis in Regional Economic Development, 1876–1915" (Ph.D. diss., Dept. of History, State University of New York at Stony Brook, 1979).

13. See Roberto Cortés Conde, *The First Stages of Modernization in Spanish America,* trans. Toby Talbot (New York: Harper and Row, 1974); Glade, *Latin American Economies,* pp. 175–289; and Sanford A. Mosk, "Latin America and the World Economy, 1850–1914," *Inter-American Economic Affairs* 2, no. 3 (1948): 53–82.

14. Glade, *Latin American Economies,* pp. 236–39; Roberto Cortés Conde, "Patrones de asentamiento y explotación agropecuaria en los nuevos territorios argentinos (1890–1910)," in *Tierras nuevas: Expansión territorial y ocupación del suelo en América (siglos XVI-XIX),* by Alvaro Jara et al. (Mexico City: Colegio de México, 1969),

pp. 105–20, indicates that the total cultivated area in Argentina expanded from 2.5 million to 24 million hectares between 1888 and 1913. Other cases were less dramatic, but significant.

15. The excellent essays in *Land and Labour in Latin America: Essays on the Development of Agrarian Capitalism in the Nineteenth and Twentieth Centuries*, eds. Kenneth Duncan and Ian Rutledge (Cambridge: Cambridge University Press, 1977) address the questions of labor recruitment in all its varieties.

16. Examples of technological change are discussed in James R. Scobie, *Revolution on the Pampas: A Social History of Argentine Wheat, 1860–1910* (Austin: University of Texas Press, 1964), pp. 81–86; and Arnold J. Bauer, *Chilean Rural Society from the Spanish Conquest to 1930* (Cambridge: Cambridge University Press, 1975), pp. 101–106. Glade, *Latin American Economies*, pp. 216–27, gives an overview of foreign investment; for the British, see J. Fred Rippy, *British Investments in Latin America, 1822–1949* (Minneapolis: University of Minnesota Press, 1959).

17. Guerra y Sánchez, *Sugar and Society*, pp. 29–99; Cortés Conde, *First Stages*, pp. 29–56.

18. Marco Palacios, *Coffee in Colombia, 1850–1970: An Economic, Social, and Political History* (Cambridge: Cambridge University Press, 1980), pp. 55–76; William H. Durham, *Scarcity and Survival in Central America: Ecological Origins of the Soccer War* (Stanford: Stanford University Press, 1979), pp. 33–36, 40–44; and Mitchell A. Seligson, *Peasants of Costa Rica and the Development of Agrarian Capitalism* (Madison: University of Wisconsin Press, 1980), pp. 22–27.

19. See the essay in this book by Vincent Peloso.

20. Luis Cossío Silva, "La agricultura" and "La ganadería," in *Historia moderna de México*, ed. Daniel Cosío Villegas (Mexico City: Editorial Hermes, 1965), vol. 7, part 1:1–178; and John H. Coatsworth, "Anotaciones sobre la producción de alimentos durante el Porfiriato," *Historia Mexicana* 26, no. 2 (Oct.–Dec. 1976): 167–87.

21. Scobie, *Revolution on the Pampas*, pp. 99–113; Aldo Ferrer, *The Argentine Economy*, trans. Marjory M. Urquidi (Berkeley: University of California Press, 1967), pp. 77–132.

22. The difficulties of assessing food production for this period are well illustrated in the case of Mexico, for which Cossío Silva, "La agricultura," using *Estadísticas económicas del porfiriato*, vol. 2: *Fuerza de trabajo y actividad económica por sectores* (Mexico City: Seminario de Historia Moderna de México, Colegio de México, 1965), argues that food production fell nearly 50 percent per capita between 1877 and 1910; Coatsworth, "Anotaciones sobre la producción de alimentos," claims that food production per capita at the end of the Porfiriato was essentially the same as at the beginning.

23. On prices, see Bauer, *Chilean Rural Society*, p. 233; Ramón E. Ruíz, *The Great Rebellion: Mexico, 1905–1924* (New York: W. W. Norton, 1980), p. 63; Roberto Cortés Conde, *Trends of Real Wages in Argentina (1880–1910)* (Cambridge: Centre of Latin American Studies, University of Cambridge, 1976). Currencies are discussed in: Fernando Rosenzweig, "Moneda y bancos," in *Historia moderna*, ed. Cosío Villegas,

vol. 7, part 2:789–885; J. F. Normano, *Brazil: A Study of Economic Types* (Chapel Hill: University of North Carolina Press, 1935), pp. 189–201; Frank Whitson Fetter, *Monetary Inflation in Chile* (Princeton: Princeton University Press, 1931); and Ferrer, *Argentine Economy*, pp. 110–15.

24. Cossío Silva, "La agricultura," p. 20.

25. John W. F. Dulles, *Anarchists and Communists in Brazil, 1900–1935* (Austin: University of Texas Press, 1973), pp. 36–70; Thomas C. Wright, "Origins of the Politics of Inflation in Chile, 1888–1918," *Hispanic American Historical Review* 53 (1973): 239–59; and Steve Stein, *Populism in Peru: The Emergence of the Masses and the Politics of Social Control* (Madison: University of Wisconsin Press, 1980), pp. 33–34.

26. Manuel Pardo et al., *Datos e informes sobre las causas que han producido el alza de los artículos de primera necesidad que se consumen en la capital* (Lima: Imprenta del Estado, 1870); and J. B. H. Martinet, *Estudio económico sobre la carestía de víveres en Lima (1875)* (Lima: Centro Peruano de Historia Económica, 1977).

27. Richard M. Morse, *From Community to Metropolis: A Biography of São Paulo, Brazil* (Gainesville: University of Florida Press, 1958), p. 233.

28. Cossío Silva, "La agricultura," pp. 16–30.

29. Wright, "Origins of the Politics of Inflation," offers an overview of the "cattle tax" question.

30. Wright, "Origins of the Politics of Inflation"; and Gonzalo Izquierdo, "Octubre de 1905: Un episodio en la historia social chilena," *Historia* 13 (1976): 55–96. The "food crisis" is discussed in Gonzalo Vial Correa, *Historia de Chile (1891–1973)* (Santiago: Editorial Santillana del Pacífico, 1981), vol. 1, part 2:455–65.

31. Ruíz, *The Great Rebellion*, pp. 79–83; Coatsworth, "Anotaciones sobre la producción de alimentos," p. 185.

32. This factor is often overlooked as a cause of political change. For the Chilean case, see Wright, "Origins of the Politics of Inflation." Witness also the role of food prices in stimulating urban rioting in Brazil, the Dominican Republic, and elsewhere in Latin America during 1984.

33. Jorge Errázuriz Tagle and Guillermo Eyzaguirre Rouse, *Estudio social: Monografía de una familia obrera de Santiago* (Santiago: Imprenta . . . Barcelona, 1903). See note 1, and for the case of Chile see Thomas C. Wright, *Landowners and Reform in Chile: The Sociedad Nacional de Agricultura, 1919–1940* (Urbana: University of Illinois Press, 1982), p. 118, note 5, and p. 120, notes 53–55.

34. Robert Morse Woodbury, *Food Consumption and Dietary Surveys in the Americas: Results—Methods* (Montreal: International Labour Office, 1942), pp. 1–6.

35. Wright, *Landowners and Reform*, pp. 105–109; the quotation is from Malaquías Concha, Democratic Party leader, in *El Mercurio* (Santiago), April 20, 1919, p. 23.

36. On early populist reform, see John J. Johnson, *Political Change in Latin America: The Emergence of the Middle Sectors* (Stanford: Stanford University Press, 1958);

and Michael L. Conniff, ed., *Latin American Populism in Comparative Perspective* (Albuquerque: University of New Mexico Press, 1982).

37. From the 1938 Popular Front campaign in Chile, in John Reese Stevenson, *The Chilean Popular Front* (Philadelphia: University of Pennsylvania Press, 1942); and from the speeches and writings of Aprista leader Andrés Townsend Ezcurra, *Pan y libertad: Ensayos y discursos en torno al Apra* (Lima: Ediciones Pueblo, 1968).

38. As examples, Chile began keeping these statistics in 1913; Mexico in 1929.

39. Although usually treated as separate issues, wages and related matters really addressed the cost of food, either to allow workers to obtain basic nutrition or to raise their standard of living by lowering the food share of household expenditure. This relationship is covered specifically by Germinal Rodríguez, "Los alimentos dentro del presupuesto obrero y su relación con los salarios," in *Política alimentaria argentina: Conferencias pronunciadas en la campaña de educación alimentaria* (Buenos Aires, Ministerio de Salud Pública de la Nación, 1951), pp. 59–90.

40. S. H. Gamble, *The Despensa System of Food Distribution: A Case Study of Monterrey, Mexico* (New York: Praeger, 1970); Morse, *From Community to Metropolis*, p. 213, indicates that SESI (Industrial Social Services) and SESC (Commercial Social Services) together set up thirty-seven "supply posts" in São Paulo in 1946 and undersold retailers by 30–50 percent, forcing food price levels down.

41. Wright, *Landowners and Reform*, pp. 105–17.

42. On corporatism, see Fredrick B. Pike and Thomas Stritch, eds., *The New Corporatism: Socio-Political Structures in the Iberian World* (Notre Dame, Ind.: Notre Dame University Press, 1974); and James M. Malloy, ed., *Authoritarianism and Corporatism in Latin America* (Pittsburgh: University of Pittsburgh Press, 1977).

43. Wright, *Landowners and Reform*, pp. 112–14. An incomplete list of surveys is found in Woodbury, *Food Consumption*, pp. 3, 62–63; Chile, Congreso Nacional, Cámara de Senadores, *Sesiones ordinarias en 1938* (Santiago, 1939), pp. 1200, 1289.

44. Wright, *Landowners and Reform*, pp. 113–14. For examples of these activities see: Uruguay, Ministerio de Instrucción Pública, *Las actividades de la Comisión Nacional de Alimentación Correcta desde su iniciación hasta la fecha* . . . (Montevideo: Peña y Cia., Imprenta, 1933); Venezuela, Ministerio de Sanidad y Asistencia Social, Instituto Nacional Pro-Alimentación Popular, *Organización y labores* . . . (Caracas: Poligráfica Nacional, 1949).

45. Fernando Berenguer, *El problema de las subsistencias en Cuba* . . . (Havana: Imprenta "El Arte," 1918); L. S. Rowe, *The Early Effects of the European War upon the Finance, Commerce, and Industry of Chile* (New York: Oxford University Press, 1918); L. S. Rowe, *El Perú y la guerra de 1914* (Lima, 1975); and Guido Di Tella and Manuel Zymelman, *Los ciclos económicos argentinos* (Buenos Aires: Editorial Paidós, 1973), pp. 129–86.

46. Ernesto Yepes del Castillo, *Perú, 1829–1920: Un siglo de desarrollo capitalista* (Lima: Instituto de Estudios Peruanos-Campodónico, 1972), pp. 267–75; Steve Stein, "Populism in Peru: APRA, the Formative Years," in *Latin American Populism in Comparative Perspective*, ed. Michael L. Conniff (Albuquerque: University of New

Mexico Press, 1982), pp. 113–19; Peru, Ministerio de Hacienda, Inspección Fiscal de Subsistencias, *Legislación y reglamentación sobre subsistencias*, 1ª parte: *1914–1918* (Lima: Imprenta Torres Aguirre, 1921); Di Tella and Zymelman, *Ciclos económicos*, pp. 129–86; Morse, *From Community to Metropolis*, pp. 207–210; Dulles, *Anarchists and Communists in Brazil*, pp. 49–51; and David Rock, *Politics in Argentina, 1890–1930: The Rise and Fall of Radicalism* (Cambridge: Cambridge University Press, 1975), pp. 125–217.

47. Retail food prices fell in 1929 or 1930 and began to climb in 1932 in Chile, in 1934 in Brazil, and in 1936 and 1937 in Mexico. See: Chile, Dirección General de Estadística, *Anuario estadístico, año 1942: Comercio interior y comunicaciones* (Santiago, 1942), p. 46; U.S., Office of Price Administration, Foreign Information Branch, "Price Control, Prices, Cost of Living, Rationing: Brazil" (Washington, D.C., 1943, Mimeographed), pp. 34–35; Guillermo Martínez Domínguez, *Intentos de control de precios en México* (Mexico City: Secretaría de Educación Pública, 1950), pp. 48–49.

48. Decree no. 1971, Nov. 3, 1931, in U.S., Office of Price Administration, "Colombia: Price Control and Rationing" (Washington, D.C., 1943, Mimeographed), pp. 19–21; Guillermo Torres Orrego, "El Comisariato General de Subsistencias y Precios de la República" (thesis, University of Chile, Santiago, 1947); Martínez Domínguez, *Intentos de control*, pp. 7–13, traces the evolution of Mexican price-regulating agencies from 1937 to 1950; Woodbury, *Food Consumption*, p. iv; Venezuela, Instituto Pro-Alimentación Popular, *Organización*, p. 13; U.S., Office of Price Administration, "Price Control . . . Brazil," p. 2.

49. On the general United States role, see U.S., Institute of Inter-American Affairs, Food Supply Division, *Paraguayan Rural Life: Survey of Food Problems, 1943–1945* (Washington, D.C., 1946). See also the Office of Price Administration reports cited above.

50. Cuba, Ministerio de Comercio, *Política de abastecimientos del Presidente Dr. Ramón Grau San Martín* . . . (Havana: Editorial Publicitas, 1947), pp. 12–15; Umberto Peregrino, *O SAPS em 1949* (Rio de Janeiro: Gráfica TUPY, 1949); Brazil, Conselho Coordenador do Abastecimento, *Balanço alimentar, 1945–1957* (Rio de Janeiro, 1961). See also the essay by Lana L. Hall in this book.

51. Rosemary Thorp and Laurence Whitehead, eds., *Inflation and Stabilisation in Latin America* (New York: Holmes and Meier, 1979) includes extensive bibliography; and Celso Furtado, *Economic Development of Latin America: Historical Background and Contemporary Problems*, trans. Suzette Macedo, 2nd ed. (Cambridge: Cambridge University Press, 1976), pp. 120–30. John Wells, "Industrial Accumulation and Living Standards in the Long Run: The São Paulo Industrial Working Class, 1930–75," *Journal of Development Studies* 19, no. 2 (Jan. 1983): 145–78, and no. 3 (April 1983): 297–328, deals extensively with food costs in a pioneering study of long-term living standards in an inflationary economy.

52. See Lana L. Hall's essay in this book.

53. Furtado, *Economic Development of Latin America*, pp. 107–30; and the essay by Lana L. Hall in this book.

54. The Chilean case is the most extreme application of controls, outside of Cuba, through 1973. See Kurt Ulrich B., *Algunos aspectos del control del comercio en la agricultura chilena, 1950–58* (Santiago, 1965); and Peter D. Bennett, *Government's Role in Retail Marketing of Food Products in Chile* (Austin: Bureau of Business Research, University of Texas, 1968). On Mexico, see Marye Tharp Hilger, "Decision-Making in a Public Marketing Enterprise: CONASUPO in Mexico," *Journal of Interamerican Studies and World Affairs* 22 (1980): 471–94; and William P. Glade, "Entrepreneurship in the State Sector: CONASUPO of Mexico," in *Entrepreneurs in Cultural Context*, eds. Sidney M. Greenfield, Arnold Strickon, and Robert T. Aubey (Albuquerque: University of New Mexico Press, 1979), pp. 191–222. The minimal policies operative in the 1950s in Central America are described in FAO, *National Food Reserve Policies in Underdeveloped Countries* (Rome, 1958), pp. 44–46. For information on food control policies in Brazil, Colombia, and Venezuela, see the essays by Lana L. Hall and Eleanor Wright in this book.

55. Peru, Junta Nacional de Alimentación y Nutrición, *Primera memoria anual de la Junta Nacional de Alimentación y Nutrición* (Lima, 1946); and Rodríguez, "Los alimentos dentro del presupuesto," p. 81.

Vincent C. Peloso

Succulence and Sustenance:
Region, Class, and Diet in
Nineteenth-Century Peru

At the end of the nineteenth century, Lima was the culinary as well as the political capital of Peru. The coastal metropolis dictated food customs far out into the provinces, influencing patterns of agricultural production and essential features of village life. A haute cuisine that had survived from the colonial period was one of the many ways in which the elites were distinguished from the popular sectors of society. Aristocratic residents of Lima enjoyed markets that were enviable for their ability to meet the diverse demands of a cosmopolitan center. As its reputation spread, the cuisine of Lima nurtured the idea that everyone in Lima ate as well as did the wealthy and powerful. This view, stimulated by the strength of agricultural commerce, prevailed in many quarters until industrialization made new demands upon the marketing of food.

Sharp distinctions between the wealthy and the poor in Peru did not become clear through dietary practices until after mid-century. Earlier, though differences in dietary customs and access to foods existed, they were not readily apparent. The marketplace abundance that enriched the cuisine of the prominent Lima families also fostered the belief that only among the provincials—Indian villagers, field hands, and landlords alike—did truly limited diets exist.

The wars of independence had interrupted food production and distribution and momentarily shattered the illusion of democratic abundance, but it soon regained currency as Lima merchants recaptured their power in the economy. By the late nineteenth century, the impoverishment of the popular diet began to attract attention. Gradually, as access to food by urban workers, plantation field hands, and Indian villagers became more limited, a general groundswell of complaints challenged the prevailing political order. The following essay describes some of the unique features of dietary customs in nineteenth-century Peru and then evaluates the social and economic patterns that brought food into the arena of politics.[1]

Relative Abundance of the Limeño Diet

The belief that both the poor and the wealthy of Lima enjoyed a more abundant and varied diet than did the provincials was based on a combination of image and reality.[2] While access by the poor to food was relatively good, common cuisine, habits, beliefs, and markets helped blur the real class distinctions in diet. Provincial diets varied greatly, but even the provincial elites were hard pressed to duplicate the variety that enhanced life for the humble of the capital.

Residents of Lima had access to a variety of seafood dishes and especially prized *ceviche,* a lime-marinated fish salad, and *parihuela,* a spicy seafood stew that enlivened urban menus in ways unknown in the highland interior of the country. While it was true that provincial centers in the highlands, notably Cuzco and Arequipa, boasted of distinctive regional specialties such as *carapulcra* (potato-thickened, chicken-pork soup), *ocopa* (crayfish-potato-peanut salad), or *papa a la huancaína* (sweet-and-sour potato salad), which were not found on the coast, variety was absent in the menu. After 1850, the introduction of Chinese cuisine into Peru accentuated the culinary leadership of Lima.[3] It was not until recently that provincial restaurants could duplicate the standard feat performed in nineteenth-century Lima *picanterías,* combining seafoods and Chinese condiments into criollo recipes for their guests. In contrast, regional variations on popular diet persisted in virtual isolation from one another until near the end of the era, but in any case few of them escaped eventual amalgamation into the capital's bill of fare.

As the center of cosmopolitan Peru in the early nineteenth century, Lima claimed that it satisfied the most varied demands of the palate.[4] With the largest, wealthiest, and most socially diverse population in the country, Lima was the preferred market for the products of coastal valley plantations and highland estates. Despite the nonstop civil wars or the hazards of bandit-plagued local travel, commentators reinforced the conviction that food was abundant by writing about the maze of stalls in the luxury food market, noting repeatedly that they always contained the ingredients needed to satisfy the most demanding formal banquet.[5]

Moderate population growth was a major factor in the abundance of the limeño diet. Observers commented with near unanimity on Lima's slow growth or actual demographic decline, trends influenced by the occurrence of epidemic disease in the early nineteenth century and by the absence of an industrial base. In 1812, ten years before independence, Lima housed an estimated 63,900 people, but by 1839 it contained only 55,627. Over the next thirty-seven years, the population grew by a modest 1200 persons annually.[6] Lima's demographic trends, then, permitted the colonial sources of urban food to continue supplying the capital with minimal strain for several decades after independence.

It was the extraordinary inventiveness of limeño recipes as well as the abundance that stimulated comment about criollo cuisine, leading foreign observers to assume a generalized alimentary well-being. Pungent *guisos* and *pucheros* of beef, pork and fowl, shell-fish *chupes, picantes* and ceviches, the last decorated with garlic, sweet potato and *choclo* (corn on the cob), arrived at the table spiked with an array of orange, red and green varieties of *ají* (hot pepper) and accompanied by unusual arrangements of potatoes, nut-flavored tubers, rice, or noodles. Needless to say, foreign guests delighted in the sweet drinks—including *chicha de jora* (corn beer) and chocolate, in addition to the strong local coffees, teas, and wines—that were served to drown the delicious pain of the ají. Thickly sweet Peruvian desserts like *mazamorra morada* (mixed fruit pudding) and others based on corn, wheat, rice, honey, quince, or tamarind preceded a cornucopia of tropical fruits. Near the close of such opulent, extended meals, diners and their hosts sank languidly into narcosis with fine rums and *aguardiente de pisco* (grape brandy). Overdosed and torpid, foreigners could be excused if they allowed their social sensibilities to be overwhelmed by the constellation of scents that flowered the evening air of Lima. No doubt they were encouraged in this direction by their hosts, who conveniently forgot that the range and strength of this cuisine was not accessible to the entire population.

Limeños of all classes shared cultural practices involving food. It was conventional wisdom that foods had "hot" and "cold" properties. No limeño in his right mind would consume rice and chocolate at the same meal, given the "cold" quality of the first and "hot" character of the second. The combination was feared to lead to all sorts of physical disorders—indigestion, fevers, perhaps even impotence or death. Above all, limeños admonished their guests to drink large amounts of water after a meal. Everyone followed this dictum religiously, and the common suspicion that everyone suffered for doing so found expression in a motto about the fountain in the central plaza of Lima: "He who drinks from this fountain will never leave Lima."[7] A romantic double entendre, it conveys a longing for Lima, but it also expressed a grim reality: diseases carried through the water system swept aside class barriers in early nineteenth-century Peru.

Similarities between elite and popular provisioning habits also had a public dimension.[8] For many years, the upper echelons of Lima shared the waters of the Rimac River with the city crowds. Nearly everyone bought water from the *aguadores*, ubiquitous vendors who ladled out portions from barrels filled at the reservoir. Those who could not buy this "fresh" liquid drank from the odoriferous common wells in the plazas. Not until the late 1850s did a private utility company extend the piping system throughout downtown Lima, making aerated water available to the upper class.[9] The food markets of the capital likewise were the object of some concern on the part of the upper class. Small and inefficient, they were not much better than the displays mounted on nearly every street corner by the casual vendors, usually slave women, whose activities were immortalized in the 1840s drawings and watercolors of the French artist Léonce Angrand.[10]

The complaints of merchants could not go forever unheeded. In mid-century the Ramón Castilla government finally addressed the marketplace issue by planning a large, airy market building to be erected on the site of the monastery of La Concepción, a massive structure bissected by a walkway. Half the monastery was appropriated for the purpose, the walkway was widened to provide street access, and plans called for a two-story facility. Building began in 1852 on 13,900 square meters of space, and periodically thereafter the facility underwent improvement. In 1905, a second floor was added.[11]

With the new marketplace came a further blurring of class distinctions. A larger number of food merchants was able to serve a socially more varied clientele, and with centralization of facilities came social mingling. Street corner marketing nevertheless retained its vigor after the central market was installed, and Ephraim G. Squier later spoke disparagingly of this persistent practice. He complained that even the government palace had been invaded by these shabby establishments, making the building look all the worse because below its balcony stood a "great number of low *chucherías, picanterías,* and what may best be described as 'junk shops.' "[12] It was easy for most people in Lima to satisfy a craving for exotic sweets. Street vendors hawked a splendid variety of candies and creams, and the crowds awaited with eager anticipation the arrival of the ice trains to fulfill the demand for *helados* (ices) of milk and essence of pineapple.[13]

A final element in the view that even poor limeños ate well was the general availability of two basic foods, wheat bread and beef. Wheat bread provided the state with an opportunity to support the notion of widespread access to the staples of survival. In the eighteenth century, when a disease apparently wiped out the wheat crop in Peru's coastal valleys, the government quickly turned to a flourishing Chilean wheat commerce to make up the difference.[14] A convenient colonial exchange (Peru sent sugar to Chile) became a liability in 1818. Independent Chile sought sugar elsewhere while Peru remained a Spanish colony, and when the exchange resumed in 1827 the Chileans held an advantage they never relinquished.[15] The lack of flexibility in Lima meant that the government had to subsidize bread prices and provide bakers with a special tax status.[16] Chilean wheat was essential for Lima. City residents consumed 9,699,679 pounds of bread in 1860, over 92 pounds per capita or roughly a quarter of a pound of bread a day. At that rate one could argue that most limeños had regular access to bread in mid-century.[17] Wheat flour also went into noodles, the basic urban staple, shaped as *fideos* or *tallarines* and sold by the case. Noodles enriched the cheapest soups found on the menus of picanterías.

Meat was even more plentiful than bread. Limeños encountered 10,195,000 pounds of meat in the Lima markets in 1860. This made 97.15 pounds per capita available through the *matadero* (slaughterhouse), an amount that allowed each person to consume a bit more than a quarter of a pound of meat per day, not including the finer grades of beef, pork, and specialty meats.[18] Bread on the whole remained constant in price from 1847 to 1870, while beef fluctuated slightly but also carried a very low price.[19] Other evidence bears out the general access to meat. Pablo Macera recently proclaimed that mid-century Lima may have consumed more beef than any other city of its day, rivaling London for the honor.[20] The infamous matadero of Lima, a monopoly and a stench-filled epidemiological disaster before 1855, was upon general complaint cleaned up and expanded considerably during the 1860s government of Ramón Castilla, ridding the city of its foulest eyesore and riskiest source of food. The slaughterhouse monopoly ended in the 1860s, but the problem of penning up increasing numbers of cattle before slaughter remained to annoy the sensibilities of urban residents until after World War I.[21]

It is no wonder that Lima residents believed that they had access to a surfeit of food with little social distinction. City markets were overflowing with a bewildering variety of edibles. The garden plantations of the surrounding Rimac valley, whence plantation owners sent slave women with products to crowd the major and minor markets of the city, supplied most of them. The capital's restaurants and picanterías did a brisk business. One had to search hard to find urban popular hunger. If the abundance that flowed to Lima from the varied sources of Peru's comestible riches was consumed more by the rich than the poor, few observers before 1860 noted any ill effects of it.

Region and Diet

By 1860, population growth rates in Lima and major provincial centers reversed earlier trends. Lima had experienced moderate growth since 1836, while provincial cities apparently lost ground over the same period. Though coastal Trujillo showed minute advances, Cuzco's population was down 0.4 percent from earlier figures. Arequipa and Huamanga (Ayacucho) followed the latter trend.[22] Yet the majority of the over one million Peruvians who required daily sustenance in the nineteenth century lived in the coastal valleys and in the highlands. When it became necessary to leave their villages for provisions before 1860, they encountered local products in the provincial market centers. Trujillo in northern Lambayeque department, the heart of the sugar plantations, and Huaraz, an ancient town in the northern highlands, competed vigorously with Lima for agricultural trade and proved stronger than other provincial centers. Jauja was at the crossroads of a highland pastoral and agricultural region that in 1826 "provided the city of Lima with an abundance of edibles."[23] Cuzco, the seat of the ancient Inca culture, and Arequipa, a stronghold of pastoral interests, provided their respective regions with wheat, but as the years passed they could not match resources with Lima suppliers.

The exaggerated geography of Peru accentuated the disadvantages faced by the outlying regions in their contacts with Lima. Remote highland population centers could not easily acquire goods from a coastal economy that favored the international market over sales in the provinces. Important towns like Tarma, Cerro de Pasco, Cuzco, and Arequipa rarely attracted coastal goods into the Andes, yet they readily sent local products to European markets. Shipping foodstuffs from Arequipa to the port of Islay and then by sea to Lima was easier than routing them from Arequipa to Huamanga or Cuzco in the nineteenth century.[24] The province of Jauja fed Lima its prime beef. Jauja supplied ice, which was carved from Andean glaciers, shaved to fit on the backs of mules, and sped down the roads to the capital on virtually the same day. It was said that insurgent armies never touched the pack animals for fear of turning the populace of Lima against their cause.[25] Similarly, the bulk of the finest wines and brandies of south coast Ica went to

Lima after mid-century, and when Chilean wheat shipments fell short of the city's needs, merchants pressed the growers of coastal Chancay province to make up the difference.

In contrast to Lima, where *alcanzadores* (monopoly creditors) dominated the major markets and *mercachifles* (petty merchants) eked out a living selling foodstuffs, highland food dealers faced more dispersed producers and consumers. Provincial landowners, their eyes on the living conditions of aristocrats in the capital, sought to emulate urban cuisine, an effort that met with mixed success. A few of them had ready access to the varied ingredients of traditional Peruvian dishes, while others paid a high price for them. Early in the century, the highland landowners' demand for expensive wines and liquor maintained an arduous commerce from the Ica vineyards to Tarma.[26] Meanwhile, in Huaraz, a northern agricultural center, such local products as sweetmeats, apricots, goats, maize, beans, garbanzos, lentils, *quinua* (a nutritious highland cereal), and wheat were available. Muscat grapes grew in Trujillo, where they were used for local wines. Nevertheless, few outsiders ventured to provincial estates, and landlords often drank alone. When the rigors of Andean trekking whetted the appetites of travelers, they rarely encountered meals worthy of comment. The standard fare they shared with landowners and clerics in highland towns consisted of corn, corn bread, beans, potatoes, and fruits such as *chirimoyas* and oranges. It was a lucky visitor who boasted that a rancher offered his guest "slightly smoked and salted mutton," a sauce of ají and vinegar, roasted potatoes, preserved apricots, and quince marmalade.[27]

Landowners approached the problem of access to foods with selfish concerns in mind, and their actions reflected these interests. Dairy belts developed around the towns of the coast where freehold peasants had little choice but to sell their produce in the nearby estates and towns rather than arrange for their barter and sale elsewhere. In Tarma, near the mines of Cerro de Pasco, demand for foodstuffs led to a catastrophic loss of communal lands. Communities that long had subsisted on potatoes, alfalfa (for mules), and the sale of their chicha found that demand for aguardiente outstripped that for corn beer. The Indians resisted a change in crops, but Tarma landlords, who foresaw high profits from the sale of mass-produced aguardiente at the mines, forced the communities into indebtedness, took their lands, and converted the basic crop from corn to sugar.[28]

Markets in and near Indian population centers served the communities in ambiguous, sometimes contradictory ways. Often goods were bartered, so Indian villagers could use their meager cash to pay rent and taxes.[29] The demands of the state were thus met while villages maintained their independence. But markets also placed the communities in jeopardy. The practice of supplying nearby towns and estates provided communities with cash, but it also weakened opposition to ambitious merchants and government officials who sought to move foodstuffs over long distances by centralizing control of rural markets. Indian desire for autonomy, not laziness as some maintained, was the reason for Indian reluctance to seek more distant markets.[30]

Regional marketing at low social cost was vital to the Indian communities. In other words, their subsistence depended in great measure on self-sufficiency and reciprocity.[31] When the communities produced surpluses, they sought out the most convenient markets on neighboring estates or in major regional towns. For example, in Huánuco province, several villages near the lowlands Loreto and Amazonas regions conducted a busy commerce with nearby estates in the 1880s, selling vanilla, coffee, cacao, and other highly desirable foodstuffs. The villagers found their taxes relatively easy to pay and avoided indebtedness. Indians in Conchucos province were not as fortunate. Villagers reluctantly turned to cash exchanges when their lands could not produce enough varieties of valuable foodstuffs to give them entry to several markets. Without alternatives, price competition from other villages forced them to use cash more than they would have liked, and village members soon found it necessary to work in the mines to subsist. In areas where land was poor, climate and topography made subsistence from agriculture a hopeless pursuit.[32]

The diet of Indian communities often was varied and substantial, and the communities struggled to keep it that way. Traditionally based upon control of the potato, whether it was boiled, roasted or freeze-dried (chuño), the Indian diet mocked the market system.[33] Alongside potatoes the highlanders grew maize and beans, and they used goat's milk, lamb, and guinea pig (cuy) to supply other nutrients. One observer noted guinea pigs so plentiful they overran the houses in villages he visited.[34] Foreign visitors could not easily adapt to the community practice of preparing *pachamanca* by baking corn, potatoes, and a whole goat on heated stones in the ground to celebrate feast days. Roast mutton "scorched to a cinder" by a hostess, who then "tore it to pieces with her dirty fingers" and served it with corn bread and potato, also offended the sensibilities of Charles Wilkes. Indian breakfast of stewed leftovers (*olla podrida*) and goat's milk hardly satisfied such travelers, but they envied Indian access to nut-flavored *olluca* (a tuber) and chupes of eggs and potatoes.[35]

Some highland foods clearly were associated with festivals, not with sustenance. Indian rituals, where community leaders wasted vast amounts of victuals in festive displays of power, provided additional evidence of the broad significance of food. In Cuzco, the festival of Corpus Christi required the consumption of *cocha yuyo* (seaweed) along with *chiri ucho,* a combination of pork, cuy, and other meats. Sapallanga, the festival of the Virgin of Cocharcas, called for a meal of *cuy con maní* (guinea pig with peanut sauce). Similar practices survive in the capital. The October celebration of Our Lord of the Miracles in Lima is not complete without *anticuchos* (grilled beef hearts) and *turrón de doña pepa* (a candy of rum and wheat biscuit).[36]

By comparison with the highland communities, laborers on the coastal plantation fields and in nearby freeholds ate meagerly. Spanish and then republican law in Peru called for a daily plantation ration of meat and vegetables for each slave, but in reality not even jerked beef was a major item of the landlord's budget.[37] Indeed, until the abolition of black slavery in 1854, the total diet of the plantation work force consisted of *menestras* (vegetables). Plantation owners sometimes supplemented the daily bowl of greens with chicha de jora and *guarapo* (cane whiskey) on the weekends and holidays. The diet of the indentured Chinese who followed the black slaves into the fields was thought to be even less adequate. Rice was not a significant food on early republican plantations, but by 1850 it was in constant demand to meet the needs of the Chinese field hands. Often rice was the only food distributed to the Asian contractees, who were fed hurriedly in the field at midday. At night, however, once the men were returned to the locked *galpón* (barracks), they were issued mind-numbing rations of opium, coca leaf, and the ubiquitous guarapo.[38]

The Widening Chasm: Diet and Class

The working classes of Lima fared little better than their provincial brethren as the demand for agricultural goods intensified after mid-century. Indeed, from the earliest days of the republic the realities of access to criollo cuisine departed significantly from the fanciful visions of plenty so easily attributed to the lives of the urban poor. Casual remarks about the city markets as well as the *comedores* of fine homes suggest that a different reality prevailed for many popular sectors. House servants, urban slaves, and unskilled elements of society found the prices at La Concepción market prohibitive. They were served in humble fashion by some of the street vendors and by the two "minor" markets that statistician Manuel A. Fuentes casually passed off as unworthy of consideration by his readers. They were located outside the fashionable downtown area, one of them in a former schoolhouse.[39]

But the Lima working class did not find it necessary to resort to minor markets until the markets were centralized. Thereafter, wages did not keep up with rises in the price of foodstuffs. A division began to emerge after 1860 visible enough to elicit comment from foreign observers. Squier described the distinction when he noted that limeño cuisine was at the time in a "transitive state." In the late 1870s it was an "incongruous mixture of foreign and native styles, the latter predominating in private meals, the former in all formal or public banquets."[40] While, Squier continued, "a puchero might because of its wide-ranging ingredients always be a universally available dish, the picantes seem to be going out of fashion with the better classes. . . . On the lower order, however, they retain their ancient hold, and in some parts of the city almost every second shop is a picantería, around which water-carriers, porters and negro and cholo laborers cluster in swarms."[41] Always popular was "chicharrón, lean pork fried in lard, cooked by zamba women over braziers on the sidewalk, one of the commonest of the viands." For the people on the streets, chupe, "a simple composition," was "a favorite breakfast dish."[42]

The free day laborer of Lima in 1864, whose wage had doubled in the preceding decade, was gratified that noodles and bread had remained fairly constant in price; but he watched in horror as the cost of rice climbed by 110 percent, butter by 53 percent, garbanzos by 110 percent, and beans by 163 percent over the same period.[43] Workers complained that high prices made these basic foods inaccessible because wages did not keep up, and by 1870 dissatisfied voices were frequently heard within the capital city. Concurrently, observers noted that agricultural production was undergoing significant and disturbing change. These issues prompted the municipality of Lima to sponsor a commission of inquiry. The commission polled a number of prominent planters in 1870 to examine the relationship between land use and the characteristics of leading crops. Their wide-ranging questions sought the cost of such items as meat, cereals, vegetables, fuel, liquor, flour, bread, and credit. In what undoubtedly was the first such effort undertaken in Peru, the commission attempted to draw comparisons between the prices of 1855 and those of 1869. Apart from the national census, no further systematic data gathering of this kind was conducted again in Peru until the turn of the twentieth century.[44]

The answers planters gave to this inquiry indicated that they were highly critical of the government. They attributed the steady rise in prices over the previous fifteen years to unnecessary government interference in the economy. The commission also showed that planters frequently abandoned food production in favor of export agriculture. They noted that in the previous decade coastal plantation owners who ordinarily helped fill Lima's need for meat "have stopped pasturing cattle and have given those lands over to the cultivation of cotton—resulting in the probability that next year there will not be sufficient meat to fill consumption needs."[45]

A persistent theme of the survey of 1869 is the disdain of the landowners for the lower class of Peru, both rural and urban. Prompted by the conviction that Indians and other nonwhites could not be educated to be rational consumers, the elites refused to encourage the formation of a domestic market. In a prize-winning essay of 1870, J. B. H. Martinet, the influential French agronomist who worked for the planter elite, warned against government involvement in the agrarian economy. If the difference between luxury imports and stable food prices was high unemployment, Martinet argued, then the government should view this as a problem for the unemployed to solve. They had, after all, no one to blame for their condition but themselves: "It is of little importance to society that those who, lacking means, refuse to work and starve to death. Society should not worry much about them."[46]

Martinet's advice reinforced a number of rarely spoken perceptions of the Peruvian masses held by urban and rural elites. One of the images that dominated their thinking was that of the coca-chewing Indian. It was said repeatedly that an Indian chewing coca leaf could work in the mines for long periods without much more nourishment than that provided by a daily ration of the leaf.[47] Another was the opium-sotted, indentured Chinese worker who likewise demanded little sustenance when he was under the influence of the drug.[48] Yet another was the black cannibal, an image that reduced blacks to an uncivilized condition. A popular tale about the 1872 uprising in Lima depicted a "brawny negro" who was a member of a Lima mob that hanged a rebel leader and burned his body. Afterwards, he was seen fighting "for a morsel of burnt flesh, which he gnawed with gusto," purportedly in vengeance against the fallen rebel.[49]

These images, accepted with little question by the powerful landowners and merchants, were the unspoken assumptions behind nineteenth-century agricultural policy in Peru. With a negative view of the consumer always before them, the elites easily could explain away the lack of a carefully managed, state-regulated domestic market. It was more convenient and profitable to trade agrarian products in European and North American markets and to seize upon those elements of the rural economy that yielded to the pressure of urban demand than to replenish provincial resources.

Alterations in the Peruvian economy continued unabated despite the 1869 survey. International cotton prices rose precipitously during the United States Civil War, convincing many coastal planters to abandon foodstuffs or fodder in favor of cotton. In the Piura-Chira region of the far north, in the area around Lima, and in the south coast Pisco-Ica region, new plantings increasingly were made in cotton, not food. Such modifications did not so much reduce the amount of food available as they affected the pattern of food allocation.[50] New markets arose and old ones disappeared, and crop changes sometimes led to bottlenecks and stimulated price rises. The diagram of marketing in Peru changed in the way the pattern of a cell is modified with adjustments of the microscope.

During the War of the Pacific, 1879–83, for perhaps the first time in the republican era, food scarcities became critical. In Lima, the government issued decrees to protect merchants and control prices, but shortages that incited looting occurred despite all efforts.[51] With the postwar recovery, the agrarian export economy returned to life, and the prices of food and other basic needs began to rise. Part of the blame for the price increases could be traced to population growth and cityward migration. The expansion of mining and the concentration of land in the hands of fewer owners sent new migrants to Lima, which contained 160,000 people in 1896.[52] A chamber of commerce survey in 1899 revealed a sharp upward movement in the cost of basic foods. Since 1892, vegetables had all but disappeared from the stalls, and food prices had doubled while wages on the plantations and in Lima remained virtually unchanged.[53]

The 1899 chamber of commerce survey highlighted two basic reasons for the cost increases: marketing problems and the impact of the world economy. Respondents specifically cited rises in the price of lard from the United States, an increase in Ecuadorean demand for Peru's goods, and damage to the previous year's rice harvest in India as causes for shortages in Peru.[54] Increased exports and reliance upon food imports were symptoms, however, rather than causes of Peru's difficulties. At the root of the sharp price increases at the turn of the century were unheeded population growth and migrations and a shift in land use from foodstuff production to export agriculture.

Lima was the center of discontent over food. Urban workers demonstrated in 1858 and in 1872 against import policies that threatened their livelihood and left them unable to keep up with high food prices.[55] Periodic bread riots hit Lima between 1861 and 1878, often necessitating the use of troops. The government cited bad weather and breakdowns in shipping schedules as the causes of shortages, but other factors may well have been involved. The rise in Lima's population to about 120,000 in the census of 1876, a 4 percent annual growth rate for a quarter of a century, may have passed unnoticed by bread merchants. In addition, for a number of years a monopoly of wheat shipped into Lima was held by José Suito, an Italian merchant who in the 1860s also controlled wheat storage in Callao. Whether he held back deliveries in order to boost prices is not clear. In any case, in several instances of mass discontent shops were stoned, and in 1867 demonstrations closed the bakeries in Lima.[56]

Within the decade after the Chilean war, bakery workers in Lima asserted their needs by forming a mutual aid society, and by 1900 they marched with textile and printing workers against rising costs.[57] In 1904, the Federación de Obreros Panaderos Estrella del Perú demonstrated repeatedly against high food prices, with beef and mutton costing over 30 centavos per kilo, flour and beans about 6.50 soles a quintal, and rice and sugar 12.50 soles per quintal. A government survey conducted in the same year supported the workers' complaints.[58]

Labor agitation later attracted the attention of presidential candidates. Among them, Guillermo Billinghurst listened intently to worker demands, and the workers showed their appreciation of his sympathy by hoisting a "pan grande" at his political rallies. Their actions symbolized the food problem on two levels. On the one hand, the "pan grande" gave an image of solidarity to the protests of workers; and on the other, it linked food prices to the electoral campaign, making food a presidential election issue. Billinghurst won the election but within two years was overthrown in a military plot. The workers in Lima and on the coastal plantations read this coup as a statement that landowner-merchant governments would ignore high food prices while they expanded nonfood agriculture.[59]

The government attempted to hold down prices in the face of market pressures and popular discontent during World War I. The flow of imported foods was often interrupted, giving rise to brief scarcities and erratic prices. In the meantime, workers on the coastal plantations argued that wartime export demands were cutting down their access to food staples.[60] A report by a leading analyst urged that production guidelines be set for "alimentary fruits" like wheat, "for which we are paying a strong tax to the foreign producer."[61] In response, the government prohibited the export of vegetables temporarily in 1917, placed controls on the marketing and price of fish, and provided for controlled public sale of beef through government markets in 1918. Various efforts to make domestic rice more widely available and to regulate its exportation suggest that conflicting interests buffeted a government too long accustomed to retreating from the marketplace.[62]

The advent of a sympathetic government under Augusto B. Leguía temporarily calmed popular fears after the World War. Leguía assumed the presidency in 1919, and in the next two years he implemented a number of existing programs to extend public service and exercise greater control over agricultural imports. His initial actions dampened working class anger, particularly when on coastal plantations the gap between wages and prices closed slightly. Very shortly, however, Leguía reverted to the standard practices of landowner-merchant governments. His reversals gave rise to new disparities between food prices and wages. The forces that had crystallized around the popular leadership of Billinghurst then turned to the newly formed American Popular Revolutionary Alliance (APRA). Its leaders spoke to the bread-and-butter issues for workers but moved cautiously to shape a sufficiently broad program.[63] It would not be easy to bridge the distance between the divisions created by the rise in food prices and growing demands for land reform.

Conclusion

Though hunger existed before the introduction of the industrial, export economy, it was not the fate of the average Peruvian. Even poor people in the highlands occasionally feasted on traditional ritual foods, practices that continued into the twentieth century. New market demands and changes in land use patterns did, however, reduce the diets of the poor by the end of the nineteenth century. Scarcity and price increases erupted into widespread discontent after 1890 in Lima. In the provinces, a complex, better-organized market system grew as urban demand expanded, leading to a breakdown of provincial subsistence farming.

Indian communities struggled to avoid the money economy that the markets introduced; success depended on agrarian versatility and their physical distance from market towns. By the early twentieth century rural resistance began to crumble as the new relationship between city and provinces took shape. The relative isolation of the nineteenth century gave way to a dynamic, though often conflicting, new system of production and distribution. Both highland Indians and the popular classes of Lima suffered as a result.

Notes

1. Key ideas for this essay came from Jack Goody, *Cooking, Cuisine and Class: A Study in Comparative Sociology* (Cambridge: Cambridge University Press, 1982), pp. 97–153; Baltazar Caravedo, "El problema del centralismo en el Perú republicano," *Allpanchis Phuturinqa* 12, no. 13 (1979): 9–50; Sidney W. Mintz, "Time, Sugar and Sweetness," *Marxist Perspectives* 8 (Winter 1979/80): 56–73; John F. Weeks and Elizabeth W. Dore, "Basic Needs: Journey of a Concept," in *Human Rights and Basic*

Needs in the Americas, ed. Margaret E. Crahan (Washington, D.C.: Georgetown University Press, 1982), pp. 133–34. I also am grateful to the following colleagues who read and rigorously criticized earlier versions of the study: Arnold Bauer, Clifton F. Brown, Harold O. Lewis, Cornelia Levine, Murdo J. MacLeod, Enrique Mayer, Sidney Mintz, Martin Scurrah, Eleanor Wright, W. R. Wright, and Thomas C. Wright.

2. William Bennet Stevenson, A Historical and Descriptive Narrative of Twenty Years' Residence in South America, 3 vols. (London: Hurst, Robinson and Co., 1829), 1:343–44; Ephraim G. Squier, Peru: Incidents of Travel and Exploration in the Land of the Incas (London: Macmillan and Co., 1877), pp. 57–59; J. J. von Tschudi, Travels in Peru, during the Years 1838–1842, trans. Thomasina Ross (London: D. Bogue, 1847), pp. 148–49.

3. An effort to recreate nineteenth-century criollo recipes is Francisca Baylón, Comidas criollas peruanas, 2nd ed. (Lima: Field Ediciones, 1959). These and other recipes identified in this essay may also be found in Baylón, Cocina y repostería, 5th ed. (Lima: Field Ediciones, 1960); Misia-Peta, Cocina peruana, 8th ed. (Lima: Editorial Mercurio, 1979). A variation on Peruvian cuisine that arose in Chile was studied by Eugenio Pereira Salas, Apuntes para la historia de la cocina chilena (Santiago: Editorial Universitaria, 1977).

4. For evocative examples in the contemporary literature, see Ricardo Dávalos y Lissón, Lima de antaño . . . , 2nd ed. (Barcelona: Montaner y Simon Editores, 1925), pp. 86–92; Ricardo Palma, Tradiciones peruanas completas (Madrid: Aguilar, 1952), pp. 86–87, 165–66, 518–21, 535–56, 618–19, 725–26, 971–76. Also see Adán Felipe Mejía y Herrera, De cocina peruana: Exhortaciones (Lima: Talleres Gráficas P. L. Villanueva, 1969).

5. Details on Lima markets appear most fully in José María Córdova y Urrutia, Estadística histórica, geográfica, industrial y comercial de los pueblos que componen las provincias del departamento de Lima (Lima: F. Moreno, 1839), pp. 37–39; Manuel A. Fuentes, Guía histórico-descriptiva, administrativa, judicial y de domicilio de Lima, 2nd ed. (Lima: Librería Central, 1861), pp. 126–28; Squier, Peru: Incidents of Travel, pp. 521–35; Stevenson, Residence in South America, 1:224–27; von Tschudi, Travels in Peru, pp. 152–53; Charles Wilkes, Narrative of the United States Exploring Expedition during the Years 1838 . . . 1842, 5 vols. (Philadelphia: Lea & Blanchard, 1845), 1:247–48.

6. Population and economic policy are discussed in several works: Francisco Graña, La población del Perú a través de los siglos, 3rd ed. (Lima: Imprenta Torres Aguirre, 1940), pp. 32–37; Pablo Macera, Las plantaciones azucareras en el Perú, 1821–1875 (Lima: Seminario de Historia Rural Andina, Universidad Nacional Mayor de San Marcos, 1972), pp. cii–ciii; Córdova y Urrutia, Estadística histórica, geográfica, p. 19; Fuentes, Guía . . . de Lima, p. 11; Wilkes, Narrative of the United States, 1:250; Francisco de Rivero, Memoria o sean apuntamientos sobre la industria agrícola del Perú y sobre algunos medios que pudieran adoptarse para remediar su decadencia (Lima: El Comercio, 1845), pp. 8–9, 14–15; Manuel A. Fuentes, Estadística general de Lima (Lima: Tipografía Nacional, 1858), pp. 40–45, 620–21, 670; Richard

M. Morse, "Trends and Patterns of Latin American Urbanization, 1750–1920," *Comparative Studies in Society and History* 16, no. 4(Sept. 1974): 416–47; Nicolás Sánchez-Albornoz, *The Population of Latin America: A History*, trans. W. A. R. Richardson (Berkeley: University of California Press, 1974), pp. 168–72; Emilio Romero, *Historia económica del Perú* (Buenos Aires: Editorial Sudamericana, 1949), pp. 259–70; Jorge Basadre, "La riqueza territorial y las actividades comerciales e industriales en los primeros años de la república," *Mercurio Peruano* 17 (1928): 5–31; Shane J. Hunt, "Growth and Guano in Nineteenth Century Peru," Discussion Paper no. 34, Research Program in Economic Development, Woodrow Wilson School (Princeton University, Feb. 1973).

7. Wilkes, *Narrative of the United States*, 1:216.

8. For comments suggesting that caution is necessary in the use of such concepts as "elite," "mass," and "popular," see Richard Graham, "Popular Challenges and Elite Responses: An Introduction," in *Elites, Masses, and Modernization in Latin America, 1850–1930*, by E. Bradford Burns and Thomas E. Skidmore (Austin: University of Texas Press, 1979), pp. 3–10.

9. Stevenson, *Residence in South America*, 1:224.

10. Léonce Angrand, *Imagen del Perú en el siglo XIX* (Lima: C. Milla Batres, 1972), pp. 45–46, 57–58, 77–78, 155–59.

11. Juan Bromley and José Barbagelata, *Evolución urbana de la ciudad de Lima* (Lima: Lumen, 1945), pp. 80–82.

12. Squier, *Peru: Incidents of Travel*, p. 46; von Tschudi, *Travels in Peru*, p. 151.

13. Ibid., pp. 136–37, 145.

14. The death of coastal Peruvian wheat remains a mystery. Mary Matossian, Department of History, University of Maryland, suggests that alimentary toxic aleukia (ata), a wheat fungus, grew vigorously in climates such as that of the coastal valleys of Peru (personal communication, 1983).

15. On the decline of wheat cultivation in Peru and the political problems occasioned by the Chile trade, see O. Febres Villareal, "La crisis agrícola del Perú en el último tercio del siglo XVIII," *Revista Histórica* 27 (1964): 133–36, who speculates that disease killed Peruvian wheat in the late eighteenth century. Also see Demetrio Ramos, *Trigo chileno, navieros del Callao y hacendados limeños entre la crisis agrícola del siglo XVII y la comercial de la primera mitad del siglo XVIII* (Madrid: Instituto "Gonzalo Fernández de Oviedo," Consejo Superior de Investigaciones Científicas, 1967); Sergio Sepúlveda G., *El trigo chileno en el mercado mundial* (Santiago: Editorial Universitaria, 1959), p. 32.

16. Basadre, "La riqueza territorial," pp. 18, 21–22.

17. Fuentes, *Guía . . . de Lima*, pp. 11, 158–59.

18. Ibid.

19. In addition to *El Comercio*, where beef prices in several grades were listed with increasing regularity over the century, the following sources give the food prices used in this study: Pablo Macera, *Trabajos de Historia*, 4 vols. (Lima: Instituto Nacional de Cultura, 1977); Alfonso Quiroz Norris, "La consolidación de la deuda interna peruana

1850–1858: Los efectos sociales de una medida financiera estatal" (thesis, Pontifícia Universidad Católica del Perú, Lima, 1980; for the use of this I am grateful to Karen Spalding); Juan R. Engelsen, "Social Aspects of Agricultural Expansion in Coastal Peru, 1825–1878" (Ph.D. diss., Dept. of History, University of California, Los Angeles, 1977); Romero, Historia económica; Lima, Municipalidad, Datos e informes sobre las causas que han producido el alza de precios de los artículos de primera necesidad que se consumen en la capital (Lima: Imprenta del Estado, 1870); Lima, Cámara de Comercio, Memoria presentada por el Consejo de Administración de la Cámara de Comercio de Lima a la Junta General del 11 de febrero de 1899, siendo presidente el señor D. Manuel Candamo (Lima: Imprenta Gil, 1899); Peter Blanchard, The Origins of the Peruvian Labor Movement, 1883–1919 (Pittsburgh: University of Pittsburgh Press, 1982).

20.   Macera, Plantaciones azucareras, p. cxxxvii.

21.   Fuentes, Guía . . . de Lima, p. 126; Bromley and Barbagelata, Evolución urbana, pp. 80–81; Engelsen, "Social Aspects of Agricultural Expansion," p. 275.

22.   Macera, Plantaciones azucareras, pp. ci–ciii; Alberto Flores-Galindo, Arequipa y el sur andino: Ensayo de historia regional (siglos XVIII–XX) (Lima: Editorial Horizonte, 1977), p. 54.

23.   José de Larrea, "Bases para la estadística del Perú, 1826," in Tierra y población en el Perú (SS. XVIII–XIX), ed. Pablo Macera, 4 vols. (Lima: Seminario de Historia Rural Andina, 1972), 3:550–52. See contemporary remarks on Jauja in Mariano Eduardo de Rivero y Ustáriz, Colección de memorias científicas, agrícolas é industriales publicadas en distintas épocas, 2 vols. (Brussels: H. Goemaere, 1857), 2:85–176, 211–17.

24.   Nelson Manrique, "El desarollo del mercado interior en la sierra central, 1830–1910 (informe de investigación)," Serie: Andes Centrales 6 (Lima: Universidad Nacional Agraria, Taller de Estudios Andinos, Dec. 1978): 23; Macera, ed., Tierra y población, 3:644; and see the discussion of Andean communication problems in Francis de Castelnau, Expédition dans les parties centrales de l'Amérique du Sud, de Rio de Janeiro à Lima, et de Lima au Pará: Exécutée par ordre du gouvernement français pendant les anées 1843 à 1847, 4 vols. (Paris: P. Bertrand, 1851), 3:399–405, 446–61.

25.   Stevenson, Residence in South America, 1:227; von Tschudi, Travels in Peru, pp. 136–37.

26.   Fiona Wilson, "Propiedad e ideología: Estudio de una oligarquía en los andes centrales siglo XIX," Análisis 8–9 (May–Dec. 1979): 46–48.

27.   Wilkes, Narrative of the United States, 1:269–70, 286.

28.   Engelsen, "Social Aspects of Agricultural Expansion," pp. 260–62; Fiona Wilson, "The Conflict over Indian Land in Nineteenth Century Peru," in State and Region in Latin America: A Workshop, eds. G. A. Banck, R. Buve, and L. van Vroomhoven (Amsterdam: Centrum voor Studie en Documentatie van Latijns-Amerika, 1981), pp. 94–103.

29.   Macera, ed., Tierra y población, 3:599–600, 629–42; 4:867–76.

30.   Ibid., 2:505–14.

31. Personal communication, Enrique Mayer, University of Illinois, 1983.

32. Macera, ed., *Tierra y población,* 4:731–37, 751–61.

33. Jorge Christiansen González, *El cultivo de la papa en el Perú* (Lima: Editorial Jurídica, 1967), pp. 17–38.The standard reference on the potato, *chuño,* and on the botanical theories about the spread of the potato to Europe from the Andes is Redcliffe N. Salaman, *The History and Social Influence of the Potato* (Cambridge: Cambridge University Press, 1949; reprinted, 1970), pp. 1–72.

34. Stevenson, *Residence in South America,* 2:44, 49–51.

35. Wilkes, *Narrative of the United States,* 1:268–69.

36. See note 31.

37. Stevenson, *Residence in South America,* 1:222, 268, 274–75.

38. Macera, *Plantaciones azucareras,* p. cxlvii.

39. Fuentes, *Guía . . . de Lima,* p. 128.

40. Squier, *Peru: Incidents of Travel,* p. 57.

41. Ibid.

42. Ibid.

43. Macera, *Plantaciones azucareras,* pp. lxxxv–lxxxix; Hunt, "Growth and Guano," pp. 81–83; Engelsen, "Social Aspects of Agricultural Expansion," p. 275; Quiroz Norris, "La consolidación," p. 288.

44. Lima, Municipalidad, *Datos e informes,* p. 4.

45. Ibid.

46. J. B. H. Martinet, *Carestia de víveres en Lima, 1875* (Lima: Centro Peruano de Historia Económica, 1875; reprinted, 1977), p. 21.

47. Stevenson, *Residence in South America,* 2:63–64.

48. See Michael Gonzales, "Cayaltí: The Formation of a Rural Proletariat on a Peruvian Sugar Cane Plantation, 1875–1933," (Ph.D. diss., Dept. of History, University of California, Berkeley, 1978), pp. 175–80; Macera, *Plantaciones azucareras,* pp. cxvi–cxx; and especially Carlos Enrique Paz Soldán, "El vicio amarillo en Lima," *La Crónica* (Lima), April 23, 1916, p. 13.

49. The story appeared in May Crommelin, *Over the Andes from the Argentine to Chili and Peru* (London: R. Bentley and Son, 1896), pp. 291–92.

50. Henry K. Slajfer, "Los enclaves de exportación y la agricultura alimenticia en el Perú de los años 1890–1920: A propósito de las tesis de R. Thorp y G. Bertram," *Histórica* (Lima) 4, no. 2 (Dec. 1980): 243–54. But also see Rosemary Thorp and Geoffrey Bertram, *Peru 1890–1977: Growth and Policy in an Open Economy* (New York: Columbia University Press, 1978), pp. 132–40; Ernesto Yepes del Castillo, *Perú, 1820–1920: Un siglo de desarrollo capitalista* (Lima: Instituto de Estudios Peruanos, 1972), pp. 32–51.

51. Macera, ed., *Tierra y población,* 4:224–27; Rolando Pachas Castilla, "Impacto de la Guerra del Pacífico en las haciendas de Ica, Chincha, Pisco y Cañete," in *La Guerra del Pacífico,* by Wilson Reátegui et al., 2 vols. (Lima, 1979), 1:197–220.

52. José G. Clavero, *Demografía de Lima en 1884* (Lima: J. F. Solís, 1885), pp. 29–30; Bromley and Barbagelata, *Evolución urbana,* pp. 90–91.

53. Lima, Cámara de Comercio, *Memoria,* pp. 36–38.

54. Ibid.; Blanchard, *Peruvian Labor Movement,* p. 52, table 8.

55. José Silva Santisteban, *Breves reflexiones sobre los sucesos ocurridos en Lima y el Callao, con motivo de la importación de artefactos* (Lima: Imprenta Calle de Jesus Nazareño, 1859, 1977), p. 24.

56. Engelsen, "Social Aspects of Agricultural Expansion," pp. 269–72; Estuardo Núñez, *Viajeros alemanes al Perú* . . . (Lima: Universidad Nacional Mayor de San Marcos, 1969), p. 87; von Tschudi, *Travels in Peru,* p. 121, noted the early involvement of Italian immigrants in the commerce of Lima.

57. Denis Sulmont S., *Historia del movimiento obrero en el Perú de 1890 a 1977* (Lima: Tarea, 1977), pp. 26–27. For details on the earliest efforts to organize sectors of labor and the prominence of food issues in this struggle, see Blanchard, *Peruvian Labor Movement,* pp. 15–28.

58. Ibid., pp. 22–24; Romero, *Historia económica,* p. 431.

59. Steve Stein, *Populism in Peru; The Emergence of the Masses and the Politics of Social Control* (Madison: University of Wisconsin Press, 1980), p. 33; Blanchard, *Peruvian Labor Movement,* pp. 84–90.

60. Bill Albert, "Yanaconaje and Cotton Production on the Peruvian Coast: Share-croppers in the Cañete Valley during World War One" (Paper delivered at the International Congress of Americanists, Manchester, England, Sept. 7, 1982), p. 9; Heraclio Bonilla and Alejandro Rabanal, "La Hacienda San Nicolás (Supe) y la Primera Guerra Mundial," *Económica* (La Plata) 2, no. 3 (June 1979): 6, 21–22.

61. Quoted in César Antonio Ugarte, *Bosquejo de la historia económica del Perú* (Lima: Imprenta Cabieses, 1926), p. 72.

62. Perú, Ministerio de Hacienda, Inspección Fiscal de Subsistencias, *Legislación y reglamentación sobre subsistencias,* first part: *1914–1918* (Lima: Imprenta del Estado, 1921), pp. 199–241, 253–55.

63. Peter Klarén, *Modernization, Dislocation and Aprismo: Origins of the Peruvian Aprista Party, 1870–1932* (Austin: University of Texas Press, 1973), chap. 5; Stein, *Populism in Peru,* chaps. 6–7. Both studies suggest the difficulties of focusing the party's program.

James W. Wilkie and
Manuel Moreno-Ibáñez

Latin American Food Production and Population in the Era of Land Reform since the 1950s

The relationship between domestic food production and population levels has always influenced political and social history. The recent "population explosion" in Latin America has underscored the crucial importance of per capita food production (food/c). It is possible to arrive at a statistical understanding of the food production/population relationship by developing long-term data series from available short-term statistics prepared by the United Nations Food and Agriculture Organization (FAO) and the United States Department of Agriculture (USDA). Thus, in this essay we construct long-term measures to estimate Latin American food/c production for 18 countries since 1952 and for 20 countries since 1955.[1] These estimates for individual countries are compared with the total food/c production for Latin America and for the United States, which is the world's most important producer and exporter of food.

Our study involves calculating rates of percentage change for each year by using published revisions of data to develop a relatively consistent view for each country. We use two approaches, procedures for which are explained in the Methodological Note at the end of the text.

In one approach, the year 1955 is taken as a standard base for assessing volume of food/c output. This is the first year for which we have the percentage-change data for all Latin American countries. During the mid-1950s an awareness of the population explosion began to develop and, with it, a growing concern about Latin America's ability to feed its people. At the same time, demands for land reform became more widespread: the United Nations issued its *Progress on Land Reform: First Report* in 1954 and its *Second Report* in 1956—years which bracket our standardized base of 1955. Analysis of production from the perspective of the 1955 standard base permits us to assess progress since the rise of food/c consciousness and the call for land reform in Latin America.

Index scores above 100 indicate the extent to which food/c production of 1955 has since been exceeded; scores below 100 indicate the extent of shortfall compared with 1955. A score of 100 in 1972, for example, would indicate that the balance between population and domestic food production existing in 1955 was replicated in the sample year.

In another approach we are interested in determining the extent to which food production has been in balance with population growth. Thus, we use percentage-change data to reveal years falling above and below the balance point, shown as a score of zero for each year in a country's food/c production history.

The concept of "balanced food/c" does not mean that all people in a country share equally in food produced or that the social distribution of food remains constant over time. Income distribution determines quality and quantity of food consumption. Nonetheless, the relationship between domestic food production and population growth has important implications for the politics and social ramifications of food, when viewed in the broader context of total per capita food availability (influenced by imports, exports, and nonconsumption uses of food as well as by food/c production).

Food production, for our purposes, includes nutritious liquids, crops, livestock, and livestock products intended for human consumption in each country. It is adjusted for livestock feed, but not for food that is imported, exported, or put to nonconsumption/industrial uses. Thus, for the FAO, food includes cereals, vegetables, starch roots, sugar cane, pulses, edible oil crops, nuts, cocoa, fruits, livestock, and livestock products such as milk and cheese. Fish are always excluded. Although the concept of "food" has varied somewhat over time (through 1960 in the data presented here, food includes coffee, tea, and linseed—items which have subsequently been removed by the FAO on the grounds that even if they are edible, they have practically no nutritive value), we presume that the changes do not appreciably distort our long-term calculations. (For further discussion, see the Methodological Note.)

Before presenting the results of the analysis, it is important to mention one problem discussed in the Methodological Note. Because the food/c production data are revised yearly and because the revisions may extend backward several years, the view developed here does not represent "final" measurement of the situation in any given country, especially for the most recent years. The case of Cuba is portrayed in table 1 to show how the FAO estimates of food/c productions for that country have changed. Estimates are shown from four issues of the *FAO Production Yearbook* (FAO-PY). For

Table 1: Evolution of FAO Short-Term Estimates for Cuba's Food/c
Production Index, 1970–80. (1969–71 = 100)[a]

	FAO-PY Index			
	Vol. 31	*Vol. 33*	*Vol. 34*	*Vol. 35*
1970	123	124	124	124
1971	91	93	94	94
1972	81	82	85	84
1973	83	83	87	88
1974	84	85	90	85
1975	88	89	90	88
1976	85	89	91	90
1977	89	98	96	96
1978	[b]	100	105	106
1979	[b]	103	111	113
1980	[b]	[b]	103	103

Source: FAO-PY, published in 1978, 1980, 1981, and 1982.

[a]Data not yet rebased as in tables 2 and 4.

[b]Data not available.

some years (as in 1970, 1975, and 1980), the FAO estimates remain relatively constant for food/c production; for other years the FAO apparently was skeptical of Cuba's food/c production. For example, the FAO-PY, volume 31 (utilizing its own 3-year index base wherein 1969 to 1971 equals 100) gave Cuba an index number of 89 for 1977; with enhanced information volume 33 raised the index score for 1977 to 98, whereas volumes 34 and 35 settled back to 96 for that year.[2] This case of Cuba, one of the more unstable countries in index scores because of Castro's aversion to complete reporting of data, reveals that data in volume 35 of the FAO-PY did not change much compared with volume 34, except in the figure for 1974, which decreased from 90 to 85 once the FAO took new information into account.

For Cuba, as for the rest of Latin America, index changes and incomplete data do not permit estimates of "exact" levels of production. Yet within certain limitations they do reveal long-term trends by country. Such indexes are a necessary point of departure for all discussion of possibilities for mass consumption of nutrients.

The Balanced View Approach

Table 2 provides the data for comparative analysis of percentage changes in food/c. It also supplies the long-term data used to calculate the level in food/c production based on the standard of 1955. Although data in table 2 show that the United States did not reach equilibrium in food/c production in 13 of the 30 years shown, apparently previous United States food production was so high that there has been more than enough production to meet both domestic and world food needs. In any case, in seven of the years when the United States output fell below zero, it did so by only 1.0%. In only two cases did food/c production fall as low as 4% (in 1957 and 1980). Similarly, the United States gains in output have not been subject to wide swings away from zero, except for three years that went over 6% (1959, 1971, and 1981). In 1981 the United States made its best gain (8.1%) after its worst loss (4.3%) in food production during the period for which we have data.

In contrast to the stable output of food/c in the United States, Latin American countries have experienced some extreme swings away from the "equilibrium" point of zero in the percentage-change data. Since Latin America's food/c output situation before 1952 was certainly not as advantageous as that of the United States, the idea of equilibrium as zero may in some ways be misleading. Disparities in income (and food) distribution in most countries of the region require that gains be well above zero in order that the masses might share in the expanded total output. The greater the percentages above zero, the greater the chance for the masses to benefit because there is extra food available to society as a whole; the farther the food/c percentage below zero, the less the possibility for society as a whole to benefit.[3]

Latin America's "normally" wide variation in gains and losses of food/c output is illustrated in Cuba's pattern. In 1970, Cuba compressed much of two crop years together in order to try to attain the 10-million-ton sugar cane crop that Fidel had promised in his propaganda oratory. The food/c gain was 49.4%, though only 85% of the magical figure of 10 million tons was reached. The cost was a collapse in food/c the following year, when production fell by 24.2%, the second-worst decline in the 30 years of data covered here. Only Nicaragua has had a worse decline: 28.3% during 1980 in the aftermath of the Sandinista victory over the dictator Anastasio Somoza in 1979.

The wide swings in the percentage changes of food/c production for Latin

America are depicted in graphs 1 through 6, which chart some of the absolute data series in table 2. Examining these graphs, we can see that the range of percentages above and below zero varies considerably (zero is indicated by a straight line across the graphs).[4] Cuba's record, seen in graph 2, for example, is presented on the computer-generated scale in a format measuring 40 points above zero and 40 points below zero—a range of 80 points.[5] In graph 4, Nicaragua's scale covers 50 points, 20 above zero and 30 below. Percentage changes do not always reach these maximum and minimum scores, of course, but the scale for each graph must provide the referenced points for reading changes shown. The differing scales in the graphs must be kept in mind; otherwise, Cuba's widest swings in percentage changes appear to be less than Nicaragua's variation.[6]

Explanations of the changes often point to either political factors or the weather. For example, critics of Fulgencio Batista's and Fidel Castro's Cuba point to the wide swings shown in graph 2 as being politically-motivated. Yet others point out that many variations in food/c production can be traced to the weather. Cuba is regularly buffeted by hurricanes, including 16 major ones between 1952 and 1971. Hurricanes in 1963 and 1964 were especially devastating: Flora hit the island in the fall of 1963 with winds of 70–100 miles per hour for more than 100 hours and left 90 inches of water in some areas; and the ninth hurricane of the 1964 season wiped out the country's tobacco crop.[7] Some observers might even blame Cuba's weather problems on politics. If the United States Central Intelligence Agency—as alleged—was able to sabotage Castro's new tractors by placing sugar in the gas tanks as they awaited shipment from European ports, then it could conceivably have seeded the clouds in the Caribbean to flood Cuba. Yet it is clear to us after consulting data on Cuba's weather that no hurricanes or other major weather problems complicated Castro's policy in 1970–71, when Cuba's widest swing took place.

Table 3 summarizes the percentage changes given in table 2. Four periods are set forth as follows: 1953–59, the 1960s, the 1970s, and 1980–81. Averages for the total 29-year period (27 years for El Salvador, Haiti, and Nicaragua) reveal that the highest score was attained by Brazil with a 1.9% yearly gain in food/c production. Bolivia, Ecuador, Mexico, and Venezuela followed with 1.7%, 1.6%, 1.5%, and 1.4% respectively. No other countries exceeded 1.0% yearly. Four countries had an average that did not keep up with the population: Haiti (−1.0%), El Salvador (−.6%), Dominican Republic (−.4%), and Honduras (−.2%). Peru was the only country where fluctuations in population neither rose above nor fell below changes in food production.

Table 2: Percentage Changes in Food/c Production, 1953–81

	Argentina	Bolivia	Brazil	Chile	Colombia	Costa Rica	Cuba
1953	−5.0	−2.0	4.3	3.1	−3.9	6.7	−22.7
1954	5.2	−2.1	4.1	0	−1.0	−6.3	−5.1
1955	−5.9	−1.1	0	4.0	3.1	−7.7	−6.4
1956	12.6	28.0	2.0	−1.0	1.0	−10.4	2.3
1957	−10.3	5.0	2.9	−4.9	−6.9	11.6	12.2
1958	6.3	8.8	.9	9.3	−1.1	−4.2	−2.0
1959	−7.8	−2.9	0	−7.5	−3.2	0	2.0
1960	−8.5	4.5	.9	−1.0	−3.1	5.4	0
1961	8.1	2.9	1.8	3.1	0	−8.2	6.9
1962	3.2	−2.8	0	−3.0	2.2	1.1	−21.3
1963	11.5	8.0	0	3.1	−5.3	0	−15.3
1964	−2.8	4.7	2.7	−4.0	4.4	−1.1	5.6
1965	−13.5	−5.8	7.0	−4.2	−1.1	4.5	21.1
1966	7.8	−1.4	−4.9	8.7	0	−4.3	−19.6
1967	7.1	0	4.3	−1.0	−2.0	−3.3	18.8
1968	−7.6	5.2	1.0	1.9	1.0	12.6	−4.4
1969	7.2	−3.9	0	−7.6	0	1.1	−2.3

continued

Table 2 continued

	Argentina	Bolivia	Brazil	Chile	Colombia	Costa Rica	Cuba
1970	-2.9	4.1	5.2	6.1	2.1	5.3	49.4
1971	-5.9	0	-1.0	-4.8	5.1	5.0	-24.2
1972	-4.2	5.9	1.0	-6.1	-1.0	0	-10.6
1973	8.8	.9	2.0	-9.8	-1.9	1.0	4.8
1974	2.0	.9	6.7	11.9	4.0	-2.8	0
1975	1.0	5.5	1.8	3.2	5.7	11.7	0
1976	7.8	.9	8.0	-3.1	3.6	.9	1.1
1977	-1.8	-7.8	.8	6.4	-1.7	0	7.9
1978	9.3	-.9	-6.5	-9.0	6.2	-1.7	11.5
1979	2.5	-2.8	3.5	6.6	2.5	0	5.6
1980	-8.3	1.9	7.6	-2.1	-3.3	-4.4	-10.6
1981	5.4	-5.7	0	4.2	4.2	-1.8	3.0

continued

Table 2 continued

	Dominican Republic	Ecuador	El Salvador	Guatemala	Haiti	Honduras	Mexico
1953	-4.9	7.3	—	0	—	0	6.8
1954	1.0	10.0	—	-3.9	—	-12.1	7.4
1955	-4.0	10.1	-6.1	-3.0	-1.8	-2.1	2.9
1956	6.3	4.6	.9	4.2	-.9	10.9	1.9
1957	1.0	5.3	-3.7	-2.0	-9.2	0	7.5
1958	0	1.7	-4.8	6.1	1.0	3.9	1.7
1959	0	9.0	-5.0	-1.9	1.0	-2.8	-4.3
1960	12.6	-4.5	4.2	0	-1.0	-2.9	0
1961	-13.8	3.9	2.0	-2.9	-2.0	5.0	3.6
1962	-3.0	.8	-2.9	10.1	2.9	0	1.7
1963	-5.2	-.8	4.0	3.7	1.0	-1.9	5.2
1964	-1.1	9.8	-4.9	-1.8	0	1.0	3.3
1965	-14.3	2.8	2.0	-9.0	1.0	5.8	1.6
1966	5.1	-5.4	3.0	1.0	-1.0	-8.2	0
1967	-2.2	-1.9	-5.0	2.2	1.0	12.5	-1.0
1968	-1.1	.9	3.2	3.2	-4.0	4.0	-1.9
1969	7.9	-6.6	-5.1	1.0	2.0	2.0	-3.0

continued

Table 2 continued

	Dominican Republic	Ecuador	El Salvador	Guatemala	Haiti	Honduras	Mexico
1970	4.2	1.0	8.5	2.0	0	−4.9	1.0
1971	2.0	−2.0	0	−1.0	0	4.1	1.0
1972	0	−6.1	−8.8	3.0	1.0	2.0	0
1973	−1.9	−1.1	9.7	2.9	−2.9	−5.8	0
1974	1.0	7.6	−2.9	−.9	−1.0	−11.3	0
1975	−6.9	0	7.1	1.9	−2.0	−17.4	−1.0
1976	4.2	0	−.9	3.7	0	11.3	−2.0
1977	1.0	0	−2.9	0	−5.2	5.1	5.1
1978	0	−5.1	11.8	−.9	2.2	3.6	5.8
1979	−2.0	−1.1	−1.8	5.5	−1.1	−7.0	−6.4
1980	2.0	6.5	−7.1	0	−6.5	0	4.9
1981	0	1.0	−6.7	0	−1.1	0	1.9

continued

Table 2 continued

	Nicaragua	Panama	Paraguay	Peru	Uruguay	Venezuela	Latin America	United States
1953	—	3.1	-2.0	4.1	15.6	3.2	-1.0	-2.0
1954	—	0	0	2.3	-8.1	3.1	2.0	1.0
1955	12.6	5.1	-1.0	-1.0	-2.9	2.0	-1.0	0
1956	.9	-2.9	0	-7.8	-5.1	-1.0	4.0	1.0
1957	-9.3	5.0	1.0	0	-1.1	2.9	-1.0	-4.0
1958	5.1	.9	4.0	4.2	-14.0	-4.8	2.0	6.2
1959	-3.9	.9	-2.9	1.0	-10.0	4.0	-3.8	-1.0
1960	-1.0	-.9	-6.9	6.1	15.3	6.7	-1.0	-1.0
1961	3.1	3.7	0	-1.0	-1.2	.9	3.0	-1.0
1962	1.1	-1.8	-3.2	-2.9	4.9	3.6	-2.0	-1.0
1963	6.3	.9	-3.3	-1.0	2.3	0	2.0	4.0
1964	3.9	-.9	11.4	2.0	12.5	6.9	1.0	-1.0
1965	-2.8	4.6	2.0	1.0	-5.1	3.2	0	0
1966	-2.9	-1.8	-1.0	3.9	-11.7	0	-2.0	2.0
1967	4.4	3.3	1.0	2.0	-11.7	1.0	2.0	5.2
1968	3.2	8.5	-4.0	-12.0	12.1	3.3	-2.0	-1.0
1969	2.0	3.9	0	10.2	8.6	5.3	1.0	-1.0

continued

Table 2 continued

	Nicaragua	Panama	Paraguay	Peru	Uruguay	Venezuela	Latin America	United States
1970	1.0	-11.3	8.4	5.2	5.0	2.0	3.0	-2.0
1971	-1.0	6.4	-1.0	-1.0	-13.1	-3.0	-2.9	7.2
1972	-4.0	-4.0	-5.9	-2.0	-3.2	-3.1	-1.0	-2.9
1973	-1.0	2.1	-3.1	0	6.7	0	1.0	1.0
1974	3.2	1.0	6.5	1.0	9.4	0	3.0	1.0
1975	7.1	2.0	-4.0	-6.0	-2.9	8.4	1.0	5.8
1976	1.0	-2.9	3.2	0	12.7	-6.8	1.9	1.8
1977	-1.9	5.1	7.1	-2.1	-14.8	5.2	1.9	2.7
1978	6.7	1.0	-5.7	-6.6	-2.0	1.0	.9	-1.8
1979	-4.5	-4.8	10.1	0	-2.1	5.9	0	3.6
1980	-28.3	1.0	5.5	-9.3	7.4	-1.9	0	-4.3
1981	2.6	4.0	-5.2	11.5	14.9	-8.5	1.9	8.1

Source: See Methodological Note, p. 101.

Graph 1. Brazil: Percentage Change in Food/c Production, 1953–81.
(0 = equilibrium between food production and population)

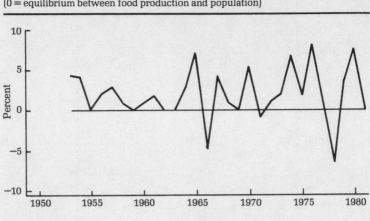

Source: Table 2.

Graph 2. Cuba: Percentage Change in Food/c Production, 1953–81.
(0 = equilibrium between food production and population)

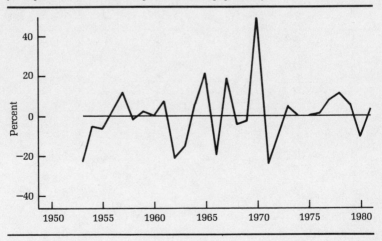

Source: Table 2.

Graph 3. Mexico: Percentage Change in Food/c Production, 1953–81.
(0 = equilibrium between food production and population)

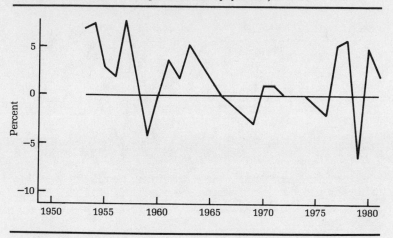

Source: Table 2.

Graph 4. Nicaragua: Percentage Change in Food/c Production,
1953–81. (0 = equilibrium between food production and population)

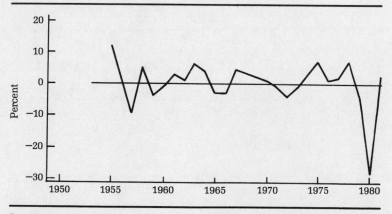

Source: Table 2.

Graph 5. Latin America: Percentage Change in Food/c Production,
1953–81. (0 = equilibrium between food production and population)

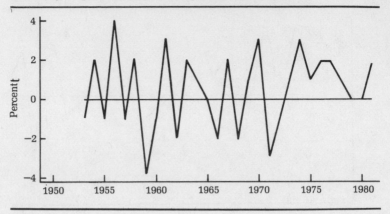

Source: Table 2.

Graph 6. United States: Percentage Change in Food/c Production,
1953–81. (0 = equilibrium between food production and population)

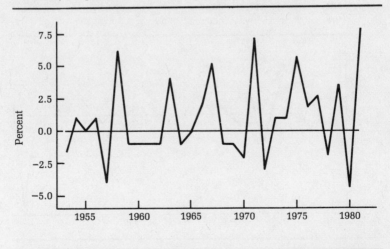

Source: Table 2.

Only Brazil and Mexico averaged positive growth in food/c in all time frames. The highest average was recorded for Ecuador (6.9%) in the 1950s; the lowest recorded was for Nicaragua in the early 1980s (−12.9%). No country had a consistently negative rate, but Haiti came close with a minus average change in all eras except the 1960s, when the rate was zero.

Does an increase or decrease in food/c production "cause" revolution? The results shown in table 3 are mixed. Cuba saw its average situation get much worse in the 1950s (prior to Castro's victory in 1959), but Nicaragua's average improved slightly during the 1970s (before the Sandinistas won in 1979), as did Peru's during the 1960s (before General Juan Velasco Alvarado began the Peruvian upheaval of 1968). Brazil's average food/c situation improved prior to the military seizure of power in 1964, but the average situation slightly worsened in Chile prior to Salvador Allende's victory in 1970. Individual year data (table 2) are equally contradictory. During the year immediately preceding upheaval, Cuba (in 1958) and Chile (in 1969) showed decreases, but Nicaragua and Peru showed increases. The year 1973, when Augusto Pinochet seized power in Chile, marked Chile's worst recorded loss, the third consecutive yearly loss in a row under Allende. Brazil's rate for 1963 was zero.

Does land reform contribute to positive or negative changes in food/c production? Here the answer is somewhat more clear. For Cuba, where land is retained by the state, table 2 shows an average annual gain of 1.3% over 23 years but also the widest and therefore most disruptive swings in production for any Latin American country. For Peru, where land was neither retained by the state nor redistributed, but administered by huge syndicates, food/c production declined an average yearly .8% over 14 years. Where much land was distributed either to communes (Mexico since 1915) or to individuals (Bolivia and Venezuela), all land holdings produced the following average yearly gains: Mexico over the 29 years from 1953 to 1981, 1.5%; Bolivia over 29 years, 1.7%; Venezuela over 24 years, 1.2%. In Chile, Eduardo Frei's land reform program (effectively 1965–70), expanded upon and revised by Allende (1970–73), yielded an average yearly 1.9% loss, but production under Frei showed a a slight gain of .7% compared with Allende's losses of 4.8%, 6.1%, and 9.8%. In the muddled Chilean case, much of the land was simply seized by workers under Allende's Revolution, whereas Frei's distribution procedures were somewhat more orderly. Both subprograms for the period 1965–73 were too short to be judged in themselves.

What happens to food/c production under the new conservative "revolutions" that have not enacted land reform? In the case of Brazil's Conservative Revolution, the military has not undertaken land reform at all since

Table 3: Average Yearly Percentage Change in Food/c, by Period, 1953–81

	1953–59 (7 years)	1960–69 (10 years)	1970–79 (10 years)	1980–81 (2 years)	Total (29 years)
Argentina	− .7	1.3	1.7	−1.5	.7
Bolivia	4.8	1.1	.7	−1.9	1.7
Brazil	2.0	1.3	2.2	3.8	1.9
Chile	.4	− .4	.1	1.1	.1
Colombia	− .8	− .4	2.5	.5	.6
Costa Rica	−1.5	.8	1.9	−3.1	.4
Cuba	−2.8	−1.1	4.6	−3.8	.3
Dominican Republic	− .1	−1.5	.2	1.0	− .4
Ecuador	6.9	− .1	− .7	3.8	1.6
El Salvador	−3.7[a]	− .4	1.2	−6.9	− .6[b]
Guatemala	− .1	.8	1.7	0	.8
Haiti	−2.0[a]	0	− .9	−3.8	−1.0[b]
Honduras	− .3	1.7	−2.0	0	− .2
Mexico	3.4	1.0	.4	3.4	1.5
Nicaragua	1.1[a]	1.7	.7	−12.9	.1[b]
Panama	1.7	2.0	− .5	2.5	1.1
Paraguay	− .1	− .4	1.6	.2	.4
Peru	.1	.8	−1.2	1.1	0
Uruguay	−3.7	2.6	− .4	11.2	.6
Venezuela	1.3	3.1	1.0	−5.2	1.4
Latin America	.2	.2	.9	1.0	.5
United States	.2	.5	1.7	1.9	.9

Source: Arithmetic averages calculated from table 2.

[a]1955–59. [b]27 years.

1964 but has averaged a 2.2% yearly gain in food/c production; from 1953 to 1963, civilian governments, also opposed to land reform, had averaged 1.5% yearly gains.[8] After 1976 Argentina's Conservative Revolution achieved a 2.5% yearly increase over the six years for which we have data. Uruguay's Conservative Revolution achieved a 2.6% yearly increase from 1972 through 1981, as did Chile's Conservative Revolution after 1973.

In the meantime, for countries under more traditional repressive governments, food/c production since 1953 has tended to do poorly. El Salvador through 1979 and Guatemala through 1981 averaged, respectively, −.1% and .8% yearly; Paraguay under dictator Alfredo Stroessner averaged .5% from 1954 through 1981; Colombia, under an almost permanent state of siege, averaged .6%.

These last figures reduce the bigger gains of countries discussed earlier, so that the total Latin American average has been about half of the United States gain since the onset of the 1960s. During the 1950s, Latin America kept pace only because the United States rate of change was a low .2% average per year.

Questions of political change cannot be investigated solely by reference to food/c production. The dynamics of food production as represented by yearly shifts, however, do underscore a variable that has been neglected for too long in explaining the political process. Careful use of these data will certainly help illuminate the nature of the political process in individual countries. By using the data of table 2 in a comparative way, grouping countries according to the number of years they rose above or fell below zero, for example, new perspectives on broader regional patterns can be introduced. Cluster analysis of percentage changes (see Methodological Note) is helpful in the same way.

Let us group, in one illustration, the countries according to the number of years food/c fell below zero. One group is formed by three countries whose food/c production did not fall into the minus level for more than 7 years out of the 29 surveyed: Brazil 3 years, Mexico 6, and Venezuela 7. Another group is made up of countries which saw their food/c production level rise above zero in 11 or fewer of these 29 years: Haiti with 9, El Salvador with 10, Paraguay with 11. In a third group, three countries saw food/c rise above zero only 12 times: Cuba, Guatemala, and Peru. Yet a fourth group of three countries can be identified where population kept up exactly with production for the most years: Brazil (6 years) and Mexico and Honduras (5 years).

A second cluster technique, which mathematically groups countries, yields quite different results. Argentina, Nicaragua, Bolivia, and Honduras form group or cluster 1 (with an average distance within the cluster of 2.4%); cluster 3 includes only Uruguay; and cluster 4 includes only Cuba.[9] The average distance within cluster 2 (which includes all other countries, Latin America's total, and the United States) is 1.1%.

These conflicting groupings in the 20 countries show the complexity of categorization. Further, they suggest that the idea of some political scientists to categorize countries simply in terms of authoritarian or nonauthoritarian regimes does not seem to be at all useful in relation to food/c policy outcomes.[10]

Groupings and the experiences of individual countries discussed to this point may be informative, but they do not answer the basic question of how far Latin America has come since 1955, the first year for which we have data on all countries and a year when land reform became an issue in politics.

The Standard-Base-Year Approach

Table 4 gives long-term index data to show the amount of change in food/c production since 1955. Index numbers in the table were calculated according to procedures discussed in the Methodological Note. Graphs 7–12 use the 1955-base-year data to show the extent to which some countries exceeded, fell below, or matched the domestic output of food in relation to the population before and after 1955.[11] The standard base of 100 is marked on the index scale with a straight line that runs across each graph from 1952 to 1981.

Countries with a positive trend in food/c production since 1955 include Bolivia (graph 7), Brazil (graph 8), Ecuador, Guatemala, Honduras, Mexico, Panama, and Venezuela. For example, Guatemala's index declined in 1953 and 1954 during President Juan José Arévalo's abortive attempt to take over United Fruit Company holdings for the purpose of land reform but subsequently surpassed pre-reform levels—continuously after 1967. Bolivia's food/c production in 1955 was also at its low point because of land reform undertaken after the Revolution of 1952.

Republics with a mixed pattern of food/c production over the 30-year period since 1955 include Argentina, Colombia, Costa Rica, Cuba (graph 9), Nicaragua, and Paraguay. For example, not until 1973 did Argentina's post-1955 index level stabilize well above 100; but only in the years 1959–61, 1965, and 1971–72 did food/c production fall below the 1955 level. In relation to the 1955 base year, Cuba has seen a decrease in its food/c production index from 145 to 100 between 1952 and 1955, an increase through 1961, a fall below 100 through 1975 (except for 1965, 1970, and 1971), and another increase since 1976. Graph 9 clearly shows Cuba's three major and two minor collapses. Major declines came under Batista in 1953 and under Castro in 1961–62 and 1971. Mini-collapses came under Castro in 1966 and 1980. For Paraguay the food/c production in relation to 1955 has hovered always around the 100 level, making strongly negative scores only in 1962–63 and strongly positive scores in 1979–81. Nicaragua stayed below the 1955 level until about 1965 and made strong positive gains only from 1975 to 1979. In 1980, it suffered the worst collapse (28.3%) in recorded Latin American food/c production history. By 1981 Nicaragua's level was again that of about 1952, as it finally overcame the results of "Tachito" Somoza's vindictive pledge to destroy what remained of the nation's economy so that the victory of his enemies in 1979 would be painful, if not irreparable.

Countries with a negative index trend since 1955 are Chile (graph 10), Dominican Republic, El Salvador, Haiti, Peru, and Uruguay. The Dominican Republic, occupying one side of the island of Hispaniola, saw its food/c production situation go far below the 1955 level after 1962 (down to 81.2 at the time of the civil war in 1965 and to 82.6 in the election year of 1968); on the other side of the island, Haiti's situation has gone almost steadily downward—from 100 in 1955 to below 80 after 1980. In Uruguay the index dropped below 100 after 1956 (except for 1976 and 1981, when it reached about 102) and declined in 1959 (to as low as about 74), 1967, 1972, and 1979. After 1955 Peru managed to well surpass the 100 level only between 1967 and 1974 (except for a 12% decline in 1968); but after 1975 Peru never again reached the 1955 level, falling to 81.7 in 1980, when disastrous mismanagement of land reform helped end 12 years of military misrule. In El Salvador the food/c production level continued a decline that began before 1955 and eventually went as low as 83.4 in 1972 before beginning to "stutter-step" upward to barely pass the 1955 level in 1978 and 1979. Perhaps the halting increase gave much of the poor population in El Salvador sufficient hope and energy to undertake guerrilla war with increasing intensity after 1980, war which caused the food/c production index to decline again. Chile's situation, shown in graph 10, compares only to the patterns of Haiti and Uruguay (ungraphed). Chile and Uruguay reached 100 in only two years. Chile (in 1973) and Uruguay (in 1959) fell below 80 even before Haiti (1980).

In spite of the countries with negative or mixed output of food in relation to population, the index for Latin America has stayed above (and usually well above) the 1955 level. After hitting a post-1962 low of 101.9 in 1966, 1968, and 1972, the total index for Latin America (graph 11) began a strong rise, passing 114 by 1981. Similarly, in 1972 the United States (graph 12) began its strong rise in food/c production over 1955 levels, but it doubled the Latin American level, reaching over 129 by 1981.

What does grouping of countries by cluster analysis show about the food/c production index data in table 4? Group or cluster 1 includes Argentina, Colombia, Costa Rica, Cuba, Latin America's total, and Nicaragua (with an average distance within the cluster of .398 points). Cluster 2 comprises Guatemala, Honduras, Panama, and the United States (with an average distance of .437 points). Cluster 3 includes Brazil, Ecuador, Mexico, and Venezuela (with an average within the cluster of .460). Cluster 4 contains Chile, Haiti, El Salvador, Uruguay, Dominican Republic, and Peru (with an average of .334). Cluster 5 has only Bolivia.[12] The mathematical separation of Bolivia is understandable given that country's rare pattern of food/c growth since 1955. Only cluster 1 seems nonsensical because Cuba's food/c output over the 29 years, although varying widely, yields a total number of points comparable to such countries as Argentina and Costa Rica. These

Table 4: Base Food/c Production: Index Data (1955=100)

	Argentina	Bolivia	Brazil	Chile	Colombia	Costa Rica	Cuba
1952	106.3	105.4	92.1	93.3	101.9	108.4	145.6
1953	101.0	103.3	96.1	96.2	98.0	115.6	112.6
1954	106.3	101.1	100.0	96.2	97.0	108.3	106.8
1955	100.0	100.0	100.0	100.0	100.0	100.0	100.0
1956	112.6	128.0	102.0	99.0	101.0	89.6	102.3
1957	101.0	134.4	105.0	94.1	94.0	100.0	114.8
1958	107.4	146.2	105.9	102.9	93.0	95.8	112.5
1959	99.0	142.0	105.9	95.2	96.0	95.8	114.7
1960	90.6	148.4	106.9	94.2	93.0	101.0	114.7
1961	97.9	152.7	108.8	97.2	93.0	92.7	122.7
1962	101.0	148.4	108.8	94.2	95.0	93.7	96.5
1963	112.7	160.3	108.8	97.2	90.0	93.7	81.8
1964	109.5	167.8	111.7	93.3	94.0	92.7	86.3
1965	94.7	158.1	119.5	89.4	92.9	96.8	104.6
1966	102.1	155.9	113.7	97.1	92.9	92.7	84.1
1967	109.4	155.9	118.6	96.2	91.1	89.6	99.9
1968	101.1	164.0	119.8	98.0	92.0	100.9	95.5
1969	108.3	157.6	119.8	90.5	92.0	102.0	93.3

continued

Table 4 continued

	Argentina	Bolivia	Brazil	Chile	Colombia	Costa Rica	Cuba
1970	105.2	164.0	126.0	96.1	93.9	107.4	139.4
1971	99.0	164.0	124.7	91.5	98.7	112.8	105.6
1972	94.8	173.7	126.0	85.9	97.7	112.8	94.4
1973	103.2	175.3	128.5	77.5	95.9	113.9	99.0
1974	105.2	176.9	137.1	86.7	99.7	110.7	99.0
1975	106.3	186.6	139.6	89.5	105.4	123.7	99.0
1976	114.6	188.3	150.7	86.7	109.2	124.8	100.1
1977	112.5	173.6	151.9	92.2	107.3	124.8	108.0
1978	123.0	172.0	142.1	83.9	114.0	122.7	120.4
1979	126.1	167.2	147.0	89.5	116.8	122.7	127.1
1980	115.6	170.4	158.2	87.6	113.0	117.3	113.6
1981	121.8	160.7	158.2	91.3	117.7	115.2	117.0

continued

Table 4 continued

	Dominican Republic	Ecuador	El Salvador	Guatemala	Haiti	Honduras	Mexico
1952	108.4	77.0	—	107.3	—	116.2	84.7
1953	103.1	82.6	—	107.3	—	116.2	90.5
1954	104.2	90.8	106.5	103.1	101.8	102.4	97.2
1955	100.0	100.0	100.0	100.0	100.0	100.0	100.0
1956	106.3	104.6	100.9	104.2	99.1	110.9	101.9
1957	107.4	110.1	97.2	102.1	90.0	110.9	109.5
1958	107.4	112.0	92.5	108.3	90.9	115.2	111.4
1959	107.4	122.1	87.9	106.3	91.8	112.0	106.6
1960	120.9	116.6	91.6	106.3	90.9	108.8	106.6
1961	104.2	121.2	89.7	103.2	89.1	114.2	110.5
1962	101.1	122.1	87.1	113.6	91.6	114.2	112.3
1963	95.8	121.1	90.6	117.8	92.6	112.0	118.2
1964	94.8	133.0	86.2	115.7	92.6	113.1	122.1
1965	81.2	136.7	87.2	105.3	93.5	119.7	124.0
1966	85.4	129.4	90.5	106.4	92.5	109.9	124.0
1967	83.5	126.9	86.0	108.7	93.5	123.6	122.8
1968	82.6	128.0	88.0	112.2	89.7	128.6	120.5
1969	89.1	119.6	84.2	113.3	91.5	131.1	116.8

continued

Table 4 continued

	Dominican Republic	Ecuador	El Salvador	Guatemala	Haiti	Honduras	Mexico
1970	92.8	120.8	91.4	115.6	91.5	124.7	118.0
1971	94.7	118.4	91.4	114.4	91.5	129.8	119.2
1972	94.7	125.6	83.4	117.8	92.4	132.4	119.2
1973	92.9	124.2	91.4	121.2	89.8	124.7	119.2
1974	93.8	133.6	88.8	120.2	88.9	110.6	119.2
1975	87.3	133.6	95.1	122.4	87.1	91.4	118.0
1976	91.0	133.6	94.2	127.0	87.1	101.7	115.6
1977	91.9	133.6	91.5	127.0	82.6	106.9	121.5
1978	91.9	126.8	102.3	125.8	84.4	110.8	128.6
1979	90.1	125.4	100.5	132.7	83.4	103.0	120.4
1980	91.9	133.6	93.3	132.7	78.0	103.0	126.2
1981	91.9	134.9	87.1	132.7	77.2	103.0	128.6

continued

Table 4 continued

	Nicaragua	Panama	Paraguay	Peru	Uruguay	Venezuela	Latin America	United States
1952	—	92.3	103.1	94.9	96.9	92.1	100.0	101.0
1953	—	95.1	101.0	98.7	112.1	95.1	99.0	99.0
1954	88.8	95.1	101.0	101.0	103.0	98.0	101.0	100.0
1955	100.0	100.0	100.0	100.0	100.0	100.0	100.0	100.0
1956	100.9	97.1	100.0	92.2	94.9	99.0	104.0	101.0
1957	91.5	102.0	101.0	92.2	93.9	101.9	103.0	97.0
1958	96.2	102.9	105.0	96.1	80.7	97.0	105.0	103.0
1959	92.4	103.8	102.0	95.1	72.6	100.9	101.0	101.9
1960	91.5	102.9	95.0	100.9	83.8	107.6	100.0	100.9
1961	94.3	106.7	95.0	99.9	82.8	108.6	103.0	99.9
1962	95.4	104.8	91.9	97.0	86.8	112.5	101.0	98.9
1963	101.4	105.7	88.9	96.0	88.8	112.5	103.0	102.9
1964	105.3	104.7	99.0	98.0	99.9	120.3	104.0	101.8
1965	102.4	109.6	101.0	98.9	94.8	124.1	104.0	101.8
1966	99.4	107.6	100.0	102.8	83.7	124.1	101.9	103.9
1967	103.8	111.1	101.0	104.9	73.9	125.3	104.0	109.3
1968	107.1	120.6	96.9	92.3	82.9	129.5	101.9	108.2
1969	109.3	125.3	96.9	101.7	90.0	136.3	102.9	107.1

continued

Table 4 continued

1970	110.4	111.1	105.1	107.0	94.5	139.1	106.0	105.0
1971	109.3	118.2	104.0	105.9	82.1	134.9	102.9	112.5
1972	104.9	113.5	97.9	103.8	79.5	130.7	101.9	109.3
1973	103.8	115.9	94.9	103.8	84.8	130.7	102.9	110.4
1974	107.2	117.1	101.0	104.8	92.8	130.7	106.0	111.5
1975	114.8	119.4	97.0	98.5	90.1	141.7	107.1	117.9
1976	115.9	115.9	100.1	98.5	101.5	132.1	109.1	120.0
1977	118.1	121.8	107.2	96.5	86.5	138.9	111.2	123.3
1978	126.0	123.1	101.1	90.1	84.8	140.3	112.2	121.1
1979	120.4	117.2	111.3	90.1	83.0	148.6	112.2	125.4
1980	86.3	118.3	117.4	81.7	89.1	145.8	112.2	120.0
1981	88.5	123.1	111.3	91.1	102.4	133.4	114.3	129.8

Source: See Methodological Note, p. 101.

Graph 7. Bolivia: 1955-Based Index of Food/c Production, 1952–81.
(1955 = 100)

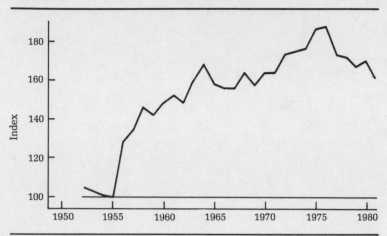

Source: Table 4.

Graph 8. Brazil: 1955-Based Index of Food/c Production, 1952–81.
(1955 = 100)

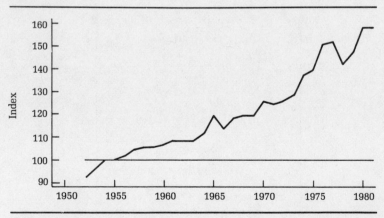

Source: Table 4.

Graph 9. Cuba: 1955-Based Index of Food/c Production, 1952–81.
(1955 = 100)

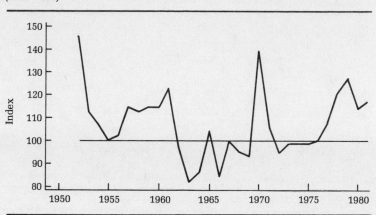

Source: Table 4.

Graph 10. Chile: 1955-Based Index of Food/c Production, 1952–81.
(1955 = 100)

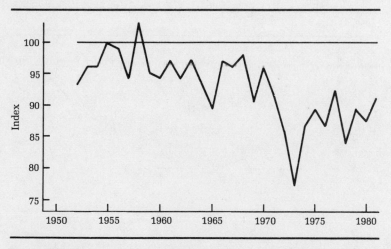

Source: Table 4.

Graph 11. Latin America: 1955-Based Index of Food/c Production, 1952–81. (1955 = 100)

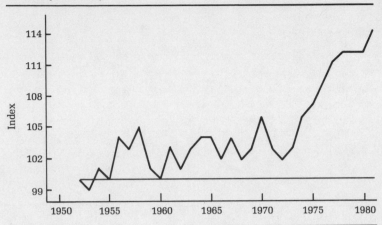

Source: Table 4.

Graph 12. United States: 1955-Based Index of Food/c Production, 1952–81. (1955 = 100)

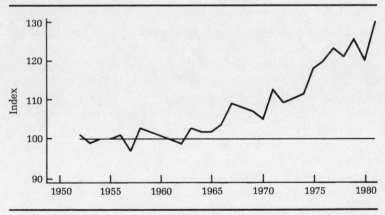

Source: Table 4.

latter countries, however, share a pattern that fluctuates above and below zero.

Problems of Analysis

We have discussed the situation of food/c production in Latin American countries since 1955 without addressing three issues. First, explicitly in relation to the index approach, how did the countries stand in relation to each other in 1955? Second, how do we rank the countries' comparative long-term output in food/c production? Third, taking into account each country's exports and imports of food, how does food/c *production* compare to food/c *supply*? Production data indicate the country's potential to be self-sufficient, whereas supply data tell what food is available for consumption after production has been adjusted for exports and imports, nonfood uses, processing wastage, etc. (see Methodological Note).

The index method used to measure food/c production up to this point is the usual one that contrasts each country's base-year situation with its performance previously or thereafter. Since the nations did not have equal bases in 1955, however, the index results may be misleading. Comparing the performance of Bolivia with that of Ecuador illustrates the problems. Bolivia's land reform, beginning in 1952, had resulted in a low food/c production index score by 1955, whereas Ecuador's index number was on the rise in 1955 from its lowest recorded point in 1952 (see table 4). Thus Bolivia's index increased as the postrevolutionary situation stabilized, especially after the beneficiaries of land reform overcame their initial inclination to merely subsist on their new holdings and began to produce for market. Bolivia had a −1.1% change in food/c production in 1955, while Ecuador enjoyed a 10.0% gain, thus influencing subsequent index changes.

These interrelated problems can be overcome by adjusting the index data for 1955 (and the following years) to "equalize" the growth rate for each country. Although we cannot work from the same levels for each country, we can work from the counterfactual position of "balance" in percentage change of food and population to measure subsequent change.

Let us show how this counterfactual adjustment to the index data can enhance analysis. In table 5 the percentage change for each country in 1955 (column 1) is added to or subtracted from the unadjusted index data for 1980 (column 2) to yield the adjusted index data (column 3). For Bolivia and Ecuador in 1980, then, we reverse the signs on the percentage changes for each country in 1955 and multiply those figures by the unadjusted index score: +1.9 points or an adjusted index of 172.3 for Bolivia in 1980 and −13.5

Table 5: Adjustment to Index Scores for Food/c Production

	1955 Percentage Change (1)[b]	1980 Index[a]	
		Unadjusted (2)[c]	Adjusted (3)[d]
Argentina	−5.9	115.6	122.4
Bolivia	−1.1	170.4	172.3
Brazil	0	158.2	158.2
Chile	4.0	87.6	84.1
Colombia	3.1	113.0	109.5
Costa Rica	−7.7	117.3	126.3
Cuba	−6.4	113.6	120.9
Dominican Republic	−4.0	91.9	95.6
Ecuador	10.1	133.6	120.1
El Salvador	−6.1	93.3	99.0
Guatemala	−3.0	132.7	136.7
Haiti	−1.8	78.0	79.4
Honduras	−2.1	103.0	104.7
Mexico	2.9	126.2	122.5
Nicaragua	12.6	86.3	75.4
Panama	5.1	118.3	112.3
Paraguay	−1.0	117.4	118.6
Peru	−1.0	81.7	82.5
Uruguay	−2.9	89.1	91.5
Venezuela	2.0	145.8	142.9
Latin America	−1.0	112.2	114.7
United States	0	120.0	120.0

[a]Index: 1955 = 100   [b]From table 2.   [c]From table 4.
[d]Column (2) times column (1) (signs reversed to equalize bases).

points for Ecuador or an adjusted index of 120.1. In relation to 1955, the differences between the two countries by 1980 were 52.2 points on the adjusted index and 36.8 points on the unadjusted index.

This discrepancy can be shown another way for Argentina and El Salvador, which had the same variation from zero to about 6% in 1955 (see column (1) in table 5). By adjusting the index base (100) by 6% (to 106) and graphing the unadjusted data for the two countries in relation to the unadjusted and adjusted bases, as in graph 13, we see how the food/c situation

Graph 13. Adjusted (106) and Unadjusted (100) Base Levels for
Comparison of Argentina and El Salvador Food/c Production
Indexes, 1955–81

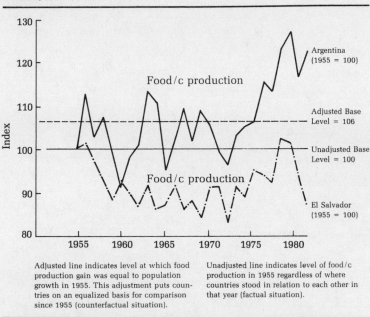

Adjusted line indicates level at which food
production gain was equal to population
growth in 1955. This adjustment puts countries on an equalized basis for comparison
since 1955 (counterfactual situation).

Unadjusted line indicates level of food/c
production in 1955 regardless of where
countries stood in relation to each other in
that year (factual situation).

Sources: Adjusted level is adapted from Table 5, column (1); all other data are
from Table 4.

differs according to real and counterfactual definitions. If the two countries
had had the same food/c production levels in 1955, Argentina would have
gone above the balance line eight fewer times and El Salvador would have
gone below the line in all years.

With regard to the second question posed at the outset of this section, how
can we rank the countries' output in food/c production? Given the three
ways presented for analyzing food/c production (unadjusted indexes, adjusted indexes, and percentage changes), how different are the views that
they afford? Table 6 gives rankings for the three different methods that cover
the cumulative pattern from the 1950s to the 1980s. Of the 20 cases, half
yield the same ranking for percentage changes as compared with either of
the two indexes. The other half of the cases show a disparity in the ranking:
the unadjusted index is closer to the percentage change ranks in seven cases,
whereas the adjusted index is nearer to percentage change ranks in only

Table 6: Three Methods of Ranking Food/c Production, 1953–81,
in the 20 Latin American Countries (1 = Highest Rank)

	Index Ranks, 1980 Average		Percentage Change Ranks	Summary Average Ranks[a]
	Unadjusted	Adjusted		
	(1)	(2)	(3)	(4)
Argentina	10	7	8	8
Bolivia	1	1	2	1
Brazil	2	2	1	2
Chile	17	17	15	17
Colombia	12	12	10	12
Costa Rica	9	5	12	9
Cuba	11	8	13	11
Dominican Republic	15	15	18	16
Ecuador	4	9	3	4[b]
El Salvador	14	14	19	15
Guatemala	5	4	7	4[b]
Haiti	20	19	20	20
Honduras	13	13	17	14
Mexico	6	6	4	4[b]
Nicaragua	18	20	14	19
Panama	7	11	6	7
Paraguay	8	10	11	10
Peru	19	18	16	18
Uruguay	16	16	9	13
Venezuela	3	3	5	3

Sources: Column (1), table 4; column (2), table 5; column (3), table 3.

[a]Columns (1) + (2) + (3).   [b]Tie rankings.

three cases. All methods indicate that Bolivia and Brazil have enjoyed the
highest rankings and Haiti the lowest. The widest differences can be seen in
the case of Uruguay, which ranks 16 on both indexes but 9 on the percentage
change. Two countries vary by 6 ranks—Ecuador and Nicaragua.

To summarize the three approaches analyzed above, all of which have
particular advantages, we developed in table 6, column (4), an average of the
three ranking methods. Hence we established the following order of comparative advantage: 1, Bolivia; 2, Brazil; 3, Venezuela; 4, Ecuador, Guatemala, and Mexico (rank 4 includes ranks 5 and 6 because of tie scores); 7,

Panama; 8, Argentina; 9, Costa Rica; 10, Paraguay; 11, Cuba; 12, Colombia; 13, Uruguay; 14, Honduras; 15, El Salvador; 16, Dominican Republic; 17, Chile; 18, Peru; 19, Nicaragua; 20, Haiti.

The answer to the third question about food/c production and supply depends on the analysis of export and import patterns and on the way food is wasted or put to nonfood uses. The question is a complicated one, largely beyond the scope of this study. It is important, nonetheless, to emphasize that food/c production is influenced by many forces. Regardless of how Cuba has fared in food/c production, its shortage of dollars since the United States economic embargo of the 1960s has caused the country to ration such staples as rice, beans, and even sugar and citrus products, which have been exported to gain foreign exchange. Brazil, different from Cuba in so many ways, has also become a major exporter of citrus products and of items such as soybeans. In contrast, Bolivia gained self-sufficiency in commodities such as rice, sugar, and milk products under its National Revolution (1952–64), a revolution that sought to meet domestic needs rather than producing food for export. Mexico and Venezuela, which have experienced extensive land reforms, often have had to import wheat, corn, milk, and eggs; Venezuela even has had to import meat and vegetables. In light of cost advantages, of course, it is often preferable for countries such as Mexico and Venezuela to concentrate on the export of oil at high prices while importing food at low prices—an argument to which we can only allude here.

The method that the FAO is developing to measure food/c supply involves adjusting production for trade and nonfood uses in order to estimate the supply of calories, fats, proteins, etc. (see Methodological Note, below). To suggest the dimensions of that emerging approach, we present in table 7 the FAO data on daily caloric supply per capita. Calorie supply increased for all 20 countries between 1965 and 1980, if only by one calorie for Haiti. The data on Bolivia tend to confirm our findings on rise of production; without export goals, the food supply could rise and the daily calories per capita could increase from 1,731 to 2,122. Certainly the analysis of food/c supply offers a useful counterpoint to the study of food/c production, especially if such components as calories, proteins, and vitamin supply could be combined to achieve a single measure of supply.

Conclusion

In offering new research perspectives for analyzing food/c production, we do not claim to have established a definitive approach or to have presented "final" data. Revisions of the data and new conceptual standards will no

Table 7: Daily Supply of Calories Per Capita, 1965–80

	1965	1970	1975	1980
Argentina	2868	3036	3048	3069
Bolivia	1731	1902	2016	2122
Brazil	2541	2613	2675	2731
Chile	2523	2540	2601	2655
Colombia	2220	2160	2195	2233
Costa Rica	2223	2344	2401	2472
Cuba	2665	2688	2726	2762
Dominican Republic	2004	2143	2177	2223
Ecuador	1848	1906	1964	2014
El Salvador	1877	1877	1934	2002
Guatemala	1952	1972	2056	2145
Haiti	1904	1896	1900	1905
Honduras	1930	2042	2123	2203
Mexico	2623	2660	2676	2698
Nicaragua	2253	2314	2371	2426
Panama	2317	2429	2551	2661
Paraguay	2732	2798	2819	2835
Peru	2255	2194	2305	2428
Uruguay	3039	3105	3136	3167
Venezuela	2392	2524	2586	2641
Latin America	2470	2524	2570	2616

Source: Octavio Paredes López and Yoja Gallardo Navarro, "La alimentación en América Latina: Una mirada al pasado, el presente y el futuro," *Comercio Exterior* (Mexico City) 31 (March 1981): 252.

doubt alter some of our findings. Nevertheless, we hope that among our alternative approaches, readers will find one or more with which they feel comfortable. In table 6 we offer three methods of ranking the Latin American countries to compare the advantages of each. Although the three methods yield somewhat different results, especially in the middle rankings, we also develop a system that combines the different methods to arrive at an average ranking.

In relation to what most scholars would hypothesize about the summary rankings before making this statistical assessment, there are some surprises. Bolivia's ranking at the top in the summary average for food/c production is unexpected, while Brazil's high position is not. That Venezuela ranks third and Mexico fourth helps sustain the argument that land reform need not mean an end to national food productivity, especially if the reform leaves plenty of opportunity for private production that is socially useful. (Socially useful production utilizes the land as fully as is wise and employs modern methods as well as many workers other than those of one family.[13]) The mismanaged Cuban and Peruvian reforms, which contributed to food/c production ranks 11 and 18, are further evidence of the inadvisability of minimizing the private role in agricultural production.

It is no surprise that countries such as Haiti and El Salvador rank poorly in summary averages (20 and 15, respectively) or that the Dominican Republic, which suffered so long under the egomaniacal dictator Rafael Trujillo (1930–61) before undergoing civil war in 1965, would rank near the bottom (16). Yet the rankings of some of the countries near the top cause one to reassess prior assumptions. Such varied countries as Ecuador and Guatemala rank fourth, with Panama following in the seventh position. Although Argentina shows little variation in the three methods of ranking and holds the summary rank 8, its neighbor Uruguay shows one of the greatest differences in subrankings (7 places), to average thirteenth in food/c production for Latin America. The other wide variation in subrankings is seen for Costa Rica (also 7 places), which stands at summary rank 9.

That Colombia, with its great size and economic activity, should rank 12, close to Honduras (14) and behind Paraguay (10), may surprise some observers, although others have portrayed Paraguay as an agricultural paradise in rather splendid isolation. In spite of Chile's problems in food/c output, the rank of 17 is lower than one might expect, but the subtotal for percentage change for the period from 1953 to 1981 improves it slightly (to rank 15).

Perhaps we have raised more questions than we have answered. At least we have presented more data and trends than can be analyzed here. In any case, the problem of understanding specific cases requires going beyond our national totals to examine what has happened to particular crops as well as to population change. Production data must also be linked to food supply data. In suggesting the parameters of measuring food/c production in Latin America for the last third of a century, our goal has been to offer baseline data as well as analytical approaches useful to other scholars and observers who seek to understand events within specific countries or in a comparative perspective.

Notes

1. Latin America is traditionally defined as the 20 countries listed in table 2. Until 1955 the yearly total per capita data excluded El Salvador, Haiti, and Nicaragua, and since 1967 the total includes Barbados, Jamaica, Puerto Rico, and Trinidad and Tobago. In 1972 the three exclusions represented only 3.8% of the Latin American population and the four inclusions represented only 3.2%.

Data for all countries are based upon United Nations Food and Agriculture Organization (FAO) sources, except figures for El Salvador, Haiti, and Nicaragua through 1961, which came from the United States Department of Agriculture (USDA). USDA comparative data for these three countries can be calculated beginning only in 1954.

2. The FAO three-year index base is converted for subsequent index tables here to a standard 1955 base, beginning in table 3.

3. Regardless of a country's total food/c production, in some tropical areas such as Haiti, the poor are not completely at the mercy of swings in output and can survive by literally picking their food off the trees.

4. For graphs showing all countries, see James W. Wilkie and Manuel Moreno-Ibáñez, "New Research on Food Production in Latin America since 1952," in *Statistical Abstract of Latin America* 23, eds. James W. Wilkie and Adam Perkal (Los Angeles: UCLA Latin American Center, 1984).

5. On the computer method of generating each graph, see the Methodological Note.

6. With regard to range in food/c percentage change for countries not graphed, Honduras, Peru, and Uruguay show a range of 30 points or more. Countries with medium swings (from 20 to 30 points above and below zero) in food/c percentage changes include Argentina, Chile, Costa Rica, Dominican Republic, and Paraguay. Those with a usual range of less than 20 points on the computer-generated scale are Colombia, Ecuador, El Salvador, Guatemala, Haiti, Panama, and Venezuela. Haiti's data show the narrowest variation (13 points).

7. Susan Schroeder, *Cuba: A Handbook of Historical Statistics* (Boston: G. K. Hall, 1982), pp. 27, 33.

8. Conservative revolutions undertaken by the military in countries such as Brazil, Argentina, Uruguay, and Chile have aimed at eliminating the "debilitating" factor of politics from the process of national development. See, e.g., Brian Lovemen and Thomas M. Davies, Jr., eds. *The Politics of Antipolitics: The Military in Latin America* (Lincoln: University of Nebraska Press, 1978), who also discuss leftist military attempts to eliminate politics.

9. Of course, clusters 3 and 4 each average a distance of 0% because each has only one country.

10. Similarly Enrique A. Baloyra has found that the authoritarian-nonauthoritarian scheme is not relevant to budgetary outcomes. Like many others, Baloyra had hypothesized that dictators sacrifice the needs of the masses, whereas democratically elected leaders do not. Baloyra found that hypothesis to be wrong in his "Democratic Versus Dictatorial Budgeting: The Case of Cuba with Reference to Venezuela and

Mexico," in *Money and Politics in Latin America,* ed. James W. Wilkie (Los Angeles: UCLA Latin American Center, 1977) (*Statistical Abstract of Latin America,* Supplement 7), Chap. 1.

11. For graphs showing all countries, see note 4.

12. The average distance within cluster 5 is, of course, zero.

13. See James W. Wilkie, *Measuring Land Reform* (Los Angeles: UCLA Latin American Center, 1974) (*Statistical Abstract of Latin America, Supplement 5*). Most of Mexico's food/c production has come from private holdings that produce for market in contrast to communal holdings that have involved mainly production for subsistence.

Methodological Note

Much of the discussion of our methodological approaches is included in the body of this chapter.

The data on percentage changes were calculated by Waldo W. Wilkie, and the indexes and graphs were produced with the assistance of the UCLA Computer Center under a special grant from the UCLA College of Letters and Science. The project was carried out under the auspices of the Historical Research Foundation.

Sources

The food/c production indexes developed in this study are based upon original data presented in various volumes of the U.N. Food and Agriculture Organization *Production Yearbook* (FAO-PY) and in the 1966 publication of the U.S. Department of Agriculture, Economic Research Service, *Indices of Agricultural Production for the 20 Latin American Countries* (ERS-Foreign 44). Data for specific years are from the following sources:

1953   FAO-PY, vol. 23 titled 1969 (All FAO-PY volumes are published one year after title date.)

1954–66   FAO-PY, vol. 24 titled 1970; El Salvador, Haiti, and Nicaragua (excluded until 1955) through 1961 are from ERS-Foreign 44 and 1962–66 from FAO-PY, vols. 26, 27, 28, 29, titled 1972, 1973, 1974, 1975

1967   FAO-PY, vol. 31 titled 1977

1968   FAO-PY, vol. 32 titled 1978

1969   FAO-PY, vol. 33 titled 1979

1970   FAO-PY, vol. 34 titled 1980

1971   FAO-PY, vol. 35 titled 1981

1972   FAO *Monthly Bulletin of Statistics,* Nov. 1982

Original Data

Raw index data that form the basis for recalculations here are taken from the most recent published revisions in the above sources for each country, for the Latin American average, and for the United States. The original, "raw" figures are divided in the sources into two periods (through 1966 and since 1967) with price-weighted bases as follows:

1953-66: Data price weighted on 1952–56 basis, except data for El Salvador, Haiti, and Nicaragua are price weighted on 1957–59 basis through 1961 and on 1961–65 basis through 1966
1967-81: Data price weighted on 1969–71 basis

The original indexes are calculated in the sources as follows: Production quantities of each commodity are price weighted and summed for each year. The aggregate for each year (including each year within the price-weighted base) is divided by the average aggregate for the multi-year price-weighted base to obtain the index number.

The effect on index data when shifting from one price-weighted basis to another is exemplified by converting the index number in both series to a percentage change for years that appear in each of the two series. Because 1967 is the year of transition from price-weighted base 1952–56 to base 1969–71, let us examine example table A, which reveals that for 1967 there is effectively no difference in percentage change of food/c production for Argentina when shifting the basis of price weights. Because 1972 is the first year after shifting to the 1969–71 price-weighted basis from the 1961–65 basis, let us again look at example table A. As above, we find that the percentage changes are

Example Table A: Effect on Percentage Changes of Shifting Price-Weighted Bases: Argentine Case. (Read down to compare percentages)

	Percentage Change	
Price-Weighted Basis	1966/67	1971/72
1952–56	7.2[a]	—
1961–65	7.0[b]	−4.1[d]
1969–71	7.1[c]	−4.2[e]

Source: Calculated from FAO-PY as follows: [a]vol. 23; [b]vol. 29; [c]vol. 31; [d]vol. 30; [e]vol. 35.

almost exactly the same between the two series. The Argentine case illustrates the fact that when original-index data do not need revising from volume to volume of the FAO-PY, the change from one price-weighted basis to another does not affect our view of the trend of food/c production.

For data presented since 1967, national producer prices are used by the FAO as weights for computing the aggregate production of each country instead of the regional wheat-based price relatives that it previously used.

"Food Production" Defined

FAO-PY (35:5) states that since 1966 "Production data used for the computation of index numbers are now, with very few exceptions, primary commodities. Therefore, production of sugar, olive oil, copra, raisins, and wine used earlier for the computation of index numbers has been substituted by production of sugar cane, sugar beet, olives, coconuts, and grapes. The processed commodities that still remain are palm oil, palm kernels, cottonseed, and cotton lint. Production of palm nuts could not be used for lack of data on production and prices, and seed cotton could not be used because it is a mixed food and non-food product. . . .

"The FAO index numbers may differ from those produced by the countries themselves because of differences in concepts of production, coverage, weights, time reference of data, and methods of calculation."

It is important to note that the FAO defines "food production" as domestic output, not adjusted for imports and exports. Thus the quantities of food produced do not relate to the amounts reaching the consumer or actually consumed, which may be higher or lower depending upon the following: (1) government trade policy in foods; (2) losses of edible nutrients put to nonfood uses as in industry; (3) losses in the household through improper storage, preparation, and cooking (these affect vitamins and minerals to a greater extent than they do calories, protein, or fats); (4) plate-waste; (5) quantities fed to domestic animals and pets or thrown away. Moreover, also according to FAO-PY (35:9), food/c production figures "do not give any indication of the differences that may exist in the diets of different population groups, e.g., different socio-economic groups, ecological zones, and geographical areas within a country, nor do they provide information on seasonal variations in the total food supply. They represent only the average . . . for the population as a whole and do not indicate what is actually consumed by individuals."

For food/c *supply* in a country, in contrast to that country's *production,* readers should consult the FAO publication entitled *Food Balance Sheets . . . and Per Caput Food Supplies . . . , 1967 to 1977* (Rome, 1980). Summaries of data given in the *Food Balance Sheets* are presented in non-index form in the FAO-PY according to the following individual and non-summed per capita nutrients (broken down where applicable into those of vegetable or animal origin): calories, protein, fats, calcium, iron, ascorbic acid, retinol, riboflavin, thiamin, and niacin. Because there is no overall index to sum up food/c supply and because coverage is only available for a limited number of years, data on food/c supply are beyond the focus of this study.

Procedures Used to Reconceptualize and Recalculate the Raw Index Data

Using the concepts of measuring percentage changes in food/c production from year to year and showing the volume of food/c production since a standardized 1955 base year led us to a two-stage methodology. First, to convert original index data from differing price-weighted bases (discussed above at example table A) to a consistent series taking into account latest revisions, we calculated percentage change (1981 over 1980, 1980 over 1979, etc.) backward in time, using the most recent published source for every country, for the Latin American total, and for the United States. These percentages, given in table 2, were then graphed to show the yearly relation to equilibrium between food production and population growth, that is, years when the percentage was zero.

Second, we selected the year 1955 as our standardized base year to develop a single long-term index by multiplying the percentage changes in table 2 backward from 1955 to 1952 and forward to 1981. Using Cuba as an illustration, example table B shows how this process was carried out.

Computer Method

Percentage changes and standard-based index data were computed for tables 2 and 4 utilizing SAS™ (Statistical Analysis System), developed by SAS Institute, Inc. Computerized graphs were prepared using the SAS graphics package. Cluster analysis of data in tables 2 and 4 was generated using the cluster procedure available from SAS. See SAS *Users' Guide* (Cary, N.C.: SAS Institute, 1979). The clustering method utilized is based on an algorithm developed in Stephen C. Johnson, "Hierarchical Clustering Schemes," *Psychometrika* 32 (1967): 241–54.

Cautions

On the one hand, recent data are subject to future revision for several reasons. Revisions of original data backward in time as more information becomes available in each country or as methods are refined for calculating past food production may change our views. Also, reestimation of population can alter figures on per capita food production. On the other hand, recalculation here to one decimal point of original index data given in whole numbers may mean that a gain or loss of 1.0 in our indexes is due to rounding rather than a change in any country's food/c production. In either case, the trend over several years should be considered more reliable than the "exact" data for any year.

Example Table B: Methodology for Development of Long-Term Food/c Production Indexes: Cuban Case

Line	Category	1952	1953	1954	1955	1956	1957	1958	1959	1960
1	Original FAO index (1952–56 = 100)[a]	128	99	94	88	90	101	99	101	101
2	Percentage change (From line 1)		−22.7	−5.1	−6.4	2.3	12.2	−2.0	2.0	0
3	Standard base (1955 = 100)				100.0					
4	Standard-based index (Line 3 × line 2)	145.6	112.6	106.8	100.0	102.3	114.8	112.8	114.7	114.7

[a]Source: FAO-PY, vols. 23, 24.

Roland Bergman

Subsistence Agriculture
in Latin America

Subsistence agriculture remains today the principal means by which
the poor survive and even achieve a measure of prosperity in rural Latin
America. In an era of instability and fluctuation in the world economy, it is
the most stable part of the Latin American economic system. From Chile to
Mexico, unemployed urban workers commonly return to live with relatives
on subsistence farms while awaiting the next upturn in construction or
industry. Despite the proliferation of plans to transform small farmers into
more active participants in the market, both as producers and consumers,
subsistence agriculture may survive for a long time because of the security it
provides. And if caution and common sense are applied, much can be done
to improve its productivity without compromising the social and economic
security that it offers to much of the population.

This essay addresses several fundamental questions about subsistence
agriculture in Latin America. How does a system so seemingly backward
work? How efficient is it? How hard must one labor to sustain a family
within this system? How well can one live by a farming technique that uses
only simple tools along with the strength of men and, in some cases, of
domestic animals? What is the future of these cultivators and their agriculture? Before turning to case studies in three different regions of Latin
America, it is important to discuss the nature of subsistence agriculture and
some questions related to labor efficiency within subsistence systems.

Subsistence Systems

A human group creates its own distinctive subsistence system by combining its values with a technology and land. Within their system and by
their own work, members obtain food, clothing, shelter, and fuel directly

from the local environment. The technology employed ranges from simple gathering to intensive wet rice agriculture. Until recently, peoples who carried on subsistence production lacked access to modern technology, yet their mode of production and advanced methods are not necessarily incompatible. Today in Mexico, subsistence farmers combine chemical fertilizers and hybrid seeds—the developments of high technology—with traditional oxen-drawn plows. Such innovations often increase the yield and the return per hour of work.

Most subsistence farmers defined in today's terms do not supply all their needs. The production unit, usually a nuclear or extended family, purchases certain things from local sources and even regional towns that import goods from distant sources. It is a question of emphasis that distinguishes the subsistence farmer. He produces most of his food, especially the staple carbohydrate and usually the main protein, and sells any surplus in local markets. He builds his own house, largely from local materials. He usually procures fuel locally, commonly from woodlands, but sometimes from agricultural waste. Clothing is increasingly obtained from outside, but this has come to pass more because of fashion than necessity.

Some two billion people, roughly half the world's population, live by subsistence agriculture today. Most are found in south and east Asia and in Indonesia, but there are large numbers in Africa and Latin America as well. In Latin America, about 70 million people, or roughly 60 percent of the agricultural population, are estimated to be subsistence farmers.[1]

Almost all the detailed quantitative studies of Latin American subsistence agriculture have been made in the last fifteen years. Because they are few and lack integrative theory, we must look for guidance to the Old World tropics, where colonial administrators began systematic studies decades ago. Most theory has emerged from African studies, although Asian and Indonesian agricultures are taken into account.[2] One of the more intriguing problems in the literature is the relationship between productivity and technology.

Despite the example of innovative Mexican peasants who increase yields and efficiency by adding new technology, there is evidence that the adoption of so-called technological improvements does not necessarily improve production. In fact, among hunters and gatherers and subsistence agriculturists, intensification and complication often correlate negatively with the return per hour of labor. In *Stone Age Economics,* Marshall Sahlins makes a case for remarkably high efficiency among hunters and gatherers. African Bushmen, Australian Aborigines, and others supply themselves with more than adequate diets by working only two to five hours per day. Leisure, not the fear of starvation, dominates their days, and the fear of losing that leisure keeps them from taking up agriculture.[3]

Richard B. Lee reports that a Bushman was asked why his people did not take up agriculture. The Bushman replied, "Why should we plant, when there are so many mongomongo nuts in the world?"[4] Evidence like this, supported by quantitative findings, suggests that agriculture was initially adopted by hunters and gatherers not because it would enable them to work less, but rather because it would enable them to support more people on the same land area.

Ester Boserup, a Danish agricultural economist, has pursued this thesis through various stages in the technology of subsistence agriculture.[5] She contends that with each added stage of agricultural development, labor efficiency declines. Like the hunters and gatherers who avoid agriculture altogether, cultivators take up a more complex system only reluctantly, since the older, simpler, and seemingly cruder system actually returns more food per hour of work. Thus a people carrying on slash-and-burn (shifting) cultivation, using axes and machetes as the only tools, take up permanent field agriculture even though the return per hour of work will be less because they have more mouths to feed.[6] Studies carried out in India during the 1950s arrived at similar conclusions: In Madras, for example, "in irrigated crops generally the output is higher than in the unirrigated crop, but the higher output is usually secured with too high a rate of input with the result that the total cost remains uncovered."[7] Boserup uses these data to argue that subsistence farmers are acting on sound economic considerations when they hang on to traditional practices.

While some information supports the theses of Sahlins, Lee, and Boserup, other data contradict them or at least cloud the issue. In Latin America, subsistence agricultures do not seem to comply with Boserup's analysis. My own work among the Shipibos, the largest Indian tribe in the Amazon basin, shows that they could easily increase the return for their labor by intensifying agriculture. They do not do so because their present methods serve well enough. A Shipibo man works an average of 1.6 hours per day procuring food and a woman only 0.3 hours. Intensification could reduce this time even further: for example, a small increase in work in the banana *chacras* (fields) could greatly enhance yields. A rise in population that would force them to farm more intensively could actually make their lives easier.[8]

There appears to be a broad overlap in efficiency among agricultures with widely varying levels of intensification and technology. A comparison of twenty-seven case studies of rice farming in Africa, Asia, and Indonesia, with technologies ranging from slash-and-burn dry rice cultivation without animal traction to intensive wet rice cultivation in paddies utilizing draft animals, shows no clear separation of the labor efficiency of these very different systems. Slash-and-burn methods appear to reach a limit at about 2.5 kilograms of rice for an hour's work.[9] The wet rice methods range in efficiency from 0.9 kilograms per hour of work in India to 2.3 kilograms in east-central China and over 4.0 kilograms in the Philippines.[10] In short, the intensive wet rice systems cover the gamut of labor efficiencies, while dry rice production concentrates in the lower half.

It is risky to compare systems in widely separated cultural and natural circumstances, yet doing so illustrates the range in efficiency. A more telling comparison can be made from cases where one group uses more than one technology, because then variables in land and culture are more nearly constant. M. R. Haswell's study of a village in Gambia, West Africa, for example, showed a marked increase in labor productivity among villagers who took up wet rice cultivation. The old dry rice cultivation system returned 0.17 kilograms of rice per hour of work, while the same people, employing equally rudimentary tools and no animal power, grew 0.65 kilograms of rice per hour using the wet rice system, quadrupling labor efficiency.[11]

An example from central Mexico again indicates the complexity of the question. In the village of Tepoztlán, Morelos, mestizos raise maize both by plow and by hoe technology. Plow cultivation takes 395 hours per hectare per year, while hoe cultivation (*tlacolol*), used especially on the steeper, stonier slopes, requires 1,554 hours. The simpler technology, hoe cultivation, yields 5,176,922 calories per hectare, more than twice the 2,243,333 calories from plow cultivation. For each hour of work the hoe cultivator has a return of 3,332 calories while the plow cultivator has 5,675.[12] Clearly, plow cultivation gives the higher return on labor in Tepoztlán. Other considerations, of course, such as the cost of draft animals and plow land in comparison with tlacolol land, enter into the economics of choice. Plow technology is the more advantageous, and mestizos choose it when they can. This case, the Gambia study, and others like them suggest that the conditions governing labor efficiency are more complex than Boserup indicates.

These ambiguities offer an important perspective for the subsistence agricultures of Latin America. There are three major agricultural regions in tropical Latin America.[13] The first is Mexico and the Pacific margins of Central America. Here, the climate is seasonally wet and dry, and maize and beans, both seed-propagated crops, provide the basic diet. These are planted at the onset of the rainy season and mature in the early dry season. The wet tropical lowlands are the second and largest of the agricultural regions. They include all of South America north of the Tropic of Capricorn, except the Andean region, and extend northward along the Caribbean margins of Central America into the Yucatán Peninsula of Mexico. Rain forests, savannas, and great rivers dominate. Man's impact has been much less here than in the Andes or Mexico, because luxuriant vegetation and rivers that change their courses work steadily to erase the marks made by man.[14] In the wet tropical lowlands the staple food is cassava, a root crop that yields large amounts of carbohydrate but contains only about one percent protein; maize is the staple in Yucatán. Since European contact, rain forest cultivators in some areas have adopted bananas as their staple, but since these are as low in protein as cassava, people have continued to rely on fish or wild game as their main protein source. The third region is the Andean highlands of South America, a region made climatically complex by temperature variations correlated with altitude differences and by mountain blockage of rainfall. Potatoes and other tuber crops are the traditional staple, while seed-bearing crops of quinoa (Chenopodium quinoa) and canihua (Chenopodium pallidicaule) add protein. Wheat and barley, both Old World crops, have become important in post-Columbian times, complementing the maize available at lower elevations.

In examining the agricultures of these regions I concentrate on a few communities where quantitative studies of subsistence agriculture have been carefully carried out. My principal interest is labor efficiency in calories and grams of protein produced per hour of work. In the following pages I will demonstrate the similarities in yields that exist in the three regions despite great differences in environments and agricultures. Since generalizing from a limited sample entails uncertainty, comparisons are made with other data from the region. Many years of field observation in the three regions indicate to me that the villages cited are representative of a large portion of subsistence agriculture in Latin America. Productivity is a complex issue, closely related to environment, technology, and social and political questions. Approaching the three regions in turn, I offer first a description of the environment, followed by an analysis of technology and output and then a discussion of social questions.

I focus on key production statistics of staple carbohydrate foods. Of these, labor efficiency is probably the most important, because with it we can determine how much time must be spent to supply the essential diet. Further, it can be used to compute the potential for surplus production and the ability of a system to absorb further stress on the food supply. Expressing labor efficiency in calories and grams of protein produced per hour of work permits comparisons of systems that depend on different crops and animals. The number of hours expended annually on one hectare of land indicates the intensiveness of the system. Finally, the hectares of food crops grown per household (or per capita) also measures the intensiveness of the agriculture and allows an estimate of the degree of food self-sufficiency. To measure labor efficiency and productivity I have worked closely with peasants and Indians, keeping diaries and weighing crops harvested and fish and game taken. I use examples from local studies because there are few reliable statistics for larger areas. This is reasonable, in any case, because subsistence agriculture operates on a village scale.

Mexico

The subsistence agriculture of Mexico and the Pacific margins of Central America has been adapted, largely through reliance on maize and secondarily on protein-rich beans, to a climate notable for its short and often unpredictable rainy season. The ability of maize to grow rapidly and to draw up moisture with its efficient root system allows it to yield a crop under drought conditions where other moisture-loving crops would fail. Even so, without some rains there can be no crop. Wherever mountains block the path of storms, corn farmers watch the sky and wonder what the scanty and whimsical rain showers hold for them. In these drier parts of the country a mood of anxiety pervades village life from the onset of planting until the harvest is assured. Heat and shortage of food add to the tension, as do late or meager rains. Even today in the villages it is in such seasons that babies and small children are said to die most often. If the maize crop fails, men who are able go off to find work in the cities, so that their families may eat. This is the situation south of the volcano Popocatepetl in the broad area draining southward from the states of Morelos and Puebla into the Rio Balsas, the country of Emiliano Zapata's stronghold in the Revolution of 1910.

Excerpts from my journal illustrate the uncertainty of rains and the campesinos' response at the onset of the dry year of 1976 in the villages of Ixtlilco, Morelos, and San Miguel, Puebla: "May 28: Each afternoon clouds gather. The villagers watch the sky and talk of rain. Today the clouds are heavier than usual, and the wind is stronger. A few drops of rain fall. Clouds come in from the east, but so far they have not been truly heavy. Lightning and thunder add to the drama, but usually the clouds soon disperse. The villagers say, 'The wind blows the rain away.' But today they are most hopeful. The señora, Doña Juanita, says if the rains do not come earlier, they will come on the day of San Juan, June 24. This had happened in 1968. The rain poured down. Soon the *quebradas* (dry stream beds) roared with water carrying off village hogs in the swift current. When the rain stopped the road was full of people going out to their fields to plow, for the heavy rain ensured a strong start for the maize."

The villagers of this area practice subsistence agriculture based on maize and beans, with pigs and cattle as the source of cash income. They follow a short-fallow system of land use that suggests an origin in medieval Europe, cropping for two consecutive years and then fallowing for two. On hill lands close to the villages they have fenced tracts, each of which contains the *milpas* (fields) of several families. During the fallow years the gates are opened and cattle graze freely, depositing dung and urine on the poor soil. Gulches and steep slopes break up this hill land so that in a fenced section roughly half of the land is never cropped. These sections support a cover of scrub timber and scant grasses that provide more grazing than do the fallowed milpas. Alternate fallowing of the entire fenced tract allows recovery of the natural pasture as well as the milpa soil. The campesino ideal is to own milpas in two different fenced areas so that one may be planted while the other recovers.

Maize farming supplies the staple food for the villagers, but sales of surplus corn are not seen as a realistic means to economic security. Rather, cattle represent security and a form of wealth readily convertible into cash. Villagers of even ordinary circumstances try to raise herds of at least half a dozen cattle. Dry years, however, take a heavy toll on cattle, as grazing the fenced tracts or the common village pasture yields little nourishment. In severe droughts scrawny cattle must be sold to prevent their starvation, eroding villagers' economic security but bringing in a little cash with which to purchase corn and beans.

Land, men, and oxen are the main costs connected with maize cultivation, with fertilizer a secondary but important factor. Land is primary. Some have access to *ejido* (community) land, others must rent in order to cultivate, and still others rent to supplement their ejido plots. The more prosperous campesinos speak more positively about renting land than do their poorer neighbors, who prefer to work as peones or under some other fixed contractual arrangement rather than incur the risks involved in cultivating. The rent for a piece of milpa land in the hills is three *cargas* of maize at harvest.[15] The size of the plot varies between twenty and forty *tareas* (one tarea equals 0.1 hectare), depending on the soil quality, slope, and stoniness. The farmer must bear the costs of commercial fertilizer, of feeding his family during the growing season, and, sometimes, of labor and oxen. There is also the uncertainty: a large and good milpa might produce forty cargas, but most harvests are considerably less.

Few villagers own oxen, but most use them. Usually the first year in which a pair is hired out, the owner charges no fee because the three-year-old bulls receive training from the renter. If he is to get any work from them, the renter must accustom them to the yoke and to the intricate work of plowing. At the end of the first season of work the bulls are castrated; rent for the second year is half the full fee. From the third year onward the full fee of six cargas of maize is charged, until at ten or eleven years the oxen are sold for slaughter.

A man with oxen, rented or owned, cannot afford to farm without a peon, because much of the work of growing maize relies on human labor. Oxen can be used only for certain tasks, but with the help of a laborer the acreage cropped can be doubled. Following plowman and oxen, the peon plants the seed, and later he weeds, straightens plants, and applies fertilizer. For the two months involved in plowing, planting, and cultivating, the hired man receives a fifty-kilo *bulto* (sack) of maize to sustain his family, a loan of more corn if needed, and six cargas at harvest. The employer also provides one tarea of land for the peon to plant in maize and one for beans. A peon's work is not as physically demanding as that of a plowman, who commands ten cargas of maize for the season's labor. The family with a strong male adult for plowman and a teenaged boy for peon avoids the heavy expense of hiring labor and thus keeps the bulk of its harvest.

The work cycle of the maize-growing season is most graphically seen through my observations of the Villanueva family of San Miguel during the summer of 1976.

Plowing, June 12: The light rain of two nights before has soaked in enough so that the plowing on the hill lands can begin. The first plowing on this rocky ground is a continual series of stops, of freeing the plow, straightening it, and jabbing the oxen in the hind legs with a sharpened prod to get them moving again. The oxen are thin, one so bony from chronic diarrhea that it can scarcely amble along.

Planting, June 28: Farther down the slope Cristóbal and his eldest son Modesto plant maize on a twenty-tarea milpa that Don Jesús allotted many years ago to Cristóbal. Modesto at eighteen has the full muscles of a strong man in prime condition. He plows. Cristóbal follows behind, glad to take the lighter work of the peon, planting in the furrow opened by the plow. Working steadily, he and Modesto plant four tareas per day. It is surprising how evenly spaced the men, using only awkward plows and clumsy oxen, are able to make the rows in this rocky land. To minimize runoff they open furrows for planting on the contour of the slope. To plant the rows as close to the natural contour as possible, they add short (point) rows wherever necessary to allow for varying slope gradients. This is sophisticated agriculture. Cristóbal wears a *huarache* (sandal) on his left foot, but leaves his right foot bare in order to feel the ground in each spot in the furrow where he will drop the seed maize. With his bare foot he can tell if there is a large stone an inch or two below. If maize seeds were placed directly above such a stone, the maize plants would not be able to send roots downward. After the maize is a couple of inches high, the men will get the milpa ready for cultivating by placing the largest stones (15–20 kilos) between the maize plants in each row, so that the plow can pass between each pair of rows to kill the weeds.

The plow, which also serves as harrow and cultivator, is the only animal-drawn implement. The first cultivating (*beneficiar*) takes place when the maize stands about six inches tall. The abundance of stones makes cultivation especially difficult. Sometimes healthy young plants break when the plow pushes a rock against them. More often the plants simply bend over. Following the plow, the peon pulls a weed here, straightens a plant there. When the maize plants are a bit more than knee-high, the campesinos cultivate for the last time. The corn is now tall enough that by prodding the oxen to a slightly faster walk and leaning the plow handle to rotate the moldboard, the farmer uses the plow to throw loose dirt around the base of the maize plants, "hilling" the maize. The dirt covers small weeds and serves as a dust mulch to conserve moisture in the soil exactly where the young maize roots are most concentrated.

This in essence is the agricultural system of much of Mexico—men and beasts with simple tools laboring on poor land, hoping for adequate rainfall and a harvest large enough to carry them through the year. One way of measuring the adequacy of the system is to look at consumption needs and productivity. Campesinos eat stacks of tortillas at every meal, yet they do get calories from foods such as beans (frijoles); and they like to buy bread now and then from a village bakery. They also eat eggs and meat occasionally, fruit and vegetables sparingly. As a rule of thumb, an adult requires an estimated 1,000,000 calories annually. This amounts to 2700 calories per day, probably too high for warm climates where people are rather small. The average consumption by a child or a teenager is about 80 percent of the adult level.[16]

A specific example of food needs and supplies is the Villanueva family (of three adults and seven children), with whom I lived and worked. If the adults consume 2200 calories per day and the children 80 percent of this amount, and if 70 percent of the calories come from maize, the Villanueva family would eat 4,830,000 calories of maize per year. Actual consumption varies. Caloric needs among men working in the milpas probably well exceed 2200 daily, yet at other seasons the work is lighter. According to an alternative estimate, setting adult intake at 2500 calories and attributing 60 percent of the diet to maize, the Villanueva family would consume 4,708,000 calories of maize per year.

Jesús Villanueva and other peasant farmers calculate that a large family needs twenty cargas, or 11 million calories, of maize annually. This is far more than either of the estimates for the Villanuevas, and the discrepancy between what campesinos say they need and what they actually eat is accounted for by the corn fed to dooryard animals (see table 1). During the tortilla-making process, the skins of maize kernels are loosened by soaking the grains in warm lime water. After soaking, the skins are removed and thrown onto the patio for hogs and chickens to eat. Villagers say, though nutritionists doubt, that nutrients from the kernels leach into the lime water during the soaking process.[17] In the evening, extra masa (tortilla dough) and old, dry tortillas are mixed with the lime water and fed to the hogs.

The energy return on labor expended is high enough to insure the continuation of the present system in Ixtlilco and San Miguel. To work a hectare of land, which normally yields 4,230,692 calories, requires some 395 hours; thus an hour's labor produces about 10,710 calories. The yield varies in other subsistence areas of Mexico. For example, for highland Mayan maize farmers in the state of Chiapas, a hectare yields an average of 3,656,000 calories and requires 486 hours of work (7,523 calories per hour's work). The cost of production was actually higher in Ixtlilco and San Miguel, however, because of the use of oxen. On lands in the tierra caliente (hot lowlands) of the Grijalva Valley, recently made accessible by new roads, the same Mayans used machete and axe methods to grow maize yielding an average of 7,834,000 calories per hectare, at a return of 15,361 calories per hour of work.[18]

Ixtlilco and San Miguel are not entirely representative, since they have benefited from government attempts at rural development.[19] The agricultural modernization, primarily irrigation, has reached only a few lucky families; those without irrigation get enough to eat when there are sufficient rains.[20] When the rains are scant, the extra maize normally fed to swine and chickens acts as an emergency buffer. In a dry year animals can be sold to conserve maize supplies and the cash obtained can be used to buy additional maize. Generally speaking, maize agriculture on these rocky hills produces remarkably good results. With a couple of months of hard work the campesino grows the staple food needed by his family for a whole year. Clearly, the standard of living is well above bare survival.

Increased population pressures now threaten the adequacy of the entire system. In the 1950s a serious landlord-peasant clash in Ixtlilco cost the lives

Table 1. Maize Consumed by the Villanueva Household in One Year

Kilocalories	Use
4,830,000	Eaten by the family
2,400,000	Fed (dry) to hogs and chickens
2,000,000	Lime water, skins of kernels, and extra tortillas and masa fed to hogs

Source: Bergman's 1976 fieldwork, with computations based on Wu Leung, *Food Composition Table*.

of fifteen men, six of them state police; more recent conflicts underline the lack of alternatives to continuing pressure on the land. In theory, small technical changes could increase yields, but peasants are innovative only within prescribed norms. The standard of living that peasants have enjoyed for so long cannot be maintained without increasing support from outside the village. The challenge for the government today is not to improve living standards but simply to maintain them in the Mexican countryside.

The Wet Tropical Lowlands

In the wet tropical lowlands the combination of abundant rainfall and year-round warm weather makes possible more continuous plant growth than anywhere else in the world. With the right domesticated plants in suitably adapted agricultural systems, these wet tropical lowlands could outproduce the best agricultures of any other climate on earth. Reality, however, falls short of theoretical promise. The wet lowlands remain virtually empty lands even today. There are almost no roads. Access is by river or air.

Seasonally flooded plains supporting dense forests tolerant of inundation for half the year stretch out for miles on either side of the rivers. Back from the floodplain stand the interfluves, old land surfaces too high to be covered by even the highest floods. In area, the interfluves comprise about 90 percent of the wet tropical lowlands.[21] They support dense rainforest, yet their soils are poor because yearlong heat and leaching by heavy rainfall have carried away most plant nutrients. Rainforests live on the nutrients released from the decaying remains of their own dead plant life. If the energy cycle is broken by clearing the forest for crops, the soil rapidly becomes useless, usually in about three years, because domesticated crops do not add enough dead plant material to sustain the energy cycle. On these soils a sparse population of peasants and Indians practices shifting cultivation, abandoning plots to nature after two or three years. The adjacent forest moves in and restores the fertility lost through burning the forest, growing crops, and exposing the soil to the sun. Overall, the interfluves support only some 10 percent of the population of the wet lowlands.

Because of the difficulties of farming on the interfluves, most people live in the floodplains or on the borders of interfluves where they meet flood-plains. A village built on the interfluve edge is safe from flooding yet has access to the rich resources of the floodplain, where each year the flooding river deposits a layer of mud that keeps the soil fertile. Periodically, the river changes its course, leaving its old meanders behind as oxbow lakes. Here fish are especially plentiful. At flood, the waters drop most of their mud load at the river's edge, gradually building up natural levees. Old levees stand high enough so that they are flooded only about every five years, and then only to depths of 20–60 centimeters. Out in the floodplain the levees are the only places suitable for habitation. Villages of houses set on stilts a meter high survive floods that occasionally inundate the levees for a month or two. It is estimated that 90 percent of the wet lowlands population lives in or on the edge of the floodplains, which constitute less than 10 percent of the area's land surface.[22]

More than the fertile soil, the abundance of fish attracts people to the floodplain. Among the Shipibos, said to be the largest tribe in the Amazon basin and numbering some 40,000 persons, hunting supplies only 14 per-cent of the protein that they consume. Most game consists of small animals, many of them arboreal. Game is so hard to find that the Shipibo seldom hunt except during February and early March, when the flood forces ground-dwelling animals to take refuge on the higher levees. Parties of four or five men paddle their canoes to levees deep in the rainforest. The hunters walk abreast along the levees, probing with their machetes in organic debris lying between the buttress roots of trees because small animals such as armadillos like to hide there. The men kill with their machetes, though someone in a party carries a bow and arrows and commonly a shotgun.

Hunting, however, is of only secondary importance compared with fish-ing. In a year, the average Shipibo man kills 121 kilograms of game, but he catches 406 kilograms of fish.[23] Because of its adaptability, the basic im-plement for fishing is the bow and arrow. In the backswamps, trees and stands of caña brava (wild cane) stand in the water from December to May, their canopies three or more meters above the highest flood waters. A Shipibo man in a small dugout canoe, just wide enough to admit his haunches, maneuvers his canoe skillfully between the trees, avoiding the cane thickets. The water is clear in the shade of the forest canopy. Often the fisherman can see the fish, especially when the sun is high. When visibility is poor the fisherman can see only the small bubbles that the fish make when just below the surface. An excerpt from my field journal indicates a high degree of skill: "The fisherman sits forward in his canoe with his bow between his legs and resting on his left thigh. His arrow lies against his right thigh. Upon sighting a fish he paddles to within 2.5 or 3 meters and lets his paddle slip quietly into the water. He takes up his bow and arrow and shoots the fish. Seventy percent of the time the arrow found its mark."[24]

Fish in the backswamp are usually small; consequently, the Shipibo brings home fewer kilos of fish for his time spent than if he fished in the rivers or lakes. But the backswamps have one outstanding advantage: fish can be found there year-round, even during high-water season, when fishing is at its worst. The Shipibos procure an average of 0.76 kilograms of fish per hour of fishing in the backswamp. This figure includes the amount of time spent traveling from the village to the fishing site. As backswamps are found almost everywhere, one need not travel far to fish. Backswamp fishing, with its low but reliable return for effort, establishes the minimum efficiency of day-to-day Shipibo subsistence. When all else fails, they can go to the backswamps and find a few small fish. Hunting returns much more, an average of 1.6 kilograms of meat per hour, but is more erratic; only during high floods can one realistically expect to bring back something to eat.

From June to December, when the river is low and the backswamps are empty, or nearly so, Shipibos fish in the rivers and oxbow lakes. Here the return for effort is higher, on the rivers 1.83 kilos per hour of work and on the lakes 1.06 kilos per hour.[25] Actually, fishing is best on the lakes, but the return per hour is less because they are more distant from the village. Shipibo fishing and hunting demonstrate two principles of subsistence: high yield may be less important than proximity to residence in determining work efficiency; and security in a subsistence system comes from an assured minimum of yield that can be depended upon when other, preferred food sources fail.

Like nearly all rainforest peoples, the Shipibos are farmers.[26] Their staple crop is bananas, which in combination with fish provide most of the carbohydrate and protein in the diet. Bananas are eaten in such large quantities that, along with a few minor crops, they supply 28 percent of the protein in the diet even though bananas contain only 1.3 percent protein.[27]

The Shipibos of Panaillo, a village of 107 persons in eastern Peru, grow 10.75 hectares of bananas. They grow well on the fertile soils but tolerate only small amounts of flooding and therefore are planted on high levees where inundations are infrequent and of short duration. Even here a high flood will loosen the roots of some banana plants and cause them to fall. More than thirty days of water at a depth of 60 centimeters will destroy all the bananas. As a result, a village like Panaillo has its banana fields strung out on higher levees at distances up to four kilometers from the village.

Soil fertility is no problem. The alluvial soil is rich and every flood brings more mud. In Panaillo, the Shipibos have been growing bananas on some of the same fields for twenty-five years without interruption and without any decline in yields. In contrast to this permanent agriculture on the flood-plains, in the interfluves bananas yield a good crop the first year, half a crop the second year, and almost nothing the third year. Clearing the rainforest is the toughest job in wet tropical lowland agriculture. The Shipibos' continuous cultivation of the same levee fields minimizes the amount of time spent at this undesirable and demanding task, increasing the return for work done.[28]

Like most peoples of this zone, the Shipibo prepare fields by chopping down the rainforest with machete and axe. The vegetation is left a few weeks during the dry season, and then the dried leaves, vines, and small twigs are burned. Felled trees, stumps, and other debris lie in the ashes cluttering the new field, because the wood is green and will not burn.

After a shower settles the ashes, the villagers plant maize, manioc, or rice. While this crop grows they interplant bananas at intervals of about four paces. In the morning before coming to weed his growing crop, a man cuts and digs a dozen or so banana rootstalks in a nearby chacra and brings them along in his canoe for planting. He places each in a hole and packs dirt around it. The bananas begin yielding one year after planting.

A man cuts the weeds in his banana field once or twice each year. He usually cuts the weeds just above the ground with horizontal machete-strokes, but if there is a dense cover of small weeds he squats and cuts them off slightly below ground level. This poses no danger to the machete because the fine alluvial soil has no stones.[29] The women harvest the bananas, skillfully cutting down the banana plants so that the fruit is unbruised and carrying the bunches home on their backs.

A Shipibo man works an average of 1.6 hours per day and a woman 0.3 hours to provide food for themselves and their children. The excellent diet they procure by this work is perhaps the best proof of the natural richness of their environment. The average adult consumes 1,856 calories per day, 84 percent of which comes from agricultural crops. He consumes 75 grams of protein per day, 58 percent from fish.[30] An hour's work growing bananas produces 13,800 calories. This figure includes the time used to clear a small amount of rainforest each year to establish new banana fields. Because of this highly efficient banana production, a Shipibo of Panaillo spends only 150 hours per year growing food crops, mainly bananas, while his wife works 117 hours at this task. In contrast, he works 359 hours fishing and 76 hours hunting. Hunting or fishing goes on every day; growing bananas requires little effort or attention, except when a high flood endangers the fields. The Shipibo then become truly worried.

The year-round nature of Shipibo bananas and fish or game minimizes the likelihood of shortage.[31] In contrast, campesino maize farmers in Mexico base their entire food supply on one harvest that is dependent on uncertain rains. On the whole, Shipibos have a more secure livelihood than the campesinos of San Miguel and Ixtlilco because the population density of only four persons per square kilometer reduces competition for natural resources. Their subsistence system demonstrates how well mankind can live with a simple technology, provided resources are abundant and population is low.[32] In past millennia, probably many peoples lived as well. The Shipibo system rewards labor well; it is outstanding in this respect, but the Shipibos use the overall potential of their environment only poorly. Far more food could be produced. Their system is a quaint anachronism surviving from a time when few people inhabited the earth.

At present, a cohesive social structure contributes much to Shipibo well-being. Each village is a large extended family where food sharing is a deeply entrenched norm. If a man does well fishing, he invites his kinsmen to eat with his family. Such sharing goes on in a village many times every day. Matrilocal residence ensures a high degree of cooperation among the women. The Shipibo recognize that they live better than "Peruvian" families living in the floodplain because the Peruvian villages do not have the general support mechanisms of the Shipibo.[33]

For the future, the Shipibos' challenge will be to provide for much greater population densities while retaining their present security and good nutrition.[34] Even now there are problems. The rapidly increasing population of towns in the tropical lowlands has created a demand for more fish. Commercial fishermen come long distances with motorized dugouts and long nets to fish out the best spots in the rivers and lakes during the dry season, straining the Shipibos' protein resources. As regional demand for commercial food increases, the Shipibo subsistence system must endure great changes. First to fail will be their sources of protein from fish and game. Animal husbandry could produce the needed meat and eventually probably will. But the Shipibos, while they are excellent fishermen, are frightfully inept animal husbandrymen, as was demonstrated by the complete failure of a recent attempt to introduce cattle among them. As long as fish remain available, the Shipibos will continue to try to supply their needs from this source.[35]

Increased population pressure will affect the cropping system more slowly. High levees suited to banana growing will gradually be taken up. Shipibo cultivation of seasonal crops in the backswamps during the dry season now utilizes a tiny proportion of the fertile backswamp land. The long-term production of food in the floodplain must eventually concentrate on the backswamps, unpromising though they may look today.[36]

So far, the Peruvian government has had little impact on Shipibo food supply. A few years ago a government commission formalized the boundaries of the village lands, ensuring the people of Panaillo plenty of space for agriculture. Village fishing rights are more difficult to establish and even harder to enforce against the commercial fisherman. The Shipibos would definitely welcome government protection of their traditional fishing grounds, but policing would be prohibitively expensive.[37] Yet as long as adequate protein can be secured, the Shipibo subsistence system will continue without major modification.

The Andes Mountains

The Andes Mountains have many climates. Mean temperatures decline with rising elevation at the rate of about 3.6 degrees per thousand feet. By this factor alone a temperature of 90 degrees Fahrenheit at 500 feet (152 meters) in the wet tropical lowlands of the upper Amazon is reduced to 57 degrees at 9,000 feet (2,743 meters) and 47 degrees at 12,000 feet (3,657 meters).[38] At the higher elevations where Inca civilization developed, sunny skies and pleasant daytime temperatures are often followed by near-freezing nights.[39] Rainfall also varies with elevation and topography. Easterly winds bring moisture-laden air from the Amazon lowland and force it up the Andean slopes, where the air cools and drops heavy rains on the east sides of the successive Andean ranges. The air stabilizes as it moves west, dropping less moisture on the leeward, western side of each range. The valleys lying in the "rainshadow" between north-south ranges are very deep.[40]

The food supply system is based on diversification rather than the specialization observed in Mexico and the wet tropical lowlands. The threat of frost, hail, and drought in the growing season makes harvests uncertain in the high Andes. Farmers minimize this risk by growing several crops and, if possible, cultivating them at different altitudes. In southern Peru the north-south ranges coalesce into vast altiplanos, where there are few adjacent valleys that enable subsistence farmers to grow crops in several ecological zones. Those living in the altiplano rely on their herd animals (llamas, alpaca, and sheep) for survival if their crops fail.[41] The situation in much of northern Peru is more favorable because varied ecological zones are within realistic traveling distances. In the northern Andes, lower population densities and greater rainfall offer other advantages.

The village of Uchucmarca, located 3,100 meters high in the Andes of La Libertad province in northern Peru, offers a case study in the workings of subsistence agriculture in the multiple ecological zones of the Andes. The village appears to have been founded in the late sixteenth century from scattered populations brought together under the *reducción* program of Viceroy Francisco de Toledo. The villagers of Uchucmarca today are primarily mestizo, both culturally and genetically. All of them speak Spanish. Quechua place names and terms for certain agricultural activities are the only evidence of the Indian language. Families provide most of their own labor, although some tasks are performed collectively, in the Andean traditional manner. Much land is rented or sharecropped. Sloping fields with stone walls at the lower edge are the norm, in contrast to the series of flat-topped terraces like those in the Urubamba valley in southern Peru, where land management practices are more intensive.[42]

The lowest ecological zone of Uchucmarca is the *kichwa fuerte* (zone of grain cultivation), lying between 1,500 and 1,900 meters, where the rain-shadow effect is strong. Because of the constant threat of drought, villages exploit the scrub forest of the kichwa fuerte mainly for firewood. In years of adequate rainfall, they also grow small plots of maize and wheat. Higher, between 1,900 and 2,450 meters, lies the kichwa zone. Here the rainshadow effect is much less, rainfall is dependable, and temperatures are milder. The rainy season is long enough to grow maize and wheat, even though in this climate both crops require seven to nine months to mature. Since the amount of kichwa land available on the valley slopes at Uchucmarca is quite limited, villagers who do not own their own plots in this staple-producing zone try to sharecrop or obtain grain through reciprocal agreements. The Spanish introduction of wheat undoubtedly increased the utility of the kichwa and kichwa fuerte zones, where probably only maize was cultivated before the conquest.[43]

The *templado* zone (2,450 to 3,100 meters) is transitional between the warmer, drier lower valley and the cooler, wetter upper valley. In the lower parts of this zone the mestizos grow maize, wheat, and barley. They raise field peas only in this zone, and potatoes appear at the upper edge. The village of Uchucmarca is located precisely at the boundary between grain and potato cultivation.[44]

Immediately above the village of Uchucmarca, one enters the *jalka* (3,100 to 3,500 meters). This is alpine tundra, called *puna* in southern Peru and *páramo* in extreme northern Peru. The jalka is the potato zone, original home of the "Irish" potato and dozens of close relatives. The land widens here, so there is no shortage of plots for cultivation in Uchucmarca. Accordingly, more land and more time are devoted to the potato and other tubers than to any other crops. Other tubers include *oca (Oxalis tuberosa)*, *mashua (Tropaeolum tuberosum)*, and *ulluco (Ullucus tuberosa)*. Ullucos are often fed to hogs. Nontuberous crops cultivable in the jalka include the edible Andean lupine called *tarwi (Lupinus mutabilis)*, broad beans (*habas*), and barley. Apart from the Spanish-introduced barley, these crops have been grown in the jalka zone of the Andes for millennia. Here, and higher up in the jalka fuerte, hundreds of relic fields give mute testimony to the earlier presence of a denser population. Today, the abundance of jalka land allows periodic fallowing. The mestizos raise potatoes on a field for one or two years and then plant ocas, ullucos, and mashuas on at least part of it for another year or two. After this the field is fallowed for at least five years to restore fertility.[45]

The jalka fuerte (3,500 to 4,300 meters) is high tundra. In this zone above Uchucmarca, the rainfall is heavy; there is no appreciable dry season, and frosts are frequent. While part of this zone was cultivated in the past, today it is pasture for Old World livestock (cattle, sheep, and horses). In southern Peru, alpacas and llamas graze at elevations even higher than Old World livestock. Livestock raising has a more prominent place in the economy of the Uchucmarca mestizos than it does among Quechua Indian farmers in southern Peru. Livestock is the main source of cash. Villagers seldom slaughter cattle, but they do butcher animals that die by falling from cliffs. They occasionally eat mutton, pork, and guinea pigs. Andean Indians have raised guinea pigs for at least two thousand years, and families commonly keep fifty to seventy-five, treating them as pets but occasionally butchering a few.[46]

Oxen and an iron-tipped wooden plow are the principal means of tilling the land. Only very small or very steep fields are worked by hand with a pick and hoe. Because of the long fallows in the kichwa fuerte and jalka zones, preparing a field for planting often begins with clearing and burning brushwood. After this, in the lower elevations the soil is worked with a hoe, and maize or beans are grown the first year or two. In following years, when the stumps are rotted enough, the land can be plowed. In the jalka the fallows run for as long as fifteen years, necessitating considerable clearing before a field can be planted again. Here after removing shrubs and bushes, farmers either turn the land by hand or plow. This task is especially difficult because of the tough tundra sod. Potatoes or ocas are planted on these newly cleared jalka fields. A furrow is opened with a plow; the wife follows behind dropping in seed tubers; and another furrow is plowed to cover the tubers. They are hoed once or twice to eliminate weeds, aerate the soil, and facilitate drainage. At harvest, potatoes and ocas are dug up with a hoe.[47]

Cereals are the main crops in the kichwa and templada zones. Fields are not fallowed except when periodic droughts cause villagers to abandon cultivation in the kichwa. Fertility is maintained by penning (folding) sheep on a field before plowing. In the templada zone lentils and field peas, both nitrogen-fixing legumes, are planted in mixed stands with barley to help maintain fertility. Wheat, barley, and legumes are sown broadcast and a final plowing covers the seed. No weeding is done after these crops are planted. Maize is planted by poking holes in the soil with a stick and dropping in seed. Cereals and legumes are harvested with a sickle. The grain is carried to a threshing floor, where eight to fifteen horses tied side by side are driven around and around to separate the grain from the straw. After maize has dried somewhat in the field, the ears are pulled from the stalks, tied in pairs, and carried home, where they are hung from the rafters.[48]

Because the yields of Andean crops vary unpredictably, the objective of each subsistence farmer is to have crops in different ecological zones so that, whatever the weather, at least one will be good. Consequently, the labor efficiency of different crops is quite varied, and farmers often experience very low yields per unit of labor in the interest of security. The diversity of yields is demonstrated by the crops at Uchucmarca in 1971, the year of Steven Brush's observation. As always, the villagers of Uchucmarca devoted more time and acreage to potatoes than to any other crop, and yet potatoes supplied only 16 percent of their caloric intake. They produced an average of 2693 kilograms per hectare (40 bushels per acre), a very low output. Wheat yielded far better by caloric measure, an average of 2217 kilograms per hectare (33 bushels per acre), which translates into almost three times the caloric value of the potato harvest. The explanation for this seemingly uneconomic emphasis on potatoes is that rains were especially heavy in 1971, harming potatoes in the jalka but producing an exceptional wheat crop in the kichwa.[49] Such unequal rewards for effort are the logical result of spreading the risk among several crops and ecological zones when one does not know which will give the best return in a particular year.

Maize production further demonstrates the spreading of risk by Andean farmers. In 1971 maize yielded 609 kilograms per hectare (10 bushels per acre), a low return. An average man-day of work produced only 6.5 kilograms of corn, compared to 34.7 kilograms of wheat. The abundant rains had been quite sufficient for the wheat but apparently had declined early, giving insufficient moisture for the critical tasseling and silking stages in maize growth.

Diversification is a rational strategy for Andean farmers even though it often appears uneconomic. In 1971, heads of households in Uchucmarca worked forty-six days to grow potatoes that provided only 16 percent of calories in the diet, thirty-three days to grow maize that supplied 10 percent of the diet, and only twenty-eight days to grow wheat that constituted 47 percent of the diet.[50] Yet in a dry year, the ratio of labor to output for each crop would be quite different. Survival in a subsistence system depends on producing enough food each year no matter what the weather; variable yields among different crops and climatic zones provide the security necessary for survival if properly managed.

Data from the altiplano of southern Peru (District of Nuñoa, Department of Puno) permit a limited comparison with Uchucmarca. At Nuñoa, in addition to wheat and barley, Andean cereals are grown at higher elevations, quinoa up to 4250 meters and canihua up to 4450 meters. Potatoes, the most important of the tubers, are grown at altitudes up to 4250 meters, and the bitter potato up to 4450 meters.[51] At Nuñoa, as at Uchucmarca, labor efficiency was greater for growing cereals than tubers. The ratio of energy expended growing cereals compared with the amount of energy produced by that food was 1:23; with tubers, the ratio was 1:10. Thus the labor efficiency of cereal production was over twice as high as for tubers, while at Uchucmarca in 1971 it was fully five times as great.[52]

The agrarian reform program of the Peruvian military government (1968–80) helped reduce one threat to the survival of Andean subsistence systems: the pressure of haciendas on village land and labor. Today, population growth threatens subsistence agriculture in large parts of southern Peru, especially in the Lake Titicaca basin. In the lake basin, 3,800 meters above sea level, local densities of 270 people per square kilometer are supported by subsistence agriculture in one of the bleaker natural environments occupied by man. Among the Aymara, the average family of five has only 1.85 hectares of land, with some villages having averages as low as 0.84 hectares per family. This leaves no land to fallow. In contrast, the average family in Uchucmarca grows 1.58 hectares of food crops per year, but they have other acreage in fallow so that fertility is maintained.[53]

The Aymara communities appear to be undergoing rapid change as population density continues to increase. Along with the Quechua communities of the Lake Titicaca basin, they manifest a tension, an energy that one does not observe elsewhere in the Andes. In 1979, I found many villagers engaged in illegal processing of coca leaves for cocaine in order to make a living, and the police were afraid to go to many communities. Disintegration of traditional subsistence systems was in full swing.

Uchucmarca and similar northern Peruvian communities, in contrast to the Lake Titicaca basin, seem capable of retaining subsistence farming for some time to come. Relying on differentiated ecological zones and low population densities, these communities will be able to preserve their way of life against the inroads of modernization if they are spared the negative features of government development projects. In the process, their people will enjoy a secure if not abundant living derived from traditional practices.

Conclusion

Similarities in the production statistics of the three groups seem far more striking than the differences. One might expect that it would be much harder to get food for a family in one environment than another, especially when natural environments vary greatly. Yet, an hour's work growing maize in Ixtlilco in central Mexico produces 10,710 calories, while an hour's work growing bananas in the wet tropical lowlands at Panaillo produces 13,785 calories. The difference in productivity is only 30 percent (table 2). An hour's work at Uchucmarca nets some 30 percent less than at Ixtlilco, but this reflects the deliberate choice of lower overall labor efficiency in the interest of diversification. Yields in calories per hectare varied only 20 percent among all three sites. Protein production varied more, yet the higher yield in protein per hectare at Uchucmarca is linked with a lower caloric yield. In all three cases, a family of five can be fed with two to three hours of work per day. This, indeed, indicates a great underlying similarity in productivity.

It appears that stable subsistence farming systems, as these three, arrive at similar returns to labor and even to land. When the subsistence farmer succeeds in providing food, while leaving himself enough time to supply needs such as housing and a few luxuries, he stops trying to further increase labor efficiency or yield per hectare.

One can easily fall into the error of thinking that these traditional systems of agriculture produce no more because they cannot. The assumption is made that hand tools and draft animals have limitations that put a ceiling on

Table 2: Production of Principal Staple Crops by Subsistence Farmers

	Ixtlilco and San Miguel, Mexico: Maize	Panaillo, lowland Peru: Bananas	Uchucmarca, highland Peru: Wheat, barley, potatoes, maize, etc.
Yield per hectare (kilocalories)	4,230,692[b]	4,324,000[c]	5,326,000[d]
Kilocalories per hour of work[a]	10,710	13,785	7,238
Hours of work per hectare[a]	395	314	736
Yield of protein per hectare per year (grams)	101,230	49,395	223,735[e]
Grams of protein per hour of work	256	157	303
Hectares of food crops per household	2.6[b]	1.0[c]	1.58[f]

[a]The length of the workday for the Mexican campesinos is from Oscar Lewis, *Life in a Mexican Village*, chap. 7. The workday for the campesino engaged in plow agriculture appears to be about eight hours. This agrees closely with the work habits of the farmers of Ixtlilco and San Miguel. Work information for the Shipibos was recorded by hours (see Bergman, *Amazon Economics*, pp. 30, 127, 296). Brush (*Mountain, Field, and Family*, p. 96) recorded the Uchucmarca data by days. I have converted his data on the basis of an eight-hour day.

[b]Based on an ordinary harvest of 20 cargas of maize from a 26-tarea (2.6-hectare) milpa.

[c]Bergman, *Amazon Economics*, p. 133. One hectare includes all food crops, some of which are sold. Each household grew an average of 0.63 hectares of bananas. Among the Shipibos, fish and meat are the primary sources of protein and bananas are a supplement.

[d]Brush, *Mountain, Field, and Family*, p. 175.

[e]Ibid. This figure seems a bit high. It is difficult to reconstruct Brush's computation, but he apparently included the broad beans and field peas with the staple crops. The beans and peas also account for the lower return in kilocalories for an hour of work.

[f]Ibid., p. 86.

productivity. They do have limits, but their limits have not been reached. Productivity remains low but the cause appears to be social, not technical. When economic well-being is maintained, there is no pressure to innovate. In all three cases, production could be increased by changes in technique requiring no more than minor cash investments, and in some cases none at all. Even with intensified labor, efficiency need not decline and in some instances could rise. These three case studies suggest that food production in Latin America can be greatly enhanced and the prosperity of subsistence farmers much improved while maintaining the traditional social framework and avoiding the costs of mechanization.

The implications of these findings for the political and social aspects of food in Latin America are profound. Planners view subsistence agriculture as an obstacle to national development, for its practitioners produce little or nothing for the market and purchase the same. Since subsistence farmers occupy land capable of producing more and can potentially consume more industrial products and modern services, their way of life is targeted for extinction.

Fortunately for the subsistence farmers of Latin America, ambitious development schemes aimed at bringing them into the "modern" sector have been only partially successful. The onset of high energy costs a decade ago and the more recent world recession have taken their toll on development funds and plans. Politicians and planners should take advantage of the present moment to rethink the role of subsistence agriculture in their countries' futures.

As our cases illustrate, a certain amount of government intervention may be desirable, even necessary, to preserve the integrity of subsistence agriculture against population pressures and outside encroachment on resources. But the more pressing question is whether the past emphasis on converting subsistence farmers to full-scale market producers and consumers should be continued, modified, or abandoned altogether. Would the additional food that might (but might not) result from modernized agriculture be worth the investment of scarce resources to produce it? Would such food be competitive in the market with cheap foreign surpluses, or would it require subsidies paid indirectly by urban consumers? Would the purchasing power of former subsistence farmers be enough to sustain or rekindle industrial development? What could replace subsistence agriculture as a refuge for the urban unemployed and as a safety valve for urban political unrest in times of economic depression?

The future of the farmers of Ixtlilco and San Miguel, Uchucmarca, and Panaillo rests on political decisions taken by Latin America's urban majorities. If the leadership of those groups can be educated to the fact that subsistence agriculture may be beneficial, not detrimental, to the national welfare, and if they adopt the appropriate policies, then subsistence agriculture will survive well into the future.

Notes

1. Clifton R. Wharton, Jr., "Subsistence Agriculture: Concepts and Scope," in *Subsistence Agriculture and Economic Development,* ed. Clifton R. Wharton, Jr. (Chicago: Aldine, 1969), pp. 18–19; Rand McNally, *1982 Commercial Atlas and Marketing Guide* (Chicago), pp. F-17, F-19, F-20; *The New Encyclopaedia Britannica* (1981), 1:316.

2. See: William Allan, *Studies in African Land Usage in Northern Rhodesia* (Cape Town and New York: Oxford University Press, 1949); William Allan, *The African Husbandman* (New York: Barnes and Noble, 1965); Pierre de Schlippe, *Shifting Cultivation in Africa: The Zande System of Agriculture* (London: Routledge & Kegan Paul, 1956).

3. Marshall Sahlins, *Stone Age Economics* (Chicago and New York: Aldine-Atherton, 1972), pp. 17–26.

4. Richard B. Lee, "What Hunters Do for a Living, or, How to Make Out on Scarce Resources," in *Man the Hunter,* eds. Richard B. Lee and Irven DeVore (Chicago: Aldine, 1968), p. 33.

5. Ester Boserup, *The Conditions of Agricultural Growth: The Economics of Agrarian Change under Population Pressure* (Chicago: Aldine, 1965), pp. 32–34.

6. "Over 200 million people, thinly scattered over 14 million square miles of the tropics, obtain the bulk of their food by the system of shifting cultivation. They form a little under 10% of the world's population, and are spread over more than 30% of its exploitable soils" (P. H. Nye and D. J. Greenland, *The Soil under Shifting Cultivation,* Technical Communication no. 51, Commonwealth Bureau of Soil Science, Harpenden [Farnham Royal, Bucks, England: Commonwealth Agricultural Bureau, 1960], p. v).

7. India, Directorate of Economics and Statistics, *Studies in the Economics of Farm Management in Madras: Report for the Year 1956–57* (New Delhi: Ministry of Food and Agriculture, 1960), p. 191.

8. Roland W. Bergman, *Amazon Economics: The Simplicity of Shipibo Indian Wealth,* Dellplain Latin American Studies no. 6 (Ann Arbor: University Microfilms International, 1980): 209, 218.

9. Harold C. Conklin, *Hanunóo Agriculture: A Report of an Integral System of Shifting Cultivation in the Philippines,* FAO Forestry Development Paper no. 12 (Rome: Food and Agriculture Organization of the United Nations, 1957): 152.

10. India, *Farm Management in Madras,* pp. 205–6; John Lossing Buck, *Chinese Farm Economy: A Study of 2866 Farms in Seventeen Localities and Seven Provinces*

in China (Chicago: University of Chicago Press, 1930), pp. 20, 203–4, 227–28; Prospero R. Covar, *The Masagana-Margate System of Planting Rice: A Study of an Agricultural Innovation* (Manila, Philippines: Community Development Council, University of the Philippines, 1960), pp. 69, 73, 141.

11.   Margaret R. Haswell, *The Changing Pattern of Economic Activity in a Gambia Village,* Department of Technical Co-operation, Overseas Research Publication no. 2 (London: Her Majesty's Stationery Office, 1963): 16, 39, 46, 102. Wet rice labor efficiency is computed from 621 hours per acre (p. 39) and 884 pounds per acre in 1949 (p. 102). The decline was from 830 to 621 hours per acre (p. 39).

12.   Oscar Lewis, *Life in a Mexican Village: Tepoztlán Revisited* (Urbana: University of Illinois Press, 1963), pp. 105, 145–47, 154.

13.   For more information on the climates of Latin America see Preston E. James, *Latin America,* 4th ed. (New York: Odyssey Press, 1969); Robert C. West and John P. Augelli, *Middle America: Its Lands and Peoples,* 2nd ed. (Englewood Cliffs, N.J.: Prentice-Hall, 1976).

14.   Donald W. Lathrap, *The Upper Amazon* (New York: Praeger, 1970), p. 57.

15.   A carga of shelled maize weighs 140 kilograms.

16.   Clara Mae Taylor, Grace MacLeod, and Mary Swartz Rose, *Foundations of Nutrition,* 5th ed. (New York: MacMillan, 1956), p. 525.

17.   Woot-Tsuen Wu Leung, *Food Composition Table for Use in Latin America* (Bethesda: The International Committee on Nutrition for National Defense, National Institutes of Health, 1961), pp. 13, 15. The nutritional content of a tortilla, dry weight, is 400 calories per 100 grams. White maize contains 403 calories per 100 grams, leaving a loss in the tortilla-making process of only 3 calories.

18.   Frank Cancian, *Change and Uncertainty in a Peasant Economy: The Maya Corn Farmers of Zinacantan* (Stanford: Stanford University Press, 1972), pp. 47, 70, 72, 74, 171, 187. Local measures used by Cancian are converted to metric measures in order to make this comparison.

19.   Peter Goldman, "Scolding in Mexico," *Newsweek,* Feb. 26, 1979, pp. 41–42.

20.   Other studies on Mexican rural life show local variations of maize agriculture but on the whole demonstrate a marked similarity to the agriculture of Central Mexico and Chiapas. See especially: Robert Redfield and Alfonso Villa Rojas, *Chan Kom: A Maya Village,* first Phoenix ed. (Chicago: University of Chicago Press, 1962), pp. 51–86; Oscar Lewis, *Pedro Martínez: A Mexican Peasant and His Family* (New York: Random House, 1964), pp. 461–69 (Appendix I, "Division of Labor and Family Budget"); William E. Carter, *New Lands and Old Traditions: Kekchi Cultivators in the Guatemalan Lowlands* (Gainesville: University of Florida Press, 1969); Campbell W. Pennington, *The Tarahumar of Mexico: Their Environment and Material Culture* (Salt Lake City: University of Utah Press, 1963); George A. Collier, *Fields of the Tzotzil: The Ecological Bases of Tradition in Highland Chiapas* (Austin: University of Texas Press, 1975).

21.   C. F. Marbut and C. B. Manifold, "The Topography of the Amazon Valley," *Geographical Review* 15 (1925): 617–42.

22.   William M. Denevan, "A Cultural-Ecological View of the Former Aboriginal

Settlement in the Amazon Basin," *Professional Geographer* 18 (1966): 346–51.

23. Bergman, *Amazon Economics,* pp. 89, 150–52, 207–8, 218.

24. Cited in Bergman, *Amazon Economics,* pp. 136–37.

25. Ibid., pp. 136–37, 161, 208.

26. For an exhaustive listing of the tribes of the wet tropical lowlands and their livelihoods, see Julian H. Steward, ed., *Handbook of South American Indians,* vol. 3: *The Tropical Forest Tribes,* Smithsonian Institution, Bureau of American Ethnology, Bulletin 143 (Washington, D.C., 1948).

27. Bergman, *Amazon Economics,* pp. 205, 233.

28. Ibid., pp. 46, 58, 75–76, 89, 127, 133.

29. Field Notes (Jan. 1971–Feb. 1972); cf. Bergman, *Amazon Economics,* pp. 97–99.

30. Bergman, *Amazon Economics,* pp. 100–101, 176, 209.

31. Ibid., pp. 87–88, 94, 126–27, 135, 204, 209.

32. Other studies on subsistence in the wet tropical lowlands include: Stephen J. Beckerman, "The Cultural Energetics of the Bari (Motilones Bravos) of Northern Colombia" (Ph.D. diss., Dept. of Anthropology, University of New Mexico, 1976); Allen Johnson, "The Energy Costs of Technology in a Changing Environment: A Machiguenga Case," in *Material Culture: Styles, Organization, and Dynamics of Technology,* eds. Heather Lechtman and Robert S. Merrill (St. Paul: West, 1977), pp. 155–67; Daniel R. Gross, George Eiten et al., "Ecology and Acculturation among Native Peoples of Central Brazil," *Science* 206 (1979): 1043–50; Robert L. Carneiro, "Shifting Cultivation among the Amahuaca of Eastern Peru," *Völkerkundliche Abhandlungen* 1 (1964): 9–18; B. LeRoy Gordon, "Anthropogeography and Rainforest Ecology in Bocas del Toro Province, Panama" (Berkeley: Department of Geography, University of California, 1969, Photocopy); Betty J. Meggers, *Amazonia: Man and Culture in a Counterfeit Paradise* (Chicago: Aldine-Atherton, 1971); William M. Denevan and Roland W. Bergman, "Karinya Indian Swamp Cultivation in the Venezuelan Llanos," *Yearbook of the Association of Pacific Coast Geographers* 37 (Corvallis: Oregon State University Press, 1975): 23–37; William M. Denevan and Karl H. Schwerin, "Adaptive Strategies in Karinya Subsistence, Venezuelan Llanos," *Antropología* (Caracas) 50 (1978):3–91.

33. Bergman, *Amazon Economics,* p. 78.

34. Ibid., pp. 212–14.

35. Ibid., pp. 203, 215–18.

36. Ibid., pp. 89, 92, 217.

37. Ibid., pp. 215–17.

38. R. Brooke Thomas and Bruce P. Winterhalder, "Physical and Biotic Environment of Southern Highland Peru," in *Man in the Andes: A Multidisciplinary Study of High-Altitude Quechua,* eds. Paul T. Baker and Michael A. Little (Stroudsburg, Pa.: Dowden, Hutchinson and Ross, 1976), p. 27.

39. Andrew Marshall, ed., *The 1971 South American Handbook,* 47th ed. (London: Trade and Travel Publications), p. 491.

40. Thomas and Winterhalder, "Physical and Biotic Environment," p. 21.

41. R. Brooke Thomas, "Energy Flow at High Altitude," in *Man in the Andes: A Multidisciplinary Study of High-Altitude Quechua*, eds. Paul T. Baker and Michael A. Little (Stroudsburg, Pa.: Dowden, Hutchinson and Ross, 1976), pp. 388–92.

42. Stephen B. Brush, *Mountain, Field, and Family: The Economy and Human Ecology of an Andean Valley* (Philadelphia: University of Pennsylvania Press, 1977), pp. 12, 49–50, 56–58, 78, 87, 92, 98.

43. Ibid., pp. 10, 77, 81, 88.

44. Ibid., pp. 12, 78.

45. Ibid., pp. 78–79.

46. Ibid., pp. 79, 99, 115–16, 176; Edward P. Lanning, *Peru before the Incas* (Englewood Cliffs, N.J.: Prentice-Hall, 1967) pp. 57–58, 63.

47. Brush, *Mountain, Field, and Family*, pp. 93–95.

48. Ibid., pp. 94–95, 99.

49. Ibid., pp. 96–97, 112, 115, 174, 177. For the caloric content of wheat and potatoes see Wu Leung, *Food Composition Table*, pp. 19, 37.

50. Brush, *Mountain, Field, and Family*, preface, pp. 99, 130, 174, 177.

51. Thomas, "Energy Flow at High Altitude," p. 389. The longer summer days in southern Peru (15° south latitude) allow crops to be grown at higher elevations than at Uchucmarca (7° south latitude). Furthermore, the present-day upper terminus of cultivation is lower at Uchucmarca than in former centuries. Brush notes (*Mountain, Field, and Family*, p. 173) that the mestizos do not grow bitter potatoes or quinoa and canihua. Probably these frost-tolerant crops were important in preconquest times. Brush observes (ibid.) that heavy rains and irregular frosts discourage the making of freeze-dried potatoes (*chuño*), yet I believe they can be made at Uchucmarca. The Quechua of Tequile Island in Lake Titicaca, for example, carry their bitter potatoes up to a mountain meadow in order to freeze them.

52. Thomas, "Energy Flow at High Altitude," p. 390; Brush, *Mountain, Field, and Family*, pp. 96, 174.

53. Ted Lewellen, *Peasants in Transition: The Changing Economy of the Peruvian Aymara: A General Systems Approach* (Boulder, Colo.: Westview Press, 1978), p. 42; Brush, *Mountain, Field, and Family*, p. 86. Other studies of Andean agriculture include: Richard N. Adams, *A Community in the Andes: Problems and Progress in Muquiyauyo* (Seattle: University of Washington Press, 1959); F. LaMond Tullis, *Lord and Peasant in Peru: A Paradigm of Political and Social Change* (Cambridge: Harvard University Press, 1970); Enrique José Mayer, *Reciprocity, Self-Sufficiency and Market Relations in a Contemporary Community in the Central Andes of Peru*, Latin American Studies Program, Dissertation Series, no. 72 (Ithaca, N.Y.: Cornell University, Aug. 1974); William B. Hutchinson, "Sociocultural Change in the Mantaro Valley Region of Peru: Acolla, A Case Study" (Ph.D. diss., Dept. of Anthropology, Indiana University, 1973); David Guillet, *Agrarian Reform and Peasant Economy in Southern Peru* (Columbia: University of Missouri Press, 1979).

Lana L. Hall

United States Food Aid and the Agricultural Development of Brazil and Colombia, 1954–73

Food aid became an explicit and continuing element of United States foreign policy toward the developing world with the creation of Public Law 480 ("Food for Peace") in 1954. Latin America has been the second-largest recipient of American food aid, after Asia. This chapter focuses on the effects of United States food aid, specifically P.L. 480 imports, on the agricultural development of Brazil and Colombia, the two major Latin American receivers.

Brazil and Colombia's reliance on food aid until 1973, when P.L. 480 imports ceased, was partly a result of imbalances in their development policies. The availability of donated food also directly affected their internal food policies. This cause-and-effect interaction of food aid is illuminated below in a discussion of the importance of food, particularly of the food grains, the relevance of food aid to general development objectives, and the effects of these imports on agricultural development.

Policies for Economic Development

The import substitution policies followed by Brazil and Colombia in the 1950s, while aimed at promoting rapid industrial growth, set the stage for the steady increase in the importation of food grains for the following two decades. Confronted by poor export market prospects for their agricultural products (especially coffee in both cases) and influenced by the Prebisch Doctrine and the Economic Commission for Latin America, the Brazilian and Colombian governments embraced industrialization through domestic production of durable consumer goods as the most promising growth path. Basic elements of the strategy included preferential exchange rates for imported industrial raw materials and intermediary goods in general, special incentives for the importation of capital goods, and public financing of the basic industrial infrastructure.

This growth model neglected domestic agriculture. Brazil and Colombia recognized that food output should increase both to keep pace with the transfer of labor to the industrial sector and to keep food prices and wages low, but they seldom encouraged domestic food production. Agricultural exports were implicitly taxed by commercial trade and exchange rate policies that favored imports of industrial raw materials, and there was little infrastructural investment in the agricultural sector.

In Colombia, for example, the availability of food generally fell below the estimated 3.2 percent population growth rate, contributing to a 12.5 percent annual rate of inflation in food prices.[1] Brazil assumed that the expansion of agricultural acreage would provide enough food for urban centers. Roads and storage facilities were constructed to facilitate this acreage expansion, but few direct incentives were offered to domestic producers.[2] The growth rate of food production was only about half that of manufacturing from 1955 through 1965 (4.5 percent as opposed to 9.1 percent). Acreage expansion helped food production keep pace with population growth, but the increase in the demand for food, associated with income growth, fueled an average increase of 44 percent per year in food prices.[3]

These high inflation rates threatened industrialization, since urban workers spent almost half their income on food (44.7 percent for a typical São Paulo worker and 48.7 percent for a laborer in Bogotá). Food price inflation generated demands for wage increases and limited workers' ability to purchase consumer durables, thus restricting markets and slowing industrialization. Further, a country cannot allow real urban wages to continue to decline without paying a political toll in terms of worker dissatisfaction, possible violent protest, and general political instability.

Both Brazil and Colombia increased food imports in an attempt to control inflation and urban real wages. Basic cereal grains—wheat, rice, and corn, so important in diets and budgets—constituted the bulk of the imports. Rural families in Colombia spent 27 percent of their food budget on cereals, urban families 18 percent.[4] In São Paulo State, 52 percent of rural and 46 percent of urban food expenditures were for cereals and beans.[5] The relative neglect of the domestic production of grains in the 1950s and 1960s did not minimize their importance in the diet or as a major expenditure.

Despite its general self-sufficiency in corn and rice, Brazil had to import over 50 percent of its wheat supply in the early 1950s. Colombia's wheat imports also were substantial, providing 27 percent of total domestic consumption. The large wheat imports drained foreign exchange reserves earmarked for importing capital goods for the industrial sector. In part to help countries like Brazil and Colombia import United States grain without exhausting their foreign exchange, the United States developed the P.L. 480 food aid program. This was, however, only one objective of a loose, complex, and at times contradictory program. A brief history of its development and provisions is essential to understanding the conflicts in the modern history of food in Brazil and Colombia.

The United States "Food for Peace" Program

High farm price supports created by New Deal legislation resulted in large surpluses of a number of key commodities, including wheat, corn, and rice. Demands generated by World War II and the Korean War enabled the United States to dispose easily of these surpluses, but after the wars another solution had to be found. At its 1952 national conference in Seattle, the American Farm Bureau Federation developed a new scheme to use commodity surpluses. United States farmers recognized the reluctance of developing nations to expend their dollar foreign exchange on agricultural products because they needed hard currency to purchase capital goods for economic development. They proposed that if the federal government accepted soft or local currency as payment for surpluses, developing countries would be able to purchase more farm products from the United States.[6] The idea became the basis of P.L. 480, signed into law on July 10, 1954.

Though the primary objective of the bill was the disposal of surplus stocks of farm commodities, humanitarian objectives entered in as well. The food imported under the P.L. 480 program would add to total food available in the importing country and would free foreign exchange for use in development goals. In addition, under Title I of the law, the local currency that the United States government acquired from the sale of surplus commodities could be used to underwrite economic development, finance research, and create educational exchange programs in the purchasing country. Title II authorized the distribution of surplus commodities for disaster relief and to voluntary assistance organizations. Title III created a barter program and sanctioned the use of surpluses to relieve domestic food shortages. Title IV, added in September 1959, allowed long-term (ten-year) dollar payments for agricultural goods. The provision for concessional sales under Title I remained by far the most important part of this program. Total exports under P.L. 480 from 1954 through 1976 had a market value of almost $25.1 billion; of these, Title I accounted for 71 percent, or $17.9 billion.

By the late 1950s, the foreign policy objectives of P.L. 480 became more pronounced. President Eisenhower's sale of surplus commodities to Communist countries signaled that food had definite political security potential. Though India remained the major recipient of United States food under the P.L. 480 program, shipments were increasingly directed toward countries perceived as important for reasons of political security. Although these considerations have probably not played as large a role in shipments to Latin America as they have to Algeria, Egypt, South Vietnam, and other countries, maintaining political stability with food aid was undoubtedly an objective in the case of Brazil and Colombia. Efforts to ensure low food prices, particularly for urban workers, pushed Brazil and Colombia to the level of the world's ninth and twenty-first largest recipients of Title I aid ($605.9 million and $120.8 million, respectively) over the period 1954–73.

The different objectives of P.L. 480—disposal of surpluses, humanitarian needs, and political security—invite conflict. For example, to meet the humanitarian objective of providing food to nutritionally vulnerable groups, the donor country must first determine which are most calorie-deficient. The lack of agreement among the Food and Agriculture Organization of the United Nations, the World Bank, and other agencies illustrates the problem of estimating the numbers and locations of the world's most malnourished populations.[7] Directing food shipments to afflicted groups within the needy countries is also extremely difficult, as most developing countries lack efficient distribution mechanisms. Port and storage facilities for receiving large quantities of grain and rail and truck transportation networks for moving the grain inland are often inadequate. Humanitarian goals are likely to clash with political objectives of food aid. Food may be distributed to the most politically vocal groups, which include urban organized labor, and rural areas may be neglected. From the recipient country's point of view, subsidizing urban food makes more sense for its program of industrialization than does supplying the economically and politically marginal rural populations.

In the long run, the surplus-disposal objective of P.L. 480 food aid is also likely to conflict with the humanitarian goal. Title I of P.L. 480 requires a country to maintain its existing level of commercial agricultural imports when receiving aid. This provision protects private grain exporters and, more important, encourages countries to increase their total demand for grain. The result is that a country may endanger the future of its own grain production sector. Large amounts of concessional grain imports drive the unit cost of a country's grain imports to levels below the world market price, depressing internal prices and decreasing incentives to domestic grain producers. If prices remain depressed long enough, grain producers will find more profitable uses for their land or leave farming altogether. The long-term effects on a country's grain sector and thus on its ability to feed itself may be irreversible.

The extent to which this disincentive influences recipient countries depends upon the quantity of P.L. 480 imports, whether P.L. 480 imports replace or supplement commercial imports, the length of time importation continues, and the technological possibilities for domestic grain production. Most important, however, the short- and long-run effects of food aid hinge on the institutional framework for distributing food aid and for providing production incentives to domestic producers. If the government distributes the food aid so that the overall demand for food expands, supports prices for domestic producers, or makes adequate credit or subsidies available to farmers, it may at least partially circumvent the disruptions caused by importing food.

The institutional context for distributing food aid and formulating policy toward domestic producers in Brazil and Colombia has been particularly important in determining the fate of their grain sectors. In the following sections, the recent history of P.L. 480 is explored separately for Brazil and Colombia, bringing out more clearly the conflicts among the objectives of the program and emphasizing the importance of specific political and economic elements in resolving conflicts.

Brazil

The Brazilian government has been directly involved in grain pricing and distribution. Since 1952, it has set import and export prices of grains by regulating exchange rates and by serving as Brazil's sole importer and exporter. In addition, the government has mandated mill and consumer prices of wheat, flour, rice, and corn and has established support prices for producers. The prices of these grains over time provide a good indication of the government's implicit and explicit policy objectives for the grain sector. Wheat policies and prices, in particular, are key elements in this assessment, as imports into Brazil under Title I of P.L. 480 consisted almost entirely of wheat and wheat flour.

Brazilian authorities controlled every aspect of the marketing and processing of imported and domestic wheat, primarily through the National Wheat Commission (CITRIN), a body belonging to the Bank of Brazil and under the direction of the National Superintendency of Food Supply (SUNAB). To achieve the political objective of low consumer prices and to support domestic agriculture, CITRIN effectively used the difference in price between imported and domestic wheat. It bought imported wheat for less than it paid for domestic wheat, selling both to millers for less than the price of domestic wheat but more than that paid for the imports. The difference between the domestic price and the price to millers constituted the subsidy to both consumers and farmers. If, for example, CITRIN bought 100 metric tons of P.L. 480 and commercial wheat for 15,000 cruzeiros (Cr.) and sold this to millers for 18,000 Cr., it was able to use the 3,000 Cr. profit to cover the difference between the purchase of 150 metric tons of domestic wheat at 200 Cr. per metric ton and its sale at 180 Cr. per metric ton.[8] The amount of subsidy to producers through price supports and to consumers through lower prices thus depended on the ability to import wheat at low cost.

P.L. 480 enhanced the potential subsidy because as the amount of imported wheat rose, the per unit import price declined. Until 1968, P.L. 480 sales were made at loan rates as low as 2.5 percent extending over a forty-year period without an exchange rate correction factor. In addition, the foreign exchange savings resulting from P.L. 480 wheat sales for local currency lowered the effective cost of the imports. Scarce dollars could be allocated to alternative imports, such as for capital goods to build production capacity.

Table 1 shows the amount of wheat imported commercially and under P.L. 480 Title I as well as Brazil's foreign exchange reserves from 1950 to 1970. Before P.L. 480 imports ceased in 1970, they amounted to 30 percent of total wheat imports. The quantity of P.L. 480 imports was particularly high during those years when foreign exchange reserves were relatively scarce, above all from 1959 through 1964. It is estimated that P.L. 480 imports reduced the effective cruzeiro cost of Brazil's wheat imports by an average of 33 percent per year from 1954 through 1967, the period when most of the P.L. 480 wheat was imported.[9]

In using the profits obtained from the domestic resale of inexpensive P.L. 480 and commercially imported wheat, government policy favored lower consumer prices over higher producer price supports. There is little doubt that Brazil's main use of the wheat imports was to keep prices of food low for workers to bolster industrialization and avoid political conflict. As wheat imports rose, the average (real) price at which the government sold wheat to the mills (which reflects the price of bread to consumers) actually decreased by 15 percent from 1955–60 to 1965–70. Though the 36 kg. per capita consumption remained fairly constant, Brazil's population explosion caused total consumption to increase by some 30 percent.

Any policy other than one of low consumer prices would have been

Table 1. Brazil: Wheat Imports and Foreign Exchange Reserves

	Total Wheat Imports (1)	Commercial Wheat Imports (1,000 metric tons) (2)	P.L. 480, Title I Wheat Imports (3)	Foreign Exchange Reserves (Millions U.S. dollars) (4)
1955	1,422.50	1,392.60	29.90	$ 168
1956	1,440.60	940.00	500.60	$ 287
1957	1,506.20	1,097.60	408.60	$ 152
1958	1,820.20	1,423.84	396.36	$ 140
1959	2,032.90	1,436.13	596.78	$ 112
1960	1,881.30	1,449.32	431.98	$ 133
1961	2,191.80	679.10	1,512.70	$ 289
1962	2,175.60	1,346.69	828.91	$ 198
1963	2,609.00	1,846.62	762.38	$ 247
1964	1,876.30	404.72	1,471.58	$ 306
1965	2,394.41	2,172.53	221.88	$ 636
1966	2,446.02	1,804.06	641.96	$ 593
1967	2,621.01	2,183.25	437.76	$ 344
1968	2,355.60	1,838.73	516.87	$ 383
1969	1,969.30	1,880.74	88.56	$ 932
1970	1,710.52	1,439.16	271.36	$1261

Sources: Columns (1) and (2) from FAO *Trade Yearbooks* (Rome), various issues; column (3) from USDA, Foreign Agriculture Service, *Title I, Public Law 480: Total Amounts Shipped* (Washington, D.C.), various issues; column (4) includes other assets of the Brazilian monetary authorities in addition to dollar convertible currencies, from International Monetary Fund, *International Financial Statistics Yearbooks* (Washington, D.C.), various issues.

politically dangerous. Since 1948, food prices had risen steadily relative to industrial prices, peaking in 1963 under the Goulart administration. When the military, with the support of industrialists, overthrew the government in 1964, the reduction of the rate of food price inflation became an important part of a renewed emphasis on keeping wages low in support of industrialization efforts.[10]

The Effects of P.L. 480 on Brazil's Grain Sector

For this analysis, the important question is whether the Brazilian government sacrificed long-run agricultural self-sufficiency, especially in wheat production, for their consumer-oriented cheap grain policy. There are indications that the Brazilian government succeeded in partially avoiding the disincentive effect of low consumer prices by using some P.L. 480 revenues to raise domestic wheat support prices. An important political force, organized wheat farmers (FECOTRIGO), was at least partially responsible for this. FECOTRIGO, formed in 1958, was especially strong in the major wheat-producing state of Rio Grande do Sul.[11] With more than sixty cooperatives and over one hundred thousand individual producers, FECOTRIGO was sufficiently integrated into government policy making to exert considerable influence on wheat-pricing policy. The Bank of Brazil relied upon FECOTRIGO to calculate the cost of production upon which wheat support prices were based, and FECOTRIGO used its share of proceeds from farmers' wheat sales to promote wheat production research and extension.[12] Thus, when the Branco administration sought in 1965 to increase domestic production by strengthening the minimum price programs, wheat farmers were in a strong position to press for higher prices.[13] From 1964 to 1970, nominal wheat support prices increased more than tenfold. Real prices remained relatively constant but nevertheless were sufficient to encourage an expansion of wheat acreage and a near tripling of wheat production.

P.L. 480 imports contributed to the expansion in wheat production. As P.L. 480 imports increased, so did CITRIN's profits and its ability to finance higher support prices for wheat producers. An increase of 1,000 metric tons of P.L. 480 wheat increased wheat support prices by 100 Cr. per metric ton and thereby raised wheat production by about 500 metric tons.[14]

Another favorable influence on wheat production was the encouragement given to growers of soybeans, which are planted after the wheat harvest. The same farm machinery and land were often used for the two crops; thus any incentives to soybean production augmented wheat output and vice versa. To take advantage of the export market for soybeans, the Brazilian government offered elaborate assistance: varietal improvements, price and credit guarantees, fertilizer and machinery subsidies, export credits, and budgetary subsidies. Soybean production in the state of Rio Grande do Sul increased from about 200,000 tons in the beginning of the 1960s to about 745,000 tons in 1969 and 1,200,000 tons in 1971. The complementary relationship between wheat and soybeans accounted for much of this growth.[15]

In contrast to the large wheat and soybean planters of Rio Grande do Sul, producers of rice and, especially, of corn were less favored by government policy. Corn farms were geographically dispersed and occupied mainly small (5–20 hectares) and medium-size (21–100 hectares) plots.[16] Corn was largely grown by peasant farmers without organized political influence. Thus, corn production lacked the price guarantees and other incentives given to wheat and soybeans. Corn exports were often restricted to keep the internal price low.

From 1955–60 to 1965–70, corn prices declined by 37 percent, and rice prices fell almost as drastically. As these rates of decline were twice that allowed by CITRIN for the price of milled wheat, consumers were encouraged to substitute corn and rice for wheat in their diets. Per capita consumption of corn and rice increased by 17 and 25 percent, while per capita wheat consumption remained constant. Because domestic production of rice and corn was usually sufficient to meet Brazil's needs, an increase in the consumption of these relative to wheat did increase the country's self-sufficiency in cereal grains.

This evaluation of the contribution of P.L. 480 wheat to Brazil's grain self-sufficiency is cautiously positive. It appears that the Brazilian government managed to use P.L. 480 wheat imports to help satisfy its industrialization and political security objectives by keeping the price of basic food grains low to urban consumers. At the same time, it avoided some of the disincentives that might have resulted from a large influx of cheap grain. Conflict between the goals of Brazilian political security and American surplus disposal, at any rate, was mitigated. Conclusions are less sanguine with respect to the humanitarian objectives of food aid.

It is doubtful that humanitarian motives influenced the distribution of P.L. 480 imports or of the revenues from them. In the first place, the wheat price support program benefited mainly the larger, more commercially oriented farms. Government credit and subsidy policies for mechanization and fertilizers tended to discriminate against the smaller, poorer, subsistence farmers.[17]

The contribution of P.L. 480 wheat to improvement in levels of nutrition is difficult to assess. Malnutrition remains, though there appears to have been some improvement in both caloric and protein intake between 1960 and 1970. The increase in corn and rice consumption, relative to that of wheat in the form of bread, is a positive result. Bread is of little importance in low income diets, providing only 17 percent of the total calories consumed by the poorest groups in Brazil. Bread is also far less important for rural dwellers than corn and rice, contributing only 3 percent of their grain calories, while corn and rice provide 20 and 34 percent.[18] To the extent that Brazilian policymakers kept wheat prices higher than those for corn and rice, they also generated positive consumption benefits.

Colombia

The distribution of food aid in Colombia was also influenced by the differing political strengths of consumer and producer groups. As in Brazil, P.L. 480 wheat was the most important component of food aid. From 1955 to 1973, wheat imports averaged 65 percent of total wheat consumption, with P.L. 480 grain averaging 26 percent of total imports (table 2).

The freeing of foreign exchange through P.L. 480 was particularly important for Colombia's industrialization and import substitution efforts in the late 1950s and 1960s. This release was particularly crucial from 1954 through 1960, when coffee prices (and thereby foreign exchange earnings) fell and the government restricted commercial imports. Food aid shipments, particularly wheat, flour, and edible vegetable oils, had an average value of $6 million annually and played a major role in offsetting the reduction in imports of consumption goods necessitated by the coffee crisis. It has been estimated that without P.L. 480, foreign exchange expenditures of $2 million annually would have been required to maintain wheat supplies at 1953–54 levels. With P.L. 480, per capita wheat consumption actually exceeded the 1953–54 level by about 19 percent.[19]

In addition, a portion of the local currency accrued by the United States from the P.L. 480 sales was loaned to Colombia and channeled into agriculture and closely related industries. Because the loans enabled Colombia to develop new production facilities and to substitute local production for imports, there was an added balance-of-payments benefit. For example, the largest P.L. 480 loans, totaling approximately 44 million pesos, were invested in the chemical fertilizer industry, saving substantial foreign exchange previously used to import fertilizers.

The balance of payments benefits have to be weighed against the possible negative effects of food aid on Colombia's agriculture. Since 1944, the Colombian government has taken an active role in coordinating the grain trade by establishing two semi-official marketing agencies: first INA (Instituto Nacional de Abastecimiento) and later IDEMA (Instituto de Mercado Agropecuario). INA attempted to promote self-sufficiency in agricultural production by setting minimum prices for rice, corn, wheat, and beans. These prices were based on average costs and ensured farmers a normal rate of return. INA restricted and controlled imports under a system of foreign exchange licensing to keep the support prices for some crops much higher than the world price; it used profits it obtained from importing certain commodities at low world prices and selling them to domestic consumers at higher prices to at least partially finance its price support program.

Table 2. Colombia: Wheat Imports

	Total Wheat Imports (1)	Commercial Wheat Imports (1,000 metric tons) (2)	P.L. 480, Title I Wheat Imports (3)
1955	90.17	67.93	22.24
1956	104.26	55.10	49.16
1957	86.23	47.65	38.58
1958	96.05	79.16	16.89
1959	86.15	11.27	74.88
1960	126.48	83.32	43.16
1961	135.29	68.96	66.33
1962	93.01	30.61	62.40
1963	158.07	128.46	29.61
1964	173.54	158.54	15.00
1965	244.29	224.21	25.08
1966	170.35	153.31	17.04
1967	228.13	200.13	28.00
1968	243.02	101.74	141.28
1969	209.19	209.19	0.00
1970	446.04	273.69	172.35

Sources: Columns (1) and (2) from Colombia, Departmento Administrativo Nacional de Estadística, *Anuario de comercio exterior* (Bogotá), various issues, and FAO *Trade Yearbooks* (Rome), various issues. Column (3) from USDA, Foreign Agriculture Service, *Title I, Public Law 480: Total Amounts Shipped* (Washington, D.C.), various issues.

In 1968, IDEMA superseded INA. IDEMA has the responsibility for integrating food price policy with overall agricultural policy and for defending the interests of both consumers and producers. It also attempts to stabilize domestic prices by regulating supplies of a wide group of crops: sorghum, soybeans, potatoes, anis, sesame, barley, rice, corn, wheat, and beans. As part of its stabilization effort, IDEMA sets support prices, which are pegged to average production costs and are announced at planting time. IDEMA attempts to buy all that is offered at these prices but purchases mostly grain crops. For example, 87 percent of its total purchases from farmers during 1968–70 were for the three major grains of corn, rice, and wheat.[20]

IDEMA has a monopoly over agricultural exports and imports. It establishes minimum export prices and is exempt from import taxes. This control over international trade constitutes the source of its operating budget and, in addition to its inventories of commodities, provides the basis for its regulation of domestic prices. For example, IDEMA is the sole purchaser and distributor of imported wheat, which it sells at a gain.[21] As in the Brazilian case, the low international wheat prices that prevailed up to 1972, coupled with the effect of P.L. 480 in lowering the average import price, meant that IDEMA could make a substantial profit and still keep consumer prices low.[22]

Although IDEMA could have supported prices to wheat producers by buying all or part of the local crops at the support price and selling the domestic and imported wheat at a lower price to consumers, as did the Brazilian government, IDEMA did not separate producer and consumer prices. The imported wheat was sold to consumers at a price approximately equal to the support level.[23]

The Effects of P.L. 480 on Colombia's Grain Sector

By selling imported wheat at a relatively low price to consumers, IDEMA discouraged domestic production. As a result, in 1973 Colombia was farther away from wheat self-sufficiency than when it first imported P.L. 480 wheat. Graph 1, illustrating wheat production, imports, and deflated wheat support prices, shows that wheat support prices and output fell and then stagnated over time. By 1973, wheat production was less than half its average annual level from 1956 to 1960 and accounted for only about 15 percent of domestic consumption.[24] Colombian wheat producers (except for a minority who switched to barley production) appear to have suffered seriously from the government's failure to circumvent the disincentive effects of food aid.[25]

IDEMA did not support wheat production because wheat producers were not organized into a sufficiently powerful pressure group to influence price policies. Wheat farming in Colombia was characterized by small farm size and a low degree of commercialization. In Cundinamarca, one of the nation's major wheat-producing states, nearly 40 percent of the wheat was grown on plots of less than ten hectares, with an average of only slightly more than one hectare of wheat per farm.[26] Further, much wheat farming was technologically primitive, with hand cultivation competing with tractors. Only about 34 percent of the wheat area was sown with tractors in 1958, and improved wheat varieties and fertilizers were used infrequently.[27] Lacking

Graph 1: Colombia: Wheat Imports, Production, and Support Prices, 1954–73

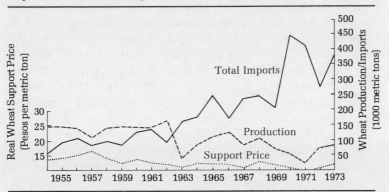

cohesion and economic clout, wheat farmers found difficulty in their bid to influence policies and call for higher wheat prices.

In contrast, rice growers were organized into a strong and politically effective National Rice Growers' Federation (FEDEARROZ). Organized in 1950 as a semi-official national institution, FEDEARROZ was the recipient of government subsidies. In 1960, while retaining full autonomy, the federation was granted public funds to cover 80 percent of expenses to develop the rice industry. Representing mainly large farmers growing rice under irrigation, principally in the department of Tolima, FEDEARROZ time and again used its power to influence national price, credit, and trade policies toward rice. It convinced the government to prohibit rice imports, lower duties on imports such as fertilizers and machinery, seek more favorable credit conditions, and obtain better support prices.[28]

FEDEARROZ preferred to emphasize cost-reducing policies. Representatives of the nascent industries, however, opposed reductions in the price of manufactured imports. A more attainable goal was to raise the amount of credit allocated to rice producers and the level of price supports offered by IDEMA. In both areas, the federation's success was affected by the availability of P.L. 480 products, as the profit made by the resale of P.L. 480 imports was shared equally by the Caja de Crédito Agrario (the agricultural bank) and IDEMA. Rice producers, especially those with irrigation, were undoubtedly successful in obtaining larger shares of the bank's credit during the years P.L. 480 wheat was imported. Credit extended to rice farmers increased sharply during the early 1960s, both in pesos and as a percentage of the total credit granted by the bank.[29]

IDEMA also used its revenues from P.L. 480 wheat to increase support prices to rice producers.[30] Each additional 1,000 metric tons of this wheat raised the rice support price by an average of 13 pesos per metric ton. (In contrast, the same increase in P.L. 480 imports decreased the wheat support price by 4.5 pesos.) By using P.L. 480 revenues to support rice and restricting rice imports, IDEMA sheltered Colombia's developing rice industry. Relatively high prices, which stimulated the adoption of new rice technologies, helped increase production from 1955 to 1973 by more than 260 percent, to a high of 1,175,000 metric tons.

As yields rose and per unit production costs fell, IDEMA gradually allowed the domestic price of rice to decline until it reached the world price. Though the wholesale price of rice dropped by over 20 percent, Colombian rice did not become competitive internationally until 1973, when P.L. 480 wheat imports and corresponding revenues ceased. Colombia now exports rice (averaging 130,000 metric tons per year since 1975) at world prices, occasionally relying on export subsidies from IDEMA. With the decline in rice prices, domestic consumption increased dramatically and at least partially alleviated the political unrest caused by the decline in real wages. Per capita consumption of rice rose 90 percent from 1955 to 1975, while sales of wheat increased only 7.5 percent per capita.

By encouraging the production and consumption of rice, the Colombian government tried unsuccessfully to circumvent the disincentive effects of P.L. 480 on the wheat sector. Under P.L. 480, wheat production declined and wheat imports increased steadily. By the late 1970s, Colombia annually imported 292,000 metric tons at a cost of about $40 million. In contrast, rice exports of approximately 90,000 metric tons earned about $33 million on the world market. Thus, even under a static cost comparison and ignoring the cost to IDEMA of supporting rice producers above the world price for so many years before 1973, the gains in rice self-sufficiency do not equal the losses in wheat production.

P.L. 480's negative economic impact was not softened by humanitarian successes. IDEMA's rice support program benefited large producers, especially those with irrigated lands. Small and medium size farms (up to 50 hectares) declined in importance, producing less rice and occupying less irrigated land. The result was a more unequal distribution of rural income. The simple but inescapable conclusion is that Colombia suffered more social and economic drawbacks from P.L. 480 than Brazil.

Conclusion

The history of food aid in Brazil and Colombia demonstrates the difficulty of meeting humanitarian, political security, and surplus disposal objectives at the same time. More important for Latin America, it illustrates the crucial importance of the national institutional framework and agricultural pricing policies of the importing country. By intervening in the marketplace, the importing country can take advantage of the low cost of food to either raise prices to producers or lower them to consumers. The policy followed depends partly on the political power of producers and consumers. Brazil used revenues from the internal resale of wheat to support politically powerful wheat producers; in contrast, Colombia used wheat revenues to support influential rice producers. Both countries used food aid to lower prices to consumers, but Brazil exercised more caution in meeting consumer demands than Colombia. The recent history of Brazil shows that the careful management of food aid can contribute to the attainment of long-run food self-sufficiency while satisfying internal political needs.

The political and economic dynamics of recipient countries influence the effect of P.L. 480 and other food aid programs as much as the conflicting objectives of the United States. Generalizations that ignore the different situations in Latin American countries distort history and mislead policy makers.

Notes

1. U.S. Department of Agriculture (USDA), Economic Research Service, *Agricultural Production and Trade of Colombia,* Foreign Agriculture Economic Report no. 343 (Washington, D.C., Feb. 1973).

2. See Fernando Homen de Mello, "Economic Policy and the Agricultural Sector in Brazil," *Luso-Brazilian Review* 15, no. 2 (Winter 1978): 195–222.

3. Getulio Vargas Foundation, *Food Consumption in Brazil: Family Budget Surveys in the Early 1960s* (Rio de Janeiro: Instituto Brasiléiro de Economia, Divisão de Estatística, Nov. 1970); *World Bank World Tables, 1980,* 2nd ed. (Baltimore: Johns Hopkins University Press, 1981).

4. Ernesto Samper Pizano, ed., *Ensayos sobre el desarrollo,* Biblioteca Asociación Nacional de Instituciones Financieras de Economía (Bogotá, 1977): 222.

5. These figures are for the three poorest groups, i.e., those with incomes of less than 249 new cruzeiros per person per year. As incomes increase, bread and rice tend to supply proportionately larger amounts of calories, and expenditures on these items increase as well. See the 1970 consumption survey from the Getulio Vargas Foundation for additional calorie and expenditure statistics.

6. See George Zacher, *A Political History of Food for Peace,* Cornell Agricultural

Economics Staff Paper no. 77–18 (Ithaca, N.Y.: Cornell University, Department of Agricultural Economics, May 1977); and Peter A. Toma, *The Politics of Food for Peace: Executive-Legislative Interaction* (Tucson: University of Arizona Press, 1967) for a political history of the development of P.L. 480 legislation.

7. Food and Agriculture Organization of the United Nations (FAO), *The Fourth FAO World Food Survey*, FAO Food and Nutrition Series, no. 10 (Rome, 1977); Shlomo Reutlinger and Marcelo Selowsky, *Malnutrition and Poverty: Magnitude and Policy Options*, World Bank Staff Occasional Papers, no. 23 (Baltimore: Johns Hopkins University Press, 1976); and Lana L. Hall, *A Critical Evaluation of Recent Attempts at Assessing World Hunger*, Cornell Agricultural Economics Staff Paper no. 79–17 (Ithaca, N.Y.: Cornell University, Department of Agricultural Economics, June 1979).

8. For more detailed discussions of CITRIN wheat operations see: Peter T. Knight, *Brazilian Agricultural Technology and Trade: A Study of Five Commodities* (New York: Praeger, 1971), pp. 89–93; Ruy Miller Paiva, Salomão Schattan, and Claus F. Trench de Freitas, *Brazil's Agricultural Sector: Economic Behavior, Problems and Possibilities* (distributed at 15th International Conference of Agricultural Economists, São Paulo, 1973), pp. 140–42.

9. This figure was obtained using parity exchange rates, which correct for the overvaluation of the cruzeiro prevailing from 1954 to 1967, and is based on an average yearly dollar value of P.L. 480 wheat and flour imports of $46,923,620. See Knight, *Brazilian Agricultural Technology*, pp. 57–63, 92–96, for discussion of the parity exchange rate and the value of P.L. 480 wheat imports.

10. Béla Kádár, *Problems of Economic Growth in Latin America*, trans. Pál Félix (New York: St. Martin's Press, 1980), pp. 195–97.

11. In 1965, the Rio Grande do Sul was producing over 90 percent of Brazilian wheat.

12. Knight, *Brazilian Agricultural Technology*, p. 41; Paiva, Schattan, and Trench de Freitas, *Brazil's Agricultural Sector*, pp. 175–79.

13. See also Donald E. Syvrud, *Foundations of Brazilian Economic Growth* (Stanford, Hoover Institution Press, Stanford University, 1974), pp. 230–31.

14. See Lana L. Hall, *The Effects of P.L. 480 Wheat Imports on Latin American Countries*, Cornell International Agriculture Mimeograph 76 (Ithaca, N.Y.: Cornell University, April 1980), for the statistical model used to derive these estimates of the effect of P.L. 480 wheat.

15. Two regions in Río Grande do Sul, Missões and Planalto Medio, were responsible for 60 percent of the wheat and almost 40 percent of the soybeans produced in Brazil in 1968 (Paiva, Schattan, and Trench de Freitas, *Brazil's Agricultural Sector*, p. 179).

16. Knight, *Brazilian Agricultural Technology*, p. 179.

17. An analysis of credit distribution in the state of São Paulo, for example, is given in Paulo F. C. de Araujo and Richard L. Meyer, "Agricultural Credit Policy in Brazil: Objectives and Results," *Savings and Development Quarterly Review* 2, no. 3 (1978): 169–94.

18. Getulio Vargas Foundation, *Food Consumption in Brazil.*

19. Theodore J. Goering, "Public Law 480 in Colombia," *Journal of Farm Economics* 44 (November 1962): 922–1004.

20. Wayne R. Thirsk, "Income Distribution Consequences of Agricultural Price Supports in Colombia," in *Economic Policy and Income Distribution in Colombia,* eds. R. Albert Berry and Ronald Soligo (Boulder, Colo.: Westview Press, 1974), pp. 203–226.

21. See Dale W. Adams et al., *Public Law 480 and Colombia's Economic Development* (East Lansing: Department of Agricultural Economics, Michigan State University, March 1964); USDA, Economic Research Service, *Agricultural Production;* USDA, Economic Research Service, *Changes in Agricultural Production and Trade of Colombia,* Foreign Agricultural Economic Report no. 52 (Washington, D.C., June 1969) for further descriptions of this policy.

22. IDEMA's profits on its wheat import operations may have averaged as high as 50 million pesos (undeflated) per year from 1954 through 1973.

23. See FAO *National Grain Policies* (Rome, various years) for consumer prices of wheat.

24. Leonard Dudley and Roger J. Sandilands conclude in "The Side Effects of Foreign Aid: The Case of Public Law 480 Wheat in Colombia," *Economic Development and Cultural Change* 23, no. 2 (Jan. 1975): 325–36, that the 1.4 million tons of wheat IDEMA imported from 1955 through 1971 could have been produced domestically at a lower opportunity cost, that is, when the value of displaced land and labor from domestic wheat production are explicitly considered.

25. There are indications that consumers as well lost from IDEMA's wheat policies. Thirsk, "Income Distribution Consequences," p. 216, found that the sale of imported wheat at prices slightly above international levels to generate revenue for IDEMA amounted to a regressive consumption tax. He speculated that consumers in all income classes would have gained if IDEMA had reduced even further its sale price for wheat.

26. See Adams et al., *Colombia's Economic Development,* for a description of wheat farming in Colombia.

27. USDA, Economic Research Service, *Agricultural Production* and *Changes in Agricultural Production.*

28. Philippe P. Leurquin, "Rice in Colombia: A Case Study in Agricultural Development," *Food Research Institute Studies* 7, no. 2 (1967): 217–303.

29. Agricultural credit in Colombia has been extensively discussed elsewhere. For credit to rice producers, see Leurquin, "Rice in Colombia," pp. 238–39.

30. See Hall, *The Effects of P.L. 480;* Grant M. Scobie and Rafael Posada T., *The Impact of High-Yielding Rice Varieties in Latin America with Special Emphasis on Colombia* (Cali, Colombia: Centro Internacional de Agricultura Tropical, April 1976).

Eleanor Witte Wright

Food Dependency and Malnutrition in Venezuela, 1958–74

After the overthrow of the Marcos Pérez Jiménez dictatorship in 1958, the new democratic regime in Venezuela faced two major problems related to the food system: food dependency and high levels of malnutrition. Heavy reliance on food imports, financed by exports of petroleum, defined the country's food dependency.[1] Food—both staples and luxury items—ranked as the third-largest category of imports. Half of the milk, three-fourths of the eggs, and almost all the wheat flour consumed in Venezuela were imported. Together, wheat flour and grains, dairy products, poultry, and eggs—all staples of the national diet—constituted 53 percent of imported food by value.[2] High levels of malnutrition, especially among children, the poor, and rural population, were associated with widely unequal levels of income and food consumption. According to 1957 health statistics, poor nutrition played a decisive role in at least 43 percent of the deaths of children between one and four years of age.[3] The rate of death due to malnutrition ranged from 48.8 per 100,000 inhabitants in Caracas to 214 per 100,000 in smaller cities of 15,000 to 40,000 inhabitants.

In 1959 the Acción Democrática party (AD), headed by Rómulo Betancourt, came into power offering a reformist solution to Venezuela's problems, including food dependency and malnutrition.[4] The AD strategy, followed by two AD administrations and the Christian Democratic (COPEI) government of Rafael Caldera (1969–74), centered on increasing domestic food production and modifying the pattern of income distribution. Despite ambitious policies and expectations for change, by the early 1970s the Venezuelan strategy had failed to eradicate food dependency or to ameliorate malnutrition significantly. The country still used revenues from petroleum exports to import large amounts of food, and malnutrition continued to take a relatively high toll. The effort of the Venezuelan government to change these fundamental characteristics of the nation's food system through import substitution industrialization did not succeed.

Conflicting objectives between the AD governments and industrial firms was only one of the aspects thwarting the intended outcome. On one hand, the AD governments committed themselves to an integral package of economic growth and income redistribution. But, as pragmatists, they planned to achieve the reform as a by-product of industrial growth. In contrast, the largest Venezuelan firms and the multinational firms such as International Milling and Ralston Purina had as sole concern the financial growth of markets and profits. As a result, multinational firms enhanced their position through changes in their structure, cooperation with other large-scale firms, support from international policy-making organizations, and the absence of a strong Venezuelan antitrust policy. These changes altered the Venezuelan agro-industrial market in unanticipated ways.

Political factionalism and wavering commitment to reform further complicated matters. After securing the necessary legislation, the government faced multiple difficulties in implementing the reforms needed to complement industrialization and to achieve the desired redistribution. Upper-income and urban groups, well represented in government and in numerous lobbies in Venezuela, were indifferent or hostile to agricultural reform. International pressures also frustrated the intention of structural change. One cannot overlook the dominant role of petroleum exports, which made possible continued food imports and attenuated the urgency of reform. As a result, neither income nor sectoral redistribution (a structural reform of the role of agriculture in the economy) was achieved in spite of strong industrial growth.

This essay examines how the increasing economic power of the multinationals and the dominant national firms, backed by international organizations, worked in conjunction with the failure of reform to undermine the goal of reducing the nation's food dependency and relatively high levels of malnutrition between 1958 and 1974.

The Challenge of Food System Reform

Although many scholars trace Venezuela's food dependency to the rise of the petroleum export industry in the early twentieth century, the roots of the contemporary situation go back at least to the late nineteenth century. The country's economy after the 1850s depended on agricultural exports, primarily coffee, cacao, cattle hides, and sugar. Several factors worked against self-sufficiency in domestic food production: use of best lands for export crops; adverse climactic conditions of torrential rains alternating with drought; regional civil wars; and a labor force debilitated by malaria and deprived of access to land ownership.[5]

By the 1920s food dependency began to take a firm hold, nourished both by decisions of the dictator, Juan Vicente Gómez, and by vagaries in the international market for agricultural exports. Assuming power in 1908, Gómez welcomed investment in petroleum exploration, especially by the United States firms of Standard Oil (Creole Petroleum), Gulf (Mene Grande), Texaco, and the British- and Dutch-owned Royal Dutch Shell. After the 1920s Venezuelan oil revenues grew; by 1955, oil accounted for 94 percent of exports by value.[6] Oil exports vastly facilitated Venezuela's capacity to import food, cementing the country's food dependency and altering the national diet.

The traditional diet evolved from a mix of native crops and European plants and animals. The diet had as a base the complementary vegetable proteins of corn, rice, black beans, squash, and root crops such as manioc and potatoes. Cheese, meat, eggs and domestic fruits such as plantains, bananas, mangoes, and tomatoes often enhanced meals, but corn provided the most common diet staple for nearly four-fifths of the population. Venezuelans usually ate corn meal in a flattened cake, the *arepa,* to which fillings of cheese or meat gave added nutritional value. A more elaborate dish served on festive occasions, the *hallaca,* used a corn dough (*masa*) filled with a delicious mixture of chicken or pork, onions, garlic, raisins, olives, and eggs, cooked wrapped in plantain leaves.

By the 1950s, food imports had altered the traditional diet of the upper and middle classes. "British biscuits, French wines, . . . Italian oils and pasta . . . and from the States "every kind of boxed or canned food," such as corn flakes and canned ham, greatly increased the variety on their tables.[7] Red apples, russet pears, and grapes were other costly imported items purchased by the well-to-do. Because of skewed distribution of income, however, only one-third of the population was estimated to consume luxury food imports regularly. The poorer half of the population, which earned only 15 percent of national income, subsisted on a little meat and inadequate amounts of vegetable proteins.[8] Only two imported items appeared regularly in their diet: government-subsidized wheat bread and canned fruit juices.

Extremes in land ownership and income in the agricultural sector were important factors in food dependency and uneven levels of consumption. Conforming to the common Latin American pattern, the majority of food producers in Venezuela owned a small fraction of the arable land. In the

1950s, close to two-thirds of the campesinos farmed their corn, beans and root crops on only 2.9 percent of cultivatable land.[9] Those without land provided labor for the large landholders and sharecropped small plots.[10] Marketable surpluses from these *minifundia* were minimal. The larger, traditional haciendas or *fincas* produced coffee, cacao, and cattle. Most commercial food production took place in a modest but growing sector of modern capitalist farms.

Uneven ownership of assets in the processing sector also prevailed by the 1950s. Three national and nine foreign firms, with capitalizations ranging from 2–11 million bolívars (Bs), dominated sales in the dairy, milling, and feed sectors.[11] Among Venezuelans, the Mendoza family controlled Protinal, a feed company; the Brangers dominated oilseed production; and the Tamayo family had large investments in processed foods. Large multinational firms, beginning in the late 1940s and early 1950s, concentrated on three areas: the Nestlé-Borden Company made powdered milk; the Venezuelan Basic Economy Corporation (VBEC), a Rockefeller subsidiary, invested in milk production and supermarkets; and Nabisco produced crackers. After 1955 several other large United States corporations invested in Venezuela, but most had barely initiated large-scale production by 1958. International Milling, Pillsbury, General Mills, and Ralston Purina established subsidiaries in the milling and feed sector, while General Foods and Standard Brands entered the diversified foods field. The vast majority of national firms were much smaller than the multinationals.

Venezuelan planners in 1959 tailored their attack on food dependency and malnutrition to the realities of Venezuelan politics and international relations. Over a decade earlier, during its brief tenure in power from 1945 to 1948, AD had attempted to alter Venezuela's food dependency by a more fundamental reform of business organization. The party had established mixed, foreign- and Venezuelan-owned food processing firms. These firms were partly capitalized by preferred stock purchases by Creole Oil and Royal Dutch Shell.[12] The government had also launched an extensive land reform program and formed strong agricultural unions. But by 1948 this regime, with its emphasis on economic nationalism and direct redistribution, fell in a coup; agrarian reform stopped, and the mixed firms were soon dissolved. Sobered by this earlier failure, AD now sought to avoid antagonizing political opponents in its food policies.

AD food policy after 1958 evolved within the general framework of import substitution industrialization as advocated by the Argentine economist Raul Prebisch and the Economic Commission for Latin America. Although planners realized that import substitution offered potential problems as a model of development, they felt that it would meet Venezuelan objectives in a pragmatic form. Import substitution did not limit consumption during the initial stages of industrialization as did the Soviet model—an important consideration, since Venezuela was a well-developed consumer society.[13] The urban bias of this model also fit Venezuela, which by 1961 was 67 percent urban. For the food system, import substitution involved stimulating national processing industries and simultaneously increasing domestic production of agricultural raw materials.

The agencies charged with implementing food policy had to work within the terms of existing trade agreements: the commercial treaty with the United States, and the International Wheat Agreement. The commercial treaty of 1939, supplemented and amended in 1952, generally set low tariffs on imports of processed foods and higher ones on raw materials. The Ministry of Development and the Venezuelan Development Corporation chose to limit imports selectively through licenses and quotas, while allowing firms to import raw materials when domestic production was insufficient.[14] They intended these imports to be a temporary phenomenon. They also employed financial aid in various forms, such as direct subsidies to dairy firms and a favorable exchange rate for milling firms importing wheat, to encourage establishment and growth of local food processing industries. The government offered credit for imports and long-term loans as well.

These measures were expected to increase gradually the proportion of locally grown and processed foodstuffs in total national consumption. Such an approach appealed to agricultural producers and processors. The policy of subsidizing basic commodities at fixed prices satisfied urban consumers. Processing firms also favored the latter policy, as it lessened the impact of international price swings on their profits.

AD planners linked import substitution industrialization and agrarian reform in effecting development through market expansion. The Agrarian Reform Law of 1960 was the basis of the AD agrarian policy designed to complement its industrial policy. The law called for resettlement of 350,000 families under the National Agrarian Institute.[15] The government intended this redistribution of land to increase supplies of raw materials as part of a modernized agricultural production and marketing system. The Ministry of Agriculture offered credit and technical aid for improved production methods. Political considerations had also helped shape this plan. Both urban consumers and processing firms would benefit in the long run from expanded agricultural production. Expropriated landowners would gain from the generous terms of indemnification and incentives for urban investment. Additionally, the promise of land ownership had made landless peasants a mainstay of AD electoral strength since the 1940s.

As the cornerstone of the 1958 import substitution plan, Betancourt's administration ratified the role of existing firms and welcomed new foreign and national investment. The AD strategy depended on large, privately owned firms as the "engine of growth" for development and indirect redistribution.[16] The United States, Venezuela's largest trading partner, backed this strategy to make the country a showcase for democratic reform and capitalist development. This emphasis on private enterprise offered an alternative to the Cuban socialist model of development for the rest of Latin America.[17] In the intensifying competition with Cuba in the early 1960s, United States aid through the Alliance for Progress flowed into Latin America along with new private investment. The favored role of United States investment in the food policy of Venezuela was undoubtedly linked to both existing large-scale private investment in the Venezuelan petroleum sector and to the international political scene.

The process of growth, or market expansion, under import substitution industrialization was envisioned as an orderly, everwidening circle. An early experiment in "supply side" economics, the strategy initiated the process by protecting industries to increase domestic supplies. This industrialization would create new jobs and enlarge the domestic market for agricultural goods. The income of agricultural producers and of workers in the domestic food processing industries would expand uniformly, generating an increase in demand for industrial goods. These purchases would stimulate further increases in production, allowing the firms to achieve economies of scale and to widen continually the circle of producers and consumers within the nation's boundaries.

Venezuelan planners thought this growth would follow naturally from the behavior of the key actors, the state and the corporations. Internal market development would not experience any adverse effects, but rather would profit from this expansion. But, certain conditions needed to exist in order to achieve this pattern. The industrial firms would have to be competitive and would have to cement strong ties to Venezuelan agricultural producers and consumers. In this manner, the corporations would increase employment and foster income redistribution.

Evolution of the Food System, 1958–74

By the early 1970s, instead of having achieved these necessary conditions, the Venezuelan food system was characterized by conditions that militated against uniform market expansion. Rather than engaging in competition, the largest national and multinational firms dominated a concentrated market. And rather than developing close links with Venezuelan agricultural producers, the dominant firms developed stronger connections to foreign sources of raw materials, especially in grains.

Sales by the largest firms indicated the existence of a concentrated market in Venezuela.[18] (A market is considered concentrated if three or four firms control at least 50 percent of sales.) Only two years after initiating flour production under import substitution, the two largest United States firms, International Milling and Pillsbury, and the United States–Argentine firm of Bunge and Born, which produced General Mills flours, dominated sales in the wheat milling sector with 90 percent of the productive worth. Soon after, three other companies—the domestic firm of Protinal and two multinationals, Ralston Purina and International Milling—controlled 80–95 percent of the market for feed. And in the dairy sector, firms with 18 percent of the assets sold 81 percent of the milk. The largest multinational firm in the powdered milk sector was Nestlé-Borden, followed by VBEC, while Kraft was a major consumer of milk for cheese production. The dominant position of these large firms prevented smaller regional firms, cooperatives, and imported products from widening the market and lowering prices in the processing and distribution of food. Thus the firms achieved only limited economies of scale and did not operate at full capacity because of the size of the market and lack of competition.

Venezuela's encouragement of industrialization by large foreign companies had contributed to the emergence of a new, dynamic form of business management, the multinational corporation, which supplanted national firms. These companies control assets to produce goods or services in several countries under the direction of a parent firm.[19] Rapid growth in this form occurred during the 1950s, when numerous developing nations encouraged industrialization through import substitution. The international corporations, predominantly based in the United States, acquired foreign subsidiaries not only in Venezuela but usually in at least three other Latin American countries as well. Most of the food processing firms investing in Venezuela were already sizable ones, having previously achieved a dominant position in their home market; they ranked among the top five hundred United States firms, with ten in the top one hundred according to sales.[20]

Four assets in this new management system enabled the firms to dominate the Venezuelan market. These were size, information, capital, and the international structure necessary to capitalize on the first three factors. Within a short period, the corporations found that larger profits came from international marketing than from processing raw materials. They restructured on an international level, "unifying" or "rationalizing" production, marketing and distribution, and management resources on a world-wide basis.

Through this process, the parent firms integrated their foreign subsidiaries into a global scheme of operations.

The development of computers contributed enormously to this growth pattern as a result of their ability to store and retrieve information on capital and commodity movements. By 1963, International Milling had installed high-speed data processing at Minneapolis and Puerto Cabello, Venezuela.[21] Ralston Purina also used computers, as did most other large firms. With such assets, the firms had an advantage over smaller firms in their ability to borrow and take advantage of import controls. The smaller Venezuelan milling firms could not compete with firms that could purchase internationally, in quantity, and at the lowest price.

These large firms also received assistance in gaining and maintaining their Venezuelan market position from other multinational corporations. In one example of such collaboration, the VBEC supermarket chain, Cada, allegedly favored multinational over smaller Venezuelan companies in selecting its merchandise. Cada originally imported 80 percent of its stock from the United States processors. As Venezuelans increasingly restricted imports of processed foods, the store continued to favor the same brand names over products of smaller Venezuelan firms; only now, the Venezuelan subsidiaries of the United States–based firms produced these foods.[22] This continuity in product lines helped the multinationals continue to dominate the Venezuelan market.

Formal contracts among the large firms aided several of the multinationals in their Venezuelan operations as well. These contracts enabled firms to enter the market in some instances and to gain a dominant position in others. For example, at the beginning of the import substitution strategy, International Milling contracted with Pillsbury, which had no Venezuelan marketing operations, to sell its imported flour in Venezuela.[23] Through this contract Pillsbury, the world's largest flour exporter, took advantage of the transitional period between easy and restricted imports, first to gain market recognition and then to establish its own Venezuelan operations. Within a few years, as Venezuelan flour imports decreased, Pillsbury ended its arrangement with International Milling and acquired its own flour mill, becoming a national producer. Another type of contract that aided in market domination was used in the feed sector by Arbor Acres, a poultry firm, as Venezuelan egg import controls took hold. Arbor Acres contracted to divide the market by supplying female broiler breeders to Protinal, the domestic firm, and by forming a separate, jointly owned company with Ralston Purina for broiler chicks.[24] This action contributed to market control through vertical integration in the feed-poultry sector.

International organizations and programs bolstered the growth of these firms at the expense of the smaller national ones. The United States Department of State supported this bias through the Alliance for Progress and the Agency for International Development (AID). United States officials promoted development through large-scale private industry, an approach expected to redistribute income, ameliorate poverty, and thereby counter the threat of communism and Castroism in Latin America. Several specific policies useful to these firms evolved from the United States position: AID financed an Industrial Resources Survey in 1962, and the government-financed Overseas Private Investment Corporation offered insurance against nationalization.[25] That same year, Venezuela and the United States signed an Investment Guarantee Agreement that eventually covered three large United States firms in the food processing sector, reducing considerably the risk of investing abroad.[26]

Finally, the Venezuelan government contributed directly to high levels of market concentration by failing to enforce any antitrust policy, even though the constitution forbade monopolies. The newness and fragility of the democratic regime in a country with historical concentration of assets, heavy presence of foreign capital, and dependence on the United States market for petroleum exports undoubtedly influenced this decision. Not until after 1975, when Venezuela had received international support for regulation of multinational corporations through the adoption of the Andean Common Market's Decision 24, did the Venezuelan Congress pass a Monopolies and Cartels Bill.

Thus, between 1958 and 1974 diversification in manufacturing and increases in capitalization had not measurably augmented the competitiveness of the agro-industrial market in Venezuela. Rather, high levels of market concentration had resulted. The corporate procedures and the policies adopted by multinational firms and a handful of national companies strongly influenced the Venezuelan food system.

The new industrialization strategy did not stimulate Venezuelan agricultural production to the degree expected. The multinationals operating with the few national firms tended to reinforce their international links in the purchase of raw materials, especially grains. The firms functioned in this manner because they had world-wide information on grains and capital movement and because enforcement of import restrictions was occasionally lax. The parent firms' research emphasis on raw materials produced in temperate zones, rather than on those suited to Venezuelan climate and soils, reinforced the subsidiaries' purchase of primary materials abroad, especially in the United States. Thus the expected stimulus to the Venezuelan agricultural producers, a basic component in the strategy to end food dependency, was diluted. Small farmers, who grew much of the country's corn, failed to benefit.

The large firms did establish selective links to the Venezuelan agricultural sector, however, through the use of contracts to control quantity, quality, and price. While these contracts aided in the introduction of new practices in chicken and milk production, they also negated the development of the free market system. Corporations set prices by arrangement rather than by competitive bidding. Other ties to domestic agriculture included corporate farming by such firms as Corn Products Corporation, International, and Heinz. The former experimented with Venezuelan production of corn, sesame, peanuts, and soybeans on 12,000 acres it purchased, while Heinz used its farms as well as contract producers to experiment with potential export crops such as peas and asparagus.[27] Ralston Purina and Protinal jointly supported the Ministry of Agriculture and the University of Zulia in 1968 in the introduction of commercial sorghum, a grain with no links to the traditional agricultural Venezuelan system.[28]

These kinds of practices resulted in integrating part of the commercial farm sector in Venezuela into a complex global food system. While the commercial farmer was directly connected to the changing market by contracts, the campesino's ability to enter the market was hindered by an increase in intermediaries, vulnerability to price fluctuations, and shortage of credit. As a result, the vast majority of food producers, those cultivating smaller plots, remained on the margin of the expanding national market.

The multinationals also strengthened international ties, circumventing the intentions of the import substitution policy. The milling and feed firms, using grains as raw materials, and the dairy firms made greatest use of practices such as intracorporate transfers, international trading and bartering, and hedging on the international market. As an illustration, International Milling exported and imported products, including those not manufactured by the company, and made a number of three-party barter deals that involved operations in as many countries and thwarted domestic market competition. This firm even expanded into a grain unloading service for the Venezuelan government, made possible by its structure and experience in international grain transport.[29] Private industry's ownership of over 70 percent of the storage capacity in Venezuela in the 1960s, combined with strategically located storage and transportation facilities in the United States, aided the large firms' ability to deal internationally.

Encouragement for the multinational subsidiaries and dominant national firms to acquire grains from abroad came from certain United States policies and programs. One influential program was the Public Law 480 (Food for Peace), established under the Department of Agriculture in 1954. In 1962, Venezuelan officials signed a treaty under P.L. 480, Title IV, to import 120,000 metric tons of corn and 6,000 metric tons of feed grains.[30] Although sales data on the Venezuelan agreement remain unavailable, no doubt exists that larger firms with access to capital and credit enjoyed advantages over most of the smaller domestic firms. The P.L. 480 grains had an adverse, lag effect on the Venezuelan production of corn. During 1962, the Venezuelan Ministry of Agriculture terminated its own corn production plan, Plan de Maíz, despite its seeming success after just one year of operation. Corn production did not regain the 1962 production level for almost four years.[31]

An organization funded under P.L. 480 legislation, Great Plains Wheat, had the explicit goal of market development for United States grains in other countries.[32] This organization, which maintained a regional office for northern South America in Caracas, convinced the Venezuelan School Lunch Feeding Program to serve wheat bread in its subsidized meals instead of using only the traditional corn arepa. Great Plains Wheat also worked with the baking industry's training program in the Venezuelan Vocational School and sponsored tours of United States milling industries and grain trade facilities for Venezuelans.

Though not specifically related to expanding the market for United States grains, the Department of State's loans under AID favored increased demand for United States goods rather than fomenting domestic agricultural production or self-sufficiency in Venezuela. AID allocated $250 million for the acquisition of goods but only $10 million for agrarian reform.[33] The Reciprocal Trade Agreement with the United States, which remained in force, also strongly reinforced established trade patterns.

As a result of this international support and their new structure, feed and milk firms found that they could operate under Venezuelan laws in ways that strengthened international ties or caused lags in national production of raw materials. In all cases, the action was contrary to the Venezuelan policy of developing local agricultural production in pursuit of self-sufficiency. In one instance, from the late 1950s through 1964, the powdered milk firms received a subsidy to maintain lower consumer prices and to stimulate local production. They also had the sole authorization to import powdered milk and took advantage of this to import over two and one-half times as much milk as they purchased from domestic producers.[34] The government eventually changed the policy, giving the subsidy directly to the Venezuelan crude milk producers instead of through the processing firms and gradually increasing the ratio of national milk purchases required in relation to imported milk. Although these policy changes caused imports to drop, lags in local production had a cumulative negative effect on Venezuelan milk production, while the processing firms benefited.[35]

The case of the feed firms also exemplifies circumvention of a Venezuelan policy aimed at self-sufficiency. Originally, the government had targeted favorable exchange rates only for the wheat milling sector, as planners had envisioned that the feed industry would stimulate national corn production. But between 1965 and 1969, instead of fulfilling this intention, the corporations turned to imports of United States wheat as a primary material for feed. Three factors contributed to this action: the existence of ample supplies of subsidized wheat in the United States; the parent firms' research finding that wheat could replace corn and other grains in feed production; and the failure of Venezuelan officials to improve the market for small-scale domestic grain producers. In turning to wheat, the dominant feed firms also received the benefit of the favorable exchange rate. The Venezuelan government claimed that it could not distinguish wheat for milling firms from that for feed firms. Finally, however, the government formulated a contingency ratio requiring feed firms to purchase a unit of national corn for every two units of imported wheat. Again, purchases on the international market caused cumulative effects on later domestic supplies and tied imports into the feed production process.[36]

The net effect of these changes was a strengthening of the large firms' international links. While it was preferable to feed animals in the country rather than import them live, many Venezuelan agricultural producers were denied the anticipated increased connections and expanded markets. In this process, cereals and grains grew to over 60 percent of imports of food and live animals by 1966 and reached 75 percent by 1975.[37] Venezuela became the leading cash market for United States agricultural products in Latin America and maintained its high level of food dependency.

Evaluation of AD's Reform Approach

The continued high level of concentration in the Venezuelan market and in international ties to food producers had a more positive effect on changes in food supplies than on intended changes in demand. From 1961 to 1975, the productive worth of the food manufacturing sector grew from Bs 1,914.5 million to Bs 9,780 million.[38] Analysts estimated that the availability of food supplies as measured by per capita calories had increased from approximately 2,246 to 2,562.[39] By the early 1960s, a corporate annual report stated that locally produced "Rice Crispies and Sugar Frosted Flakes had made it to the Venezuelan table"; Cheez Whiz, Miracle Whip, Kool-Aid, Royal puddings and Heinz' spaghetti sauces soon arrived as well.[40] Urban shoppers now found most supermarket shelves stocked with as many new processed foods as were found in the United States.

At the same time, the strategy failed to achieve the intended changes in sectoral and income distribution. The Venezuelan emphasis on industrialization as the "engine of development" did not induce the changes that planners had anticipated. Examination of the role of agriculture in the economy, of land ownership, and of income reveals this failure.

During the years after 1958, the agricultural sector continued to suffer from relative neglect. In relation to the ambitious goals that planners had set for it—complementing the growth of industry and achieving self-sufficiency in food production—the agricultural sector remained underfinanced. The Ministry of Agriculture received less than 10 percent of the national budget most years. The Agricultural Bank, the government's main agricultural credit institution, had particularly serious financial and administrative problems. It had to turn to large United States banks for funds in the early 1960s and continually suffered a low recovery rate on loans, as many farmers defaulted. Between 1963 and 1968, the bank financed only 11 percent of campesino farms and 21.9 percent of commercial farms, leaving the majority to obtain funds at prevailing high interest rates in the private lending sector.[41] Underfinancing was a major reason why the agricultural sector contributed only 6–7 percent of the gross national product through 1974.

Additionally, the land reform program did not make major changes in the concentration of landholding. One analysis of the period 1961–71 found only a 0.03 decrease in the index of concentration.[42] Low levels of funding combined with the required generous payment to expropriated landowners limited the number of private holdings redistributed. Furthermore, by 1963, shortly after receiving the $10 million agrarian reform loan under AID, Venezuelan policy shifted from redistribution of private agricultural properties to settlement of campesino families on public lands. It has been alleged but not established that AID loans often came with strings attached.[43] The political power of the country's urban majority, often directed toward other objectives, may also have weakened the government's commitment to agrarian reform. For whatever reasons, the badly needed agrarian reform program floundered by 1973. Approximately half of the 350,000 projected new landowners and their families remained at their new homestead. Some 30 percent of the settlers had abandoned their farms, discouraged by difficulties in acquiring land titles, credit, and technical aid. Many of those left practiced subsistence agriculture or produced only marginally for the market and hence consumed few manufactured goods.[44]

The economic bias in Venezuelan policies that favored large, private landowners and large-scale industries reinforced existing inequalities in Venezuelan income distribution. The failure of agrarian reform worked to sustain income inequalities among the rural populace, as did the food processing firms' selectivity in establishing links to agricultural producers. The firms' direct agricultural operations did not expand the rural market uniformly by increasing remunerative employment, as planners had anticipated. Heinz, for instance, used mechanized transplanters in its Venezuelan tomato fields. The integrated chicken operations run under contract by Ralston Purina and Protinal reduced the number of individuals employed in the process: from 1961 to 1972 there was a relatively substantial drop in the number of small producers while the owners of larger flocks increased slightly.[45] The Venezuelan business sector as a whole further influenced the failure of income redistribution in the country by successfully opposing tax reforms throughout the 1960s.

Although the percentage of population in the top income sector rose, extremes of income persisted. The poorer 50 percent made nominal gains in their share of private national income, increasing it from 19 percent in 1957 to 20 percent in 1970.[46] One observer estimated that as many as 75 percent of all families fell below the minimum subsistence level (Bs 1,500 for a family of five or six).[47] Geographic concentration of income continued, with Caracas, home of 17–20 percent of Venezuelans, receiving 40 percent of private income. The largest gap in income distribution was found between agricultural and nonagricultural workers: between 1961 and 1971, agriculture was the only occupational category to experience an increase in the proportion of its members below the poverty level. A high population growth rate of 3.5 percent compounded these divisions.[48]

The failure of sectoral and income redistribution meant that the ability to purchase foods remained uneven despite overall growth in income. This nature of food demand elicited unforeseen responses from the dominant food firms and contributed to the continuation of high levels of malnutriton.

According to Engels' Law, as incomes increase, a smaller proportion is spent on food. In order to counter this tendency and to profit from consumers with the greatest increase in income, the firms developed more expensive luxury and convenience foods. The success of this marketing approach diverted the firms from concentrating on cost-effective production of food staples, as envisioned by government planners.[49] The Venezuelan policy of subsidizing lower food prices contributed to this effect, as it made subsidized foods available to all consumers rather than reaching only the poor.

Sophisticated research and advertising aided the firms in changing production patterns to take advantage of the higher income market. Venezuelan subsidiaries of big United States advertising companies—Young and Rubicam, J. Walter Thompson, Grant Advertising, and S. J. and Kettery Grey—aggressively sought to presell and to differentiate products by brand name through television, radio, and printed advertising.[50] Some firms also made use of United States–style supermarket promotions such as Heinz' "Tomato Festival."

The multinational subsidiaries and dominant national firms researched and marketed three new categories of foods. Some products—including Kraft's Philadelphia Brand Cream Cheese, marketed in the familiar silver-and-blue box, Miracle Whip, and Cheez Whiz; Nestlé's chocolate milk; General Foods' Kool-Aid; and Standard Brands' Royal puddings—were direct transplants from the United States production lines. A second category of product, either a new raw material or processed food, was developed in Venezuela and linked to effective demand in other countries, usually by the international corporate structure. Two examples include precooked corn flour suitable for export under new technology and packaging, and new crops such as the peas and asparagus grown by Heinz. The third type of product resulted from a blend of international research in Venezuela and in the United States for Venezuelan consumers. Two particular products—Bingo, a beverage developed by Heinz, and *pan de jamón,* a bread developed by International Multifoods (formerly International Milling)—illustrate the internationalization of research, production, and marketing.

Heinz managers in Venezuela began market research for Bingo by noting a high consumption of fruit drinks in Venezuela, trying almost two hundred recipes, and conducting consumer tests.[51] Next, they turned to the United States home office, convincing skeptical corporate executives with taste test results that Venezuelans preferred very sweet drinks. The Venezuelan subsidiary then produced and marketed the product using United States merchandizing methods of displays and samples placed in a concentrated market area in the supermarkets of Maracaibo, with a greatly increased advertising budget. Heinz officials considered the launching of Bingo a great success.

Pan de jamón also typified international research and marketing. The firm wanted a product to compete during the Christmas season with corn flour, used in the traditional hallacas, and to offset the seasonal decline in wheat flour sales. The company researched customs and found the "apparent tradition" of a ham bread that existed "many, many years ago in Venezuela" and had become "more and more obscure."[52] International Multifoods then adapted recipes for industrial preparation of a wheat flour bread dough, spread with slices of ham and raisins—both imported items—and rolled into a loaf. By contrast, the traditional hallaca was prepared mostly from nationally produced foodstuffs.

The firm's merchandising methods focused on two groups, the baking industry and the consumer. Salesmen canvassed the numerous, predominantly small-scale bakers, giving them two or three recipes and an explanation of the promotion. At the same time, the firm reached the consumer through television and newspaper ads with the theme of "let's get back to our traditions," a campaign to which many consumers are susceptible at the Christmas season. Not until the last line did the ad identify International Multifoods subsidiary as the sponsor of the Christmas message. The success of this merchandising approach is indicated by the fact that heads of government agencies ordered pan de jamón as an *aguinaldo,* or Christmas bonus, for employees. By the mid-1970s, bakers sold the bread year around at a high cost of Bs 15, or over three dollars for half a long loaf.[53]

These details depict the process of introducing only two new food products into the Venezuelan market; actually, a plethora of new foods increased variety and added novel tastes for the higher-income consumers. Large numbers of lower-income groups, however, continued to suffer from undernourishment. Uneven income distribution affected the outcome in two ways. First, the poor could not afford adequate food. Second, the dominant firms failed to improve mass production, economies of scale, and lower staple prices.

Although domestic production of processed foods had expanded, the availability of basic vegetable proteins did not grow proportionately. From 1961 to 1970, the national output of animal protein increased by 6.9 percent per year, but vegetable production by only 3.7 percent.[54] Soon after, food price inflation became a feature of life in a country accustomed to relative price stability. Between 1960 and 1970, Venezuelan food prices had increased only 10 percent, but after 1970 both raw staples and prepared foods climbed rapidly.[55] The poor were especially vulnerable as a result of their low incomes, the lag in national production, and increases in international prices of raw materials and processed goods.

Even after fifteen years of governmental reform efforts, malnutrition clearly did not decrease in proportion to increases in available food supplies. Relatively high levels of generalized protein calorie malnutrition continued to afflict the rural and urban poor, and those under fourteen years of age most severely. Two indices depict this fact: rates of death due to malnutrition, and height and weight deviations from the norm among school-age children.

By 1974, the rate of death from malnutrition for the total population stood at 10 per 100,000, the approximate level of 1950.[56] Specific causes of death varied in incidence between these two periods: anemia-caused deaths increased among young children, while the incidence of deaths from vitamin deficiency and diarrhea declined.[57] The geographic breakdown indicates an increase in malnutrition in the least populated rural areas and on the fringes of Caracas. Although severe forms of malnutrition such as beriberi and pellagra had declined by the mid-1970s, the proportion of school-age children found deficient in height and weight had risen since 1960. Third grade malnutrition, the most severe, declined from 1.6 percent to 0.8–1.2 percent; second grade malnutrition from 13.4 to 10 percent; but first grade malnutrition, the least severe category, had risen from 40 to 54 percent.[58] Overall, this suggests a slight easing of the most extreme cases of malnutrition, with no improvement or a slight decline in general levels of nourishment among Venezuela's poor.

Conclusion

In its pragmatic attempt after 1958 to reform the food system in Venezuela, the two AD administrations and the successor COPEI government used international capital as the prime tool of an import substitution industrialization strategy. This strategy permitted rapid growth of new, large-scale multinational and dominant national firms. Supplies of domestic processed and semi-processed foods that had formerly been imported increased as well. But the dilemma of this growth pattern has been the continued inability to foster wider, more uniform economic participation. Both food dependency and malnutrition remain as characteristics of the food system.

Failure to eradicate these problems resulted from the attempt to achieve income and sectoral redistribution as a by-product of other policies and from unforeseen changes in industrial practices. Instead of taking complementary roles, industry and agriculture remained in hierarchical positions in the economy. Within the agricultural sector, the smaller-scale food producer did not become a dynamic element in the market, and land reform did not make radical changes in ownership. Nor did the Venezuelan government limit domination in the market by large firms; rather, it encouraged their growth.

The rise of new purchasing practices and changes in the firms and markets also affected income flows and supplies of foods. In the process, links to international raw material producers became stronger than the desired links to national grain suppliers. The present food system provides sufficient food to higher income, urban consumers. The government achieved substantial progress in industrialization between 1958 and 1974 without a major reorganization of agriculture and industry and without improving domestic employment and income distribution.

However, fundamental changes did take place in the nature of food dependency. Once simply an importer of foods, Venezuela now participated in an international network. The change involved three groups: the raw material producers, the industrial processors, and the consumers. As before, Venezuela relied on major imports of agricultural goods in exchange for petroleum. But now these imports were raw materials instead of processed and semiprocessed foods. International capital had supplanted Venezuelan capital in the key milk and flour sectors and to a large degree in feed, poultry, and eggs. In addition, government subsidization of milk and wheat bread meant that higher-income consumers increased demand for more highly processed goods, those inappropriate for the nutritional needs of low-income consumers.

In order to make the country's food system more equitable, in 1974 the AD administration of Carlos Andrés Pérez adopted new policies of direct redistribution. With petroleum income soaring as a result of OPEC strategy, the government committed substantial amounts of capital to nationalizing firms and to improving income and sectoral distribution.[59] It launched these reforms in the hopes that not only corn flakes and Bingo but also staples such as arepas, milk, and eggs could be served in greater quantities on more Venezuelan tables. With this change in direction, planners intended to make the new international food system responsive to the nation's needs. The next few years will bring the verdict on the current phase of Venezuela's struggle to feed its people.

Notes

1. In addition to specific references, general supporting material is found in Eleanor Witte Wright, "The Political Economy of Venezuelan Food Policy: 1958–1978" (Ph.D. diss., Dept. of Government and Politics, University of Maryland, 1982). For references to the political aspects of food dependency see: Sarta Aziz, "The World Food Situation and Collective Self-Reliance," *World Development* 5, nos. 5–7 (1977): 651–60; Aziz El Sherbini and Radha Sinha, "Arab Agriculture: Prospects for Self-Sufficiency," *Food Policy* 3, no. 2 (May 1978): 84–95; Frances Moore Lappé and Joseph

Collins, *Food First: Beyond the Myth of Scarcity* (New York: Random House, 1977), part 10; John P. Lewis, "National Self-Sufficiency and International Dependency," in *Proceedings: The World Food Conference of 1976* . . . (Ames: Iowa State University Press, 1977), pp. 211–12; Heather Johnston Nicholson and Ralph L. Nicholson, *Distant Hunger: Agriculture, Food and Human Values* (West Lafayette, Ind.: Purdue University Press, 1979), p. 208–11; and Thomas W. Wilson, "Hunger, Politics and Security," in *Food and People,* eds. Dudley Kirk and Ellen K. Eliason (San Francisco: Boyd and Fraser, 1982), pp. 364–70, 390–96. For food dependency and trade see: Raymond F. Hopkins and Donald J. Puchala, *Global Food Interdependence: Challenge to American Foreign Policy* (New York: Columbia University Press, 1980), pp. 11–13; David P. Harmon, Jr., "Return to World Grain Surpluses: Trends and Implications for Agricultural Self-Sufficiency," in *Critical Food Issues of the Eighties,* eds. Marylin Chou and David P. Harmon, Jr. (New York: Pergamon Press, 1979), pp. 326–28; and Howard Wagstaff, "Food Imports of Developing Countries," *Food Policy* 7, no. 1 (Feb. 1982), p. 57. Most works on food dependency concentrate on the effect on food supplies without acknowledging the effect on employment and income distribution, which in turn affect levels of malnutrition.

2. Constance H. Farnworth and Leon G. Mears, *U.S. Farm Products Find Market and Competition in Venezuela,* Foreign Agricultural Economic Report no. 1 (Washington, D.C.: U.S. Department of Agriculture [USDA], Economic Research Service, 1961): 6, 19; Reynaldo F. Rodriguez, *A Market for U.S. Products: Venezuela,* (Washington, D.C.: U.S. Department of Commerce, Bureau of International Commerce, 1964), p. 24.

3. Pablo Liendo Coll, *Nutrición* (Caracas: Instituto Venezolano de Acción Comunitario, 1962), p. 13.

4. John Osgood Field, "The Soft Underbelly of Applied Knowledge: Conceptual and Operational Problems in Nutrition Planning," *Food Policy* 2 (1977): 228–39, covers the various approaches to conceptualizing strategies: reformist, radical reform from above, etc.

5. Most scholars highlight the effect of civil wars and prices of export crops, as for example William M. Sullivan, "Situación económica y política durante el período de Juan Vicente Gómez 1908–1935," in *Política y economía en Venezuela, 1810–1976* (Caracas: Fundación John Boulton, 1976), pp. 252–56; Nikita Harwich Vallenilla, "El modelo económico del liberalismo amarillo: Historia de un fracaso, 1888–1908," in *Ibid.,* pp. 219, 234–35; Raymond E. Crist and Charles M. Nissly, *East from the Andes* . . . (Gainesville: University of Florida Press, 1973), pp. 19, 29; John V. Lombardi, *Venezuela: The Search for Order, The Dream of Progress* (New York: Oxford University Press, 1982), pp. 33–34, 199. See also Luis Troconis Guerrero, *La cuestión agraria en la historia nacional,* Biblioteca de Autores y Temas Tachirenses 29 (San Cristóbal, Venezuela, 1962); Edwin Lieuwen, *Venezuela,* 2nd ed. (New York: Oxford University Press, 1965), pp. 43–44, 117–18; and Guillermo Morón, *A History of Venezuela,* ed. and trans. John Street (New York: Roy, 1963), p. 88.

6. International Bank for Reconstruction and Development, *The Economic Devel-*

opment of Venezuela (Baltimore: Johns Hopkins Press, 1961), p. 482.

7. Erna Fergusson, *Venezuela* (New York: Alfred A. Knopf, 1943), p. 68.

8. Lourdes Urdaneta, *Distribución del ingreso: Análisis del caso venezolano* (Caracas: Banco Central, Colección de Estudios Económicos, 1975), p. 81.

9. Harry E. Wing, *Land Reform in Venezuela* (Washington, D.C.: Agency for International Development, June 1970), pp. 1, 7.

10. For descriptions of debt labor see Thomas Russell Ybarra, *Young Man of Caracas* (New York: Ives Washburn, 1941), pp. 124–25; and P. L. Bell, *Venezuela: A Commercial and Industrial Handbook . . . ,* Special Agents Series no. 212 (Washington, D.C.: U.S. Department of Commerce [and Labor], Bureau of Foreign and Domestic Commerce [Manufactures], 1922): 33.

11. Cámara de Industrias de Caracas, *Anuario industrial de Caracas* (Caracas, 1958), p. 687. The bolivar in 1950 was valued at thirty-one cents (U.S.) at the year-end exchange rate (James Wilkie and Stephen Haber, *Statistical Abstract of Latin America* 22 [Los Angeles: UCLA Latin American Center, 1983]: 330).

12. Wayne G. Broehl, Jr., *The International Basic Economy Corporation* (Washington, D.C.: National Planning Association, 1968), p. 18.

13. Robert J. Alexander, *A New Development Strategy* (Maryknoll, N.Y.: Orbis Books, 1976), p. 34.

14. Reynaldo F. Rodriguez, *A Market for U.S. Products: Venezuela*, pp. 24, 40–44; and Robert J. Alexander, *The Venezuelan Democratic Revolution . . .* (New Brunswick, N.J.: Rutgers University Press, 1964), pp. 196–99.

15. Alberto Micheo and Luis Ugalde, *La agricultura en la economía venezolana,* Formación Socio-política no. 17 (Caracas: Centro Gumilla, 1977), pp. 20–30.

16. Francisco J. Rincón, *Estudio preliminar sobre un sistema de prioridades de inversión para la CVF* (Caracas: Corporación Venezolana de Fomento, División de Estudios Generales, 1965).

17. José A. Gil, "Entrepreneurs and Regime Consolidation in Venezuela" (paper delivered at the Fifth National Meeting of the Latin American Studies Association, San Francisco, Nov. 14–18, 1974), pp. 31, 49; and John A. Clements Associates, *Report on Venezuela* (New York, n.d.).

18. William Robbins, *The American Food Scandal . . .* (New York: Wm. Morrow, 1974), p. 117; and A. V. Krebs, "A Galloping Oligopoly in Food," *Business and Society Review* 28 (Winter 1978–79), p. 64. For reference to percentage of sales held in the particular sectors see, respectively: Antonieta Monasterio C., *Industria harinera en Venezuela*, pub. no. 9 (Caracas: Corporación Venezolana de Fomento, División de Estudios Generales, 1962): 18; Juan Mújica Marcano, *La industria de alimentos concentrados para animales* (Caracas: Corporación Venezolana de Fomento, División de Estudios Generales, 1964), p. 11; and Venezuela, Ministerio de Fomento, Dirección General de Estadísticas y Censos Nacionales, *V encuesta industrial: Resultados nacionales* (Caracas, 1976), p. 49.

19. Thomas J. Biersteker, *Distortion or Development?: Contending Perspectives on the Multinational Corporation* (Cambridge: MIT Press, 1978), p. xii. For favorable

assessments of multinational corporations in food processing see: James E. Austin, *Agribusiness in Latin America* (New York: Praeger, 1974); Raymond Goldberg, *Agribusiness Management for Developing Countries* (Cambridge, Mass.: Ballinger, 1974); David P. Harmon, "The Multinational Corporations: A Buffer in the Food-Climate System," in *Critical Food Issues of the Eighties,* eds. Marylin Chou and David P. Harmon, Jr. (New York: Pergamon Press, 1979), pp. 347–66; and George C. Lodge, "Food Processing: Key to Economic Development," *Harvard Business Review* 44, no. 5 (Sept.–Oct. 1966), pp. 6–20. Critical assessments include: Richard Barnet and Ronald Muller, "How Global Corporations Compound World Hunger," in *Food for People, Not for Profit . . . ,* eds. Catherine Lerza and Michael Jacobson (New York: Ballantine Books, 1975), pp. 248–53, 351–406; Susan DeMarco and Susan Sechler, *The Fields Have Turned Brown* (Washington, D.C.: Agribusiness Accountability Project, 1975); Germán Briceño et al., *Agricultura y agro-industria en Venezuela* (Caracas: Centro de Estudios del Desarrollo, Universidad Central de Venezuela, 1978); Ernst Feder, "Agribusiness and the Elimination of Latin America's Rural Proletariat," *World Development* 5, nos. 5–7 (1977), pp. 559–73; Susan George, *How the Other Half Dies* (Montclair, N.J.: Allanheld, Osmun, 1977); Keith Griffin, "Multinational Corporations and Basic Needs Development," *Development and Change* 8, no. 1 (Jan. 1977): 61–77; Jim Hightower, *Eat Your Heart Out . . .* (New York: Crown, 1975); Lappé and Collins, *Food First,* part 8; Robert Ledogar, *Hungry for Profits: U.S. Food and Drug Multinationals in Latin America* (New York: IDOC [International Documentation on the Contemporary Church]/North America, 1975). See also Weine Karlsson, *Manufacturing in Venezuela . . .* (Stockholm: Almqvist and Wisksell, 1975).

20. *Fortune* 58, no. 1 (July 1958): 131, 148–50.

21. International Milling, *Annual Report, 1963* (Minneapolis, 1963), p. 12.

22. Broehl, *International Basic Economy Corporation,* p. 123.

23. International Milling, *Annual Report, 1958,* p. 2; International Milling, *Annual Report, 1959,* p. 2; Pillsbury, *Annual Report, 1961* (Minneapolis, 1961), p. 2.

24. Broehl, *International Basic Economy Corporation,* p. 240.

25. U.S., House of Representatives, 87th Congress, 2nd Session, Committee on Appropriations, Subcommittee on Foreign Appropriations, *Foreign Operations for 1963* (Washington, D.C., 1963), part 3, p. 1, states that the survey cost $104,000.

26. See *Business International,* Sept. 22, 1967, p. 292; Sept. 15, 1967, p. 302; and Sept. 20, 1968, p. 301.

27. Heinz, *Annual Report, 1972* (Pittsburgh, 1972), p. 22; Heinz, *Annual Report, 1966,* p. 15; Corn Products Company, International, *Annual Report, 1964* (Englewood Cliffs, N.J., 1964), p. 19; Corn Products Company, International, *Annual Report, 1968,* p. 17; *Business Latin America,* Sept. 25, 1969, p. 307.

28. Venezuela, Ministerio de Agricultura y Cría, *Memoria y cuenta, 1968* (Caracas, 1969), p. 61.

29. International Multifoods, *Annual Report, 1975,* p. 17 (formerly International

Milling); for ownership of storage in Venezuela see Louis E. Heaton, *The Agricultural Development of Venezuela* (New York: Praeger, 1969), p. 82.

30. U.S., Department of State, "Venezuela—Agricultural Commodities: Sales under Title IV," in *U.S. Treaties and Other International Agreements* no. 5068, vol. 13, part 2 (Washington, D.C., 1962): 1231–40. By 1965, the United States and Venezuela had signed three agreements at a value of $13.6 million according to U.S., Department of State, *Resources Survey for Latin American Countries* (Washington, D.C., 1965), p. 537.

31. Venezuela, Ministerio de Agricultura y Cría, Dirección de Economía y Estadística Agropecuaria, *Anuario estadístico agropecuario, 1972* (Caracas, 1973), p. 48.

32. See issues of *Foreign Agriculture,* such as 4, no. 36 (Sept. 5, 1966), p. 8; and 6, no. 22 (July 15, 1968), p. 51.

33. U.S., Department of State, Office of Media Services, *Venezuela, Background Notes, 1976* (Washington, D.C., 1976), p. 7.

34. Instituto Venezolano del Consumidor, *El problema de la leche en Venezuela* (Caracas: Centro de Estudios Técnicos y Información Pública, July 1973), p. 30, gives the figures of 222,550 metric tons of imports and 83,670 metric tons produced locally.

35. Venezuela, Presidencia, Oficina Central de Estudios e Información, *Anuario estadístico, 1975* (Caracas, 1978), p. 631. Imports were 154,521 metric tons for the period 1962–65 and dropped to 79,222 metric tons for 1966–69.

36. The dominant grains used by the feed companies included: alfalfa and corn, 1960–64; wheat, 1964–69; and sorghum and soy, 1969–74 (Venezuela, Ministerio de Agricultura y Cría, *Anuario estadístico agropecuario, 1972* [Caracas, 1973], pp. 48, 71, 709; *Anuario estadístico agropecuario, 1973* [1974], p. 51; and *Anuario estadístico agropecuario, 1978* [1979], p. 76).

37. United Nations, *World Trade Annual, 1966* (New York: Walker, 1967), I-249; *World Trade Annual, 1975* (1977), I-246, I-281–82.

38. Venezuela, Oficina Central de Coordinación y Planificación, *Encuesta industrial* (Caracas, Nov. 1963), p. 37; Venezuela, Ministerio de Fomento, *V encuesta industrial,* p. 43.

39. Sociedad Venezolana de Planificación, *Nutrición, agricultura y dependencia,* cuaderno 133 (Caracas, 1977), p. 58. Though another estimate varies in the amount, both show an increase in calories (kcal) (Thomas E. Weil et al., *Area Handbook for Venezuela* [Washington, D.C.: GPO, 1971], p. 98).

40. General Foods, *Annual Report, 1962* (White Plains, N.Y., 1962), pp. 9–10; Kellogg, *Annual Report, 1962* (Battle Creek, Mich., 1962), p. 2.

41. Ramón Losada Aldana, *La tierra venezolana en la dialéctica del subdesarrollo,* vol. 2: *El pasado del presente* (Caracas, Universidad Central de Venezuela, Facultad de Ciencias Económicas y Sociales, 1976): 304.

42. Paul Cox, *Venezuela's Agrarian Reform at Mid-1977* (Madison: University of Wisconsin Land Tenure Centre, Feb. 1978), pp. 1–2.

43. For criticism of AID see Teresa Hayter, *Aid as Imperialism* (Middlesex,

England: Penguin Books, 1974), p. 78; and Charles D. Hyson and Alan Stuart, "Impact of Foreign Aid on U.S. Exports," *Harvard Business Review* 46, no. 1 (Jan.–Feb. 1968): 64–68 and note 25.

44. Micheo and Ugalde, *La agricultura en la economía venezolana*, p. 28.

45. Venezuela, Ministerio de Agricultura y Cría, División de Economía y Estadística, *Encuesta avícola, 1961* (Caracas, 1962), p. 28, and Venezuela, Ministerio de Agricultura y Cría, División de Estadística, *Encuesta avícola nacional, 1972* (Caracas, 1974), pp. 24–25, illustrate that the number of the smallest producers decreased by 575 while the largest producers increased by only 94.

46. James F. Petras, Morris Morley, and Steven Smith, *The Nationalization of Venezuelan Oil* (New York: Praeger, 1977), p. 33; and Urdaneta, *Distribución del ingreso*, p. 181.

47. Klaus Esser, *Oil and Development: Venezuela* (Berlin: German Development Institute, 1976), p. 18. The reader needs to consider the extremely high cost of living in Venezuela when looking at these figures. See also James W. Wilkie and Peter Reich, eds., *Statistical Abstract of Latin America* 18 (Los Angeles: UCLA Latin American Center, 1977): 26, 331.

48. Kenneth Ruddle and Kathleen Barrows, eds., *Statistical Abstract of Latin America, 1972* (Los Angeles: UCLA Latin American Center, 1974), p. 5.

49. The income elasticity was higher than might be expected on unprocessed foods because of the high prices and low consumption levels. See Instituto Venezolano del Consumidor, *Los problemas de la economía pecuaria en Venezuela: Causas de los altos precios de la carne de res*, Serie Costo de la Vida no. 2 (Caracas: Centro de Estudios Técnicos y de Información Pública, 1973): 13, 70.

50. Federico Brito Figueroa, *Venezuela contemporánea: ¿País colonial?* (Caracas: Ediciones Teoría y Praxis, 1972), p. 52; and *Venezuela Up-to-Date* 10, no. 5 (Nov.–Dec. 1960), p. 13.

51. For more details of the corporate campaign and methods of advertising see *Wall Street Journal, How They Sell: The Successful Marketing Techniques of 13 Major American Corporations* (New York: Dow Jones Books, 1965), pp. 122–27; and for corporate advertising expenses see Heinz, *Annual Report, 1965*, p. 13.

52. For details of product research and advertising see International Multifoods, *Annual Report, 1972*, p. 2.

53. Eleanor Witte Wright, personal observation in Caracas, Sept. 1978–July 1979.

54. Esser, *Oil and Development*, p. 13.

55. Asociación Pro Venezuela, *La inflación: Un problema de nuestra época* (Caracas, 1975), p. 126, states that the price of wheat, corn, and meat jumped over 60 percent from just 1970 to 1972; also see Loring Allen, *Venezuelan Economic Development* (Greenwich, Conn.: Jai Press, 1977), p. 292.

56. *La Extra* (Caracas) 1, no. 95 (May 13, 1964), p. 6; and José María Bengoa, *Salud, nutrición y calidad de vida: Reflexiones 1936–76* (Caracas: I Congreso Venezolano de Conservación, 1978), p. 58.

57. Miguel A. Osio et al., *Hacia una política nacional de alimentación y nutrición* (Caracas: Instituto Nacional de Nutrición, 1976), appendix 6; Venezuela, Ministerio de Sanidad y Asistencia Social, Departamento de Demografía y Epidemología, *Anuario de epidemología y estadística vital, 1959,* 2 vols. (Caracas, 1960), 1:616, and *Anuario de epidemología y estadística vital, 1974,* 3 vols. (1975), 3: 78–79.

58. Reinaldo Grueso, *Informe sobre los problemas y programas de nutrición de Venezuela* (Washington, D.C.: Organización Panamericana de la Salud, Reunión de Asesores de Nutrición, 1970), p. 5; and "Un drama nacional de la desnutrición infantil," *Resumen* (Venezuela) 133 (May 23, 1976): 26.

59. Concerning the nationalization of firms see *The Market for Food Processing and Packaging Equipment in Argentina, Brazil, Mexico and Venezuela* (New York: Frost and Sullivan, #E273, April 1978), p. 229; and for reference to agricultural sector and income redistribution see Gustavo Pinto Cohén, *Hechos y logros de la agricultura venezolana,* supplement to *Memoria y cuenta, 1978* (Caracas: Ministerio de Agricultura y Cría, 1979), p. 27; and U.S., Department of Commerce, *Foreign Economic Trends and Their Implications for the U.S.: Venezuela* (Washington, D.C., May 1977), p. 5.

**Nancy Forster and
Howard Handelman**

Food Production and
Distribution in
Cuba: The Impact
of the Revolution

Virtually all the major political and economic changes brought about by the Cuban Revolution have engendered significant controversy and heated debate.[1] The nation's agricultural and nutritional policies have been no exception. During the early years of the Revolution, Leon Mears, an American agricultural analyst, charged that "the Cubans have gone from being among the best fed people in Latin America to a diet below the area's minimum nutritional standards."[2] More recently, many émigrés who left Cuba in the 1980 spring exodus complained about allegedly inadequate diets in their homeland. Yet, many foreign observers who have visited the island have insisted that the new regime has eradicated malnutrition—a rare accomplishment in the developing world. For example, economist David Barkin and his colleagues returned from Cuba in the mid-1970s hailing the Revolution's record in "making equitable and nutritious diets available to all Cubans."[3]

This chapter analyzes the effects of two decades of revolution on Cuban agriculture, stressing the relationship between government policy, food production, and mass nutritional levels. Any meaningful discussion must first briefly describe pre-Revolutionary agriculture and assess Cuban nutritional standards under the old order. Following such a review, we examine the manner in which agrarian reform and the introduction of a socialist economic order altered the traditional agrarian structure. Similarly, we discuss the effects of government agricultural production decisions, income policy, and rationing mechanisms on food consumption. Ultimately, we argue that popular nutritional levels in Cuba can be properly evaluated only through an analysis encompassing the effects of distribution and equity policies as well as levels of food production.

Food Production and Consumption before the Revolution

Blessed with rich soil and a relatively benevolent climate, Cuba has long been able to farm a large proportion of its surface area. Data collected in the nation's 1946 agricultural census (the only complete census of this type in Cuban history) indicate that farm land accounted for nearly 80 percent of the island's total area of 28,287,428 acres. Of that farm land, approximately 43 percent was devoted to pasture (cattle) and some 22 percent was cultivated.[4]

Traditionally, sugar cane dominated the agricultural economy. During the 1950s, Cuba was the world's leading sugar producer, contributing more than 15 percent of international output in some years. In 1958, sugar accounted for well over half the value of Cuba's entire agricultural production, with meat and other livestock products (largely for domestic consumption) a distant second. Tobacco, coffee, and rice followed in that order.[5] In addition to sugar (which dominated the export sector), tobacco, bananas, pineapples, cacao, and winter vegetables were also grown for export. Rice, corn, beans, sweet potatoes, yams, yuca (cassava), malanga (taro), potatoes, citrus, and tomatoes were cultivated primarily for domestic consumption.

As in most Latin American nations, land ownership was highly concentrated. The 1946 census revealed that 0.5 percent of the nation's farms accounted for more than a third of total agricultural area. Conversely, 80 percent of the units controlled only 20 percent of the farm land (one-third of these plots were less than 2 hectares in size).[6] Most agricultural land (about 70 percent of all farms) was managed or worked by persons who did not own it, with approximately 63 percent of the holdings cultivated by share-croppers, tenants, or squatters. These figures slightly overstate absentee ownership, since tenant sugar farmers (some 20 percent of the total tenant population) had obtained fairly secure tenure on their plots in the ten to fifteen years following passage of the Sugar Coordination Act of 1937 (as long as they paid their rent and met their cane delivery quotas to the sugar mill that owned the land).[7]

Despite the generally propitious climatic and soil conditions, agricultural productivity before the Revolution was relatively low.[8] In 1945, only 3 percent of the cultivated land was irrigated, and as of 1959 the figure was still only 10 percent.[9] Cultivation of coffee and cacao was backward and produced low yields, while productivity was higher in rice (which was mechanized and irrigated) and tobacco (which was also irrigated and intensively farmed). A 1950 study by a mission of the International Bank for Reconstruction and Development (IBRD) observed that the Cuban sugar industry showed "a conspicuous lack of technical progress." The mission cited in-

adequate utilization of irrigation and fertilizer as well as the virtual absence
of research aimed at increasing output. Concurring with these findings,
Chilean agronomist Andrés Bianchi noted the lack of research and extension
programs and the inadequate number of trained agricultural technicians.[10]

While Cuba's agrarian sector was not producing up to its potential capacity, production per se was not the major food problem. Nation-wide statistics suggested a relatively high average level of food production and consumption (by third world standards). Scattered data indicated that per capita
caloric intake during the 1950s ranged from 2,700 to 2,900 calories daily.
These figures far exceeded the estimated required level of 2,460 calories,
giving Cuba one of the highest average consumption levels in Latin America.[11] But, in a society with highly skewed income distribution—characteristic of prerevolutionary Cuba and of most of Latin America today—
average figures are highly misleading. For while Cuba's large urban middle
class and even many skilled urban workers could afford a fairly abundant
diet, low-income Cubans were inadequately fed. Poverty and the accompanying under-nutrition were particularly prevalent in the countryside.

The most widely cited study of pre-Revolutionary rural living standards
was conducted in 1956 by Havana's Catholic University Association, which
surveyed the families of one thousand agricultural workers in all of Cuba's
126 municipalities.[12] Numbering perhaps four hundred thousand, landless
agricultural workers constituted the bulk of the rural lower class. With more
than two million dependents, these workers and their families represented
over 35 percent of Cuba's entire population. Most of them labored on the
nation's sugar plantations, where they secured regular work only four to six
months of the year—from December's planting season until May's harvest.
During the *tiempo muerto* (dead season) between harvest and planting,
agricultural unemployment levels often reached 50 percent.[13] Lacking food
supplements from subsistence farm plots (an option open to the nation's one
hundred thousand or so smallholders and the approximately equal number
of tenant farmers), these families suffered most severely from nutritional
deficiencies.

The 1956 rural survey, accepted as valid by major scholars of all persuasions, indicated that 91 percent of the respondent families consumed inadequate quantities of calories and protein. Only 4 percent of the families ate
meat with any regularity; just 2.2 percent ate eggs more than once weekly
and only 11.2 percent drank milk regularly.[14] The principal foods consumed
by this population were rice (24 percent of caloric intake), beans (23 percent),
and root crops (22 percent). On the whole, rural workers received some 33
percent fewer calories than the estimated number required for the kind of

intensive labor they performed. Not surprisingly, the rural population, and particularly agricultural workers and their families, were on the average considerably smaller in stature than the typical urban Cuban.

Another 1956 survey, this one of more than two thousand sixth grade school children, reinforces the evidence that malnutrition was more widespread in the countryside than in the cities and far more prevalent among the lower income strata of both the urban and rural populations. The students surveyed attended both public and private schools and about half were urban and half rural. Nearly 44 percent of the children in the public schools were underweight—a figure more than four times the level in the private school sample—and over 10 percent of the entire group suffered from skeletal deformities due to low calcium consumption.[15] Rural children were more likely than their urban counterparts to have deficiencies of calcium, vitamin A, thiamine, and riboflavin.

Compared with northern Brazil, several Andean nations, and most of the countries in Central America, Cuba's nutritional problems in the 1950s were not severe. Starvation and severe malnutrition were not a problem. However, significant portions of the population had deficient diets. According to the 1950 study of the IBRD Mission, approximately 30–40 percent of Cuba's urban population and over 60 percent of the rural populace were undernourished. "Nutritional deficiencies [were] manifested in small bone structure, overweight [due to starch-based diets], general physical weakness, anemia, and low resistance to disease."[16]

The fundamental cause of these nutritional problems was not inadequate production, although many critics insisted that agriculture was too skewed toward sugar exportation with inadequate cultivation of food crops. Rather, the main problem was the low purchasing power of the salaried agricultural work force and the urban poor. Dudley Seers notes that in the years before the Revolution, 60 percent of the total population (and a far greater proportion of the rural sector) had incomes of less than seventy-five dollars (U.S.) per month. Families in that group spent some two-thirds of their income on food.[17] The aforementioned 1956 survey of agricultural workers showed that this important sector of the population was allocating an average of only seventeen cents (U.S.) per person daily for food (with an average family size of six).[18] Indeed, the typical agricultural worker and his family ate less than comparable Cuban families twenty-two years earlier.[19]

The Revolution and the First Agrarian Reform (1959–60)

The victory of Fidel Castro and his revolutionary forces in January 1959 ushered in a series of far-reaching policy changes that profoundly affected patterns of food production and consumption in Cuba. Soon after the guerrilla army seized the reins of power, the new government promulgated a national land reform act calling for the expropriation of most estates over 30 caballerías (402 hectares or 993 acres).[20] From 1959 to 1961, the reform law affected about 37 percent of Cuba's agricultural land. Wherever tenant farmers worked the land in small units (particularly common on tobacco and rice estates), the law gave the tenants title to their plots, thereby augmenting the ranks of Cuba's approximately one hundred thousand smallholders with an almost equal number of new owners.[21] The bulk of the expropriated crop land, sugar and rice estates that did not have tenant farming, was transformed into cooperatives under the administration of the National Agrarian Reform Institute (INRA). Finally, another portion of the affected land— primarily cattle estates—was converted to state farms. In 1961, following a vote by cooperative workers, the INRA-affiliated sugar and rice cooperatives were also incorporated into the state farm sector.[22]

As is often the case with radical changes of this nature, the land reform brought with it a certain degree of disorder and many dislocations in production. On the one hand, landlords often decapitalized as they awaited or anticipated expropriation. In the case of the cattle ranches, this included the slaughtering and selling of herds. On the other hand, many landless laborers on unexpropriated plantations and ranches became impatient with what they felt was the excessively slow rate of expropriation. In a number of cases, these agricultural workers petitioned INRA to expand the scope of expropriations or engaged in spontaneous land seizures.[23]

Despite these disruptions and INRA's inconsistent policies in agricultural management, production of food during the first three years of the revolution rose for several crops (see table 1). These increases resulted largely from greater consumer demand and the accompanying higher crop prices. Reduction (or even elimination) of rent for urban housing, guaranteed full employment, and higher minimum wages all increased the disposable income of lower-class Cubans and raised the demand for food.

By the 1961–62 harvest, however, growing chaos in the countryside began to affect production adversely. The imposition of a trade embargo by the United States deprived Cuba of its usual source of chemicals, fertilizers, and spare parts for American-built farm machinery. Also, as owners of middle-sized plantations and farms (50–400 hectares) worried about further

Table 1. Production of Selected Food Crops, 1957–78 (1000 metric tons unless specified)

	Eggs (million units)	Milk	Rice	Yuca (Cassava)	Sweet Potatoes	Malanga (Taro)	Dry Beans	Citrus	Tomatoes
1957	275	806	167	186	161	91	36	91[d]	44
1959	341	770	282	224	183	240	14	70	65
1962	530	690	229	162	181	60	56	117	140
1964	830	715	129[b]	73[b]	89[b]	43[b]	14[b]	119	112
1967	1,178	565	94	50	88	42	15	144	164
1970	1,403	520	291	22	22	12	5	164	62
1973	1,586	550[a]	237	73	87	20	3	177	101
1975	1,851	591	338	83	90	33	5	182	184
1977	1,846	722	334	83	62	45[c]	2.4	178	146
1978	1,927	782	344	86	54		2.4	198	132

[a] 1974 data.

[b] The drops partly reflect different bases of compilation after 1963.

[c] 1976 data.

[d] Average for 1957–58.

Sources: Archibald R. M. Ritter, *The Economic Development of Revolutionary Cuba: Strategy and Performance* (New York: Praeger, 1974); Comité Estatal de Estadísticas, *Anuario Estadístico* (Havana), 1967–76 issues; Comité Estatal de Estadísticas, *Compendio del Anuario Estadístico de Cuba* (Havana, 1977 and 1978); Carmelo Mesa-Lago, "Economic Policies and Growth," in *Revolutionary Change in Cuba*, ed. Carmelo Mesa-Lago (Pittsburgh: University of Pittsburgh Press, 1971).

expropriations, they reduced investment or decapitalized. Moreover, as the state socialized a sizable portion of rural production, it offered fewer agricultural inputs (fertilizer, insecticides, etc.) to private farmers.

In response to growing problems in the production and distribution of food, INRA introduced the *acopio,* an agency charged with collecting agricultural produce, processing it through central warehouses, and distributing it to the populace. The acopio facilitated the equitable distribution of foods while increasing state control over the agricultural sector and the food marketing process. INRA, however, had nowhere near the means to carry out its assignment. For example, because of a lack of trucks in 1961–62 (due both to the United States embargo and to poor Cuban maintenance and management) the acopio collected only about half of Cuba's harvested fruits and vegetables.

The situation was further complicated by the acopio's irrational pricing policies. The agency established uniform commodity prices across the country for each crop regardless of local conditions or situations of comparative advantage. It failed to make price adjustments during different seasons or to stimulate production in more difficult growing periods. The relation of individual commodity prices to each other was often irrational, causing excesses of items such as watermelons and papayas and shortages of beans and malanga. [24] Frequent changes in prices together with a lag in production responses caused great fluctuations in the quantities of farm products supplied to the consumer. Fidel Castro stated the problem succinctly and humorously: "During a period of the Revolution in which carrots were scarce, it happened that the *acopio* . . . raised the price of carrots; and the next year there were many carrots and no turnips; then they raised the price of turnips and then one could have carrots and turnips, but no malanga. . . . This was a never ending situation." [25]

The Shift from Sugar and the Second Agrarian Reform Law (1961–63)

Soon after initiating the changes in land tenure mandated by the 1959 Agrarian Reform Law, the revolutionary leadership sought a second fundamental change in Cuba's agricultural production, reduction of sugar cultivation and diversification of crops. Castro and his advisers criticized Cuba's excessive dependence on sugar exports, viewing the crop as a symbol of the neocolonical economic relationship which the island had maintained with the United States. In July 1960 the issue came to a head when the Cuban government expropriated American sugar companies and President Eisenhower eliminated the United States sugar quota for Cuba.

While the decision to de-emphasize sugar was intimately related to trade policy and the desire for rapid industrialization through import substitution, it also involved some commitment to a limited "food first" policy. To fulfill increased government quotas for rice, milk, fruit, and vegetables, state farms began to dig up cane fields and plant alternative crops. But most agricultural workers and farm managers were accustomed to raising sugar (a crop needing only moderate attention) and were ill prepared for the labor-intensive cultivation of vegetables and fruits. INRA's lack of experience in management and logistics compounded the problem. Although large quantities of fertilizer were imported during this period, all too often transportation foul-ups prevented these or other materials from reaching farms on time. Bianchi quotes a letter from a local INRA official to his superiors in early 1962: "We have had many difficulties because of the delay in applying fertilizers, because of the lack of transport, . . . because of sending them without appropriate directions, because much fertilizer was lost due to the type of container, because it gets too hard during excessively long storage, or because it is applied during the dry season without prospectives of improvement in the humidity of the soil." [26]

In one region, 78,000 hectares of state farm land were prepared for sowing of malanga before it became apparent that there was only enough seed for half that area. In the province of Camagüey, INRA officials estimated that about 60 percent of the area set aside for yams was never planted. Another problem was that unchecked increases in mass consumption of certain commodities (due, again, to the greater purchasing power of the poor) began to endanger the supply of seeds available for planting. In Oriente province, more than 20,000 hectares of land were left uncultivated because of the shortage of peanut and black bean seeds. [27]

Difficulties in the private agrarian sector paralleled those on the state farms. Smallholders hesitated to invest for fear of expropriation. Their anxieties intensified following the defeat of the Playa Girón (Bay of Pigs) invasion in 1961, when the government expropriated the farms of many suspected counterrevolutionaries. [28] In late 1961 and early 1962, some five hundred small and medium-sized landowners in the south of Matanzas province and the southeast of Las Villas undertook armed insurrection against the revolutionary government. [29] The resistance, fueled by fear of expropriation and the government's alleged favoritism toward agricultural workers in their conflicts with middle-sized farm owners, spread in 1962–63. Indiscriminate measures sometimes used to contain the insurrection exacerbated tensions. The government expropriated without compensation all smallholders who lent direct aid to the rebellion and all "middle-sized" landowners (200–400 hectares) who lent "indirect aid" (a rather nebulous and ill-defined category). Castro later criticized local officials who indiscriminately applied these measures. Some confiscated land was even returned. Yet the anxieties of middle-sized farmers and even many small-holders in Matanzas remained. French agronomist René Dumont, who served as a top agricultural adviser to the Cuban government, maintained that "peasant confidence in the regime had been shaken and the peasantry withdrew somewhat within itself, thus contributing to [growing food shortages] in 1962."[30]

Increased political tension between the government and the remaining rural landlord class (with estates of under 400 hectares) contributed to the enactment of the second Agrarian Reform Law in the fall of 1963. The new law expropriated all holdings of over five caballerías (67 hectares) with promised compensation of 250 pesos (roughly $250) per month for a period of ten years.[31] The second reform law affected some 11,215 landowners with 2.1 million hectares of land. As a result, the state soon controlled about 70 percent of the nation's cultivatable land.[32]

Unfortunately, the new expropriations increased the discomfort of Cuba's middle peasants (with holdings of 25–67 hectares), who feared that their lands would be seized next. Seeking to quell those anxieties, the government had already formed the National Association of Small Farmers in 1961. During the early 1960s, ANAP articulated the peasants' and private farmers' concerns (for example, by lobbying for higher crop prices) in a socialist economy. In later years, however, ANAP increasingly became a vehicle for conveying the government's point of view to the farmer, as well as a distributor of government-controlled benefits such as credit, technical assistance, and capital inputs.

The Return to Sugar and the Continuing Food Crisis (1963–70)

By 1962, only a year after the state farms had embarked upon a program of crop diversification, Castro and INRA leaders concluded that factors of comparative advantage dictated a return to sugar cultivation and that the attempt at overnight diversification had been a mistake. The area of land in sugar cane, which had just been cut back, was increased by 169,000 hectares of new plantings. To ensure centralized planning for sugar, the cooperatives created by the first Agrarian Reform Law were transformed into state farms. INRA officials, feeling that the cooperatives had been poorly managed, wanted to exercise greater control. The sugar workers on the co-ops, aware that state farm workers received better salaries and benefits than they did, apparently voluntarily converted their co-ops to state farms.[33] Despite the renewed emphasis on sugar exports, INRA continued some efforts at diversifying state farm production, with particular stress on citrus and rice.

Another important change in 1962 was the assumption of the directorship of INRA by Communist Party economist Carlos Rafael Rodríguez. Under his leadership, INRA began to emphasize the need for efficiency and profitability on the state farms, considerations which had been downplayed during the early revolutionary euphoria. The institute initiated better record keeping on the state enterprises and attempted to raise productivity by linking each worker's wages, housing, and other material rewards to individual output levels.

INRA's growing use of profitability criteria and material incentives for the work force was soon undercut, however, by a radical political thrust that viewed such pragmatic considerations as compromising socialist values. From the mid-1960s to 1970, the ascendent Cuban leadership, disciples of Che Guevara, believed that Cuba's "new socialist person" should be motivated by the "moral incentive" of a commitment to the betterment of society. The reflected glory of being named a "worker hero" was to replace material rewards.[34] During the radical push, mass mobilization campaigns induced large numbers of urban Cubans to undertake volunteer agricultural labor in the countryside. Although most of these brigades worked on the sugar harvest, they also helped in the harvesting of food crops for local consumption.

Much has been written and said about the revolutionary elan of the late 1960s, culminating in the 1969–70 mass mobilization aimed at achieving a record 10-million-ton sugar harvest. The fact is, however, that much of the volunteer labor used during this period was not very productive. Inexperienced city dwellers were often inefficient farm laborers and occasionally even had a demoralizing effect on the regular agricultural work force. Workers on one state farm told us that the volunteers, unused to the tedious labor of picking coffee beans, would break the branches off the coffee plants and then sit down by the side of the road to remove the beans. Ironically, at the very time the government mobilized city dwellers to work in the countryside, it failed to use full-time state farm workers efficiently. On some enterprises, workers received wages for an eight-hour day but worked only six.[35] Others, prompted perhaps by the lack of material incentives for intensive labor, chose to "stay home" periodically. During the spring planting of 1969, a number of state farms reported average daily absentee rates among their permanent work force of over 35 percent. During the 1970 sugar harvest, while thousands of urban volunteer brigades were exhorted to give up their Sunday holidays to cut cane, overall absenteeism among state farm workers reached 29 percent.[36]

Finally, like many "forced march" economic efforts, the quest for a record sugar harvest was marred by mismanagement and inefficiencies. State farm workers focused their energies on planting, all too often neglecting the more difficult, labor-intensive task of nurturing the crop during the growing season.[37] In other instances, well-intentioned volunteers arrived at state farms to cut cane only to find that the tools they needed had not arrived.[38]

While the state sector suffered from poor management, worker absenteeism, and ineffective volunteer efforts, Cuba's private farms suffered from inadequate inputs, low crop prices, and hostile government attitudes. Cuba more than doubled its imports of fertilizers and tractors during the mid-1960s and tripled its investment in irrigation, but few of these inputs went to the private smallholders who still grew most of the nation's vegetables, root crops, and tobacco.[39]

In 1967 the government initiated an active campaign to eliminate some of the last vestiges of private enterprise in Cuba. The attack reached its height during the Revolutionary Offensive of 1968. At that time, remaining artisan enterprises, small shops, and restaurants were nationalized, leaving the nation's one hundred thousand smallholders as the only surviving private producers. Clearly the regime could not afford to nationalize the private farms, since the cost in terms of peasant opposition and reduced food production would have been far too high. However, Guevarist policymakers anticipated "gradual euthanasia" for the smallholder sector, viewing individual property as incompatible with the "new socialist person."

Throughout the 1960s efforts were made to organize peasant smallholders into "credits and services cooperatives" designed to channel credits, machinery, and technical assistance to private farmers while at the same time serving as a mechanism for imposing acopio production quotas. Not surprisingly, given the scarcity of machinery, fertilizers, and insecticides actually delivered to smallholders during the middle and late 1960s, peasants were skeptical and thus slow to join the government-sponsored cooperatives. As of 1967, only 37 percent of all private farmers had become members.

In 1967–68, as the government's radical policies surged forward, the acopio lowered the prices paid to private farmers for their crops. At the same time, it restricted private sales to urban consumers (beyond the acopio production quotas). Government regulations forbade smallholders from selling their produce through middlemen and limited direct commercial transactions between the farmer and individual consumers to a volume of 25 pounds, at controlled prices higher than the acopio levels but below "free market" prices. In 1968, thirty-seven hundred street vendors—essential in the private sale of smallholder produce—were put out of business.[40] The consequences for private production were twofold. First, deliveries of vegetables and root crops to the acopio dropped sharply (table 1). At the same time, black market activity (sales through middlemen or beyond the 25-pound limit) surged. One authority estimates that during the late 1960s, the proportion of private sector vegetables, fruits, and tubers sold on the black market ranged from 25 percent for some crops to 70 percent for others.[41] In response, the government imposed stricter punishment for black market sellers and purchasers and stepped up enforcement efforts, including roadblock checks of taxis and private autos entering the cities from the countryside.

From 1967–68 on, faced with a combination of government hostility toward the private sector and inducements to sell their plots to the state, some 12,000 private farmers sold their land.[42] In all, the late 1960s marked a low point in relations between the revolutionary regime and the private farm sector. Although most peasants had benefited from rural health and educational programs or from the agrarian reform, they still clung to their private plots and the right to sell their produce on the free market. Such "bourgeois values" were obviously anathema to the Guevarist policymakers of that period.

The Revolutionary Offensive against private sales and private ownership, the volunteer labor mobilization, the lowering of crop prices and of material incentives to state farm workers, and the push for 10 million tons of sugar all combined to reduce substantially output of most basic food items in the late 1960s. Unfortunately, it is impossible to gauge the exact magnitude of this decline because of the peculiarities of Cuban food statistics. Figures covering the chaotic early years of the Revolution often represented educated guesses rather than hard data. Since 1964 government production statistics have reflected only government collection of produce from private and state farms by the acopio. These figures, then, understate total national production by excluding all private farm output consumed by the owners and their families as well as all legal or black market private sales by smallholders.

Thus, the sharp drops that table 1 shows from 1962 to 1964 in rice, cassava, sweet potato, taro, and dry bean production are partly statistical artifacts. Before 1964, government figures estimated *total* production (including private farm consumption and sales), while the data since 1964 report only acopio collection. The statistics from 1964 through 1970, however, were calculated in a consistent manner and the production declines that table 1 indicates for that period are real. During those years acopio milk collection fell by more than 27 percent, yuca by nearly 73 percent, malanga by 72 percent, sweet potatoes by 75 percent, and dry beans (a critical source of protein in the Cuban diet) by 64 percent. Supplies of other foods not reported in table 1, such as meat, also fell sharply. Only eggs and citrus steadily gained strength during those years.

The Origins of Food Rationing in the 1960s

The food production crisis of the late 1960s intensified the shortage of food relative to consumer demand. Interestingly enough, shortages first became apparent in 1960–61, a time when agriculture was doing quite well. In 1960, production of rice, tomatoes, sweet potatoes, malanga, cassava, and dry beans was higher than during any prerevolutionary year of the 1950s. Yet, consumer demand had risen at a far higher rate. As noted earlier, the virtual elimination of unemployment, higher minimum wages, and the reduction of certain basic costs of living such as rent had all significantly raised the disposable income of the poor. Since it is precisely those people who have the highest marginal propensity to consume food and other basic necessities, demand for food staples increased sharply.

By 1961–62 speculation was already driving up the price of many foods. Had the Cuban government continued to allow the market mechanism to adjust to increased demand (as in the rest of Latin America), costs would have risen rapidly, thereby effectively distributing food in correspondence to family income. Rather than recreate the prerevolutionary pattern in which only the more well-off members of society could afford to eat satisfactorily, the regime initiated rationing as a means of guaranteeing social equity. Mandatory rationing of a small number of food items, particularly meat and animal fats, was introduced in July 1961. In March of the following year, the government began distribution of ration cards (libretas) on a household-by-household basis. It also extended rationing to most of Cuba's basic foods: rice, beans, poultry, beef, fish, pork, milk, and eggs as well as various legumes, fruits, vegetables, and tubers.

Over the years the number of goods that have been rationed has varied according to the availability of supplies. Many basic staples—rice, black beans, butter, lard, meat, poultry, bread, milk, most produce, and coffee— have remained fairly permanently rationed. Other items have been sold freely when plentiful. For example, when we visited Cuba in early 1980, eggs and many types of fish were sold "off the libreta." While milk was still rationed at that time, yogurt was not. Fruits, vegetables, and sausage may be rationed at some times and sold freely at others.

The underlying objective of the rationing system is that all Cubans, regardless of income, be guaranteed equal access to a core diet. Because the prices of rationed foods are low relative to the purchasing power of even unskilled workers, the quantity of staples available through the libreta represents not only the maximum that can be purchased but also a minimum for those who wish to avail themselves of their quota. Of course, some individuals or families may choose not to purchase particular items. We were told that a certain amount of trading also goes on.

More Balanced Production and Reconciliation with Private Farmers (1970–82)

As Cuba's revolutionary leaders assessed the state of the nation's economy—including agriculture—in the wake of the 1970 sugar harvest, they could scarcely avoid recognizing the grim picture facing them. The government had mobilized a massive volunteer effort designed to produce a world record in cane output. The failure to reach the symbolically critical goal of 10 million tons had a demoralizing effect. Exhausted by the exhortations of the Guevarist mobilization and desirous of more food and consumer goods, the Cuban people expressed their discontent through high rates of absenteeism at work. In his traditional July 26 oration, commemorating the anniversary of the start of the revolutionary struggle, Castro frankly admitted government failures and noted that the push for a record sugar harvest had caused serious dislocations in other sectors of the economy, including a severe crisis in food production.

In response to the apparent excesses of Guevarist radicalism, Castro embarked on a more pragmatic economic program. For the agricultural sphere the new policies stressed more diversified production goals. To be sure, sugar continued to dominate state farm output during the 1970s. Given sugar's primacy as a source of badly needed foreign exchange, the regime had little choice but to leave most of the nation's largest agricultural estates as they had been before and after the 1959 Revolution, devoted largely to cane production. Through the mid-1970s some 80 percent of state farm land remained in either sugar cane cultivation or pasture.[43] But, in contrast to the policies of the late 1960s, the state farms now place more emphasis on growing food for domestic consumption. A substantial amount of new land was planted with citrus trees, leading to a steady, if unspectacular, growth in production. State milk and rice output, which had dropped sharply in the middle and late 1960s, returned to their prior levels in the 1970s. Finally, egg production, long the major success story of the state farm sector, continued its dynamic growth (table 1).

But the state farms, even with more rational management and material incentives for their workers, could not meet the nation's food needs. Only 12 percent of the state sector's land was devoted to the cultivation of fruits, vegetables, tubers, and grains. For these crops, Cuba continued to depend on private farm production. In 1976 private farms contributed 58 percent of the total dry bean crop collected by the state acopio, 59 percent of the cabbage, 76 percent of the malanga, 48 percent of the coffee, 51 percent of the tomatoes, 61 percent of the cassava, and 40 percent of the sweet potatoes.[44] With an average size of approximately one caballería (13.5 hectares), private smallholdings currently control only 21 percent of Cuba's agricultural and livestock area. However, their proportion of the nation's crop land—particularly the highest-yielding acreage—is considerably higher.[45]

Through the early and mid-1970s, the government continued to encourage farmers to sell their holdings to the state. Altering its policies of the Guevarist period, the regime relied on positive inducements rather than accusatory rhetoric. Farmers who turned their land over to the state received a monthly stipend of 80 pesos (about $80 U.S.), regardless of farm size, for life. Elderly peasants could couple that sum with their retirement pensions. Many former smallholders who moved onto state farms after selling their plots to the government were housed in relatively modern apartment complexes with nominal rents and free amenities such as a television set. By 1977 the state controlled 79 percent of all Cuban farm land, up from 70 percent at the time of the 1963 agrarian reform.

At the same time, the remaining smallholders were organized into Credits and Services Cooperatives. Through these, the government offered credit at little or no interest, depending on the prevailing policy. Subsidized farm machinery, fertilizer, and other supplies become more available to private farmers than they had been in the 1960s. By the mid-1970s, virtually all the nation's smallholders had joined cooperatives and were, in turn, incorporated into the National Association of Small Farmers (ANAP).

In May 1977, at the opening of ANAP's Fifth National Congress, the government opened a new, more positive phase in its relations with Cuba's private farmers. Addressing the delegates, Castro admitted that neglecting private cooperatives while overemphasizing the development of state farms had been a mistake. Henceforth, he promised, the government would reduce pressures on smallholders to join state farms. Subsequently, the Ministry of Agriculture (replacing INRA) increased tractor allocations to the private cooperatives from eighty to five hundred per year. Acopio prices were also revised to reflect regional production costs.

More recently, the government initiated a particularly significant change in policy toward private producers with the establishment of the farmers' free market (*mercado libre campesino*) in May 1980. Once farmers have fulfilled their quota of deliveries to the acopio, they can deliver surplus produce to cities and towns to sell to the public at whatever price they can negotiate. It appears that the free market has undercut the black market and also encouraged farmers to produce more. For example, one small credits and services cooperative in Matanzas province had sold only 5 *quintales* (500 lbs) of garlic to the state in 1979. However, in 1980 its members fulfilled their acopio commitment of 120 *quintales* for the first time in years and freed themselves for farmers' market sales. Similarly, in 1980 their sale of beans to the acopio was nearly four times the previous year's level.[46] In general, free market prices are higher than those in state stores but lower than those prevailing on the black market.

In contrast (and perhaps contradiction) to policies that encourage private production, the government, since 1977, has also promoted "production cooperatives," a new form of land tenure merging elements of state farms and co-ops. This latest effort to integrate the private sector into socialism involves the merging of smallholders' plots and machinery into collective production units. The production cooperatives offer members wages comparable to those of state farm workers. In addition, they receive a monthly stipend to reimburse them for land and machinery contributed to the enterprise and will share in the additional profits that accrue once the capital investments have been paid off. Finally, the state offers production cooperatives lower interest rates on loans than credits and services co-ops receive and gives them priority access to machinery and technical education.

Food Production in the 1970s: A Modest Recovery

Following the severe declines in food output during the first decade of the revolution, Cuban agriculture rebounded in a number of areas during the 1970s. We have noted the growth of state farm milk and rice output from the low points of the late 1960s. At the same time, smallholders apparently responded to more hospitable government policies by increasing production of vegetables and root crops. From 1970 to 1978, acopio purchases of tomatoes increased by 112 percent, sweet potatoes by 145 percent, yuca by 290 percent, and malanga (through 1976) by 275 percent. While it is not always clear what portion of these increases came from the private sector, yields per acre for most of these crops are far higher on private smallholdings than on state farms.[47] It is too early to know the extent to which the recent opening of farmers' free markets will stimulate further smallholder production. While initial reports indicate a burgeoning of truck farm output near Havana, official production figures do not cover private sales such as these.

Despite the agricultural gains recorded in the 1970s, Cuba's overall food production record in the first two decades of the revolution has not been impressive. Official statistics show that as of 1978 (the latest available data), acopio purchases of dry beans, yuca, malanga, and sweet potatoes were all less than half of 1957 production figures (table 1)—down over 90 percent in the case of dry beans—and comparably lower than 1952–56 harvest averages (not shown in table 1). Milk output had not risen appreciably over 1950s levels, and rice tonnage was up only 21 percent since 1959.

Unfortunately, comparisons between current acopio statistics and prerevolutionary production data are somewhat misleading. As noted earlier, Cuban statistics since 1964 include only the portion of agricultural production that the government acopio purchases from the state farms and private cooperatives. Thus, private farm output consumed by the producers themselves and sold directly to urban consumers is excluded. In the case of crops such as black beans, with considerable black market sales in the past and free market sales currently, this seriously understates total production. However, even when allowances are made for such factors, per capita outputs of milk, rice (neither of which are sold privately in significant quantities), meat, and most vegetables are still probably below prerevolutionary averages.

Nutritional Levels since the Revolution

Our discussion to this point has concentrated on Cuba's record in food production. What ramifications has the nation's rather modest performance in agriculture had for food consumption and for popular nutrition since the revolution? Table 2 indicates the findings of a series of nutritional surveys conducted in Cuba from the early 1950s through 1979. In the decade before the revolution, the average Cuban consumed some 2,730–2,740 calories daily. After holding steady for the first two years of the revolution, per capita daily consumption apparently declined about 15 percent between 1961 and 1964, dropping below 2,300 calories. As of 1975, the average caloric intake was still below prerevolutionary levels, and not until 1979 did the national average pass the mean figures for the 1950s. Even today, Cuba's caloric

Table 2. Per Capita Calorie, Protein, and Fat Consumption: 1951–79

	1951–57	1959–61	1962–64	1965	1970	1975	1979	Goals
Calories	2,740	2,730	2,200–2,300	2,552	2,565	2,645	2,759	2,900
Protein (gms.)	—	—	—	66.4	68.8	72.9	73.0	80.0
Fats (gms.)	—	—	—	56.5	60.4	70.7	72.3	—

Sources: 1951–64: Ricardo Leyva, "Health and Revolution in Cuba," in Cuba in Revolution, eds. Rolando E. Bonachea and Nelson P. Valdés (New York: Anchor, 1972), p. 463; 1965–79: unpublished data from the Institute of Internal Demand (Cuba), which for the most part are supported by the 1980 Statistical Yearbook for Latin America (Santiago, Chile: Economic Commission for Latin America, 1981), p. 90.

consumption is probably below that of Argentina or Uruguay and may even be lower than in Brazil or Mexico.[48]

If we turn our attention from overall caloric intake to consumption of specific food items—particularly dietary staples—a similarly negative impression emerges. Table 3 indicates the quantities of selected foods that Cubans have been able to purchase since general rationing was imposed in 1962 and compares those quantities to average consumption levels in 1958. The data show that 1980 ration book quotas for fresh beef and cooking fat were half as large as in the lean years of the 1960s and were even further below prerevolutionary (1958) consumption averages, particularly in the case of beef. Allowances for rice and dry beans, staples of the Cuban lower-class diet, were also less in 1980 than in 1963 and were half the 1958 levels.

Figures such as these (and the data in table 2) seem to support the contention of many critics of the revolution, including recent Cuban exiles, that government policies under Castro have adversely affected the availability of food. To be sure, the typical Cuban's diet today is quite bland and spartan, featuring heavy dosages of starches, particularly rice, bread and tubers, and little of the beef, pork, black beans, or coffee so dear to most people's hearts. In our 1978 and 1980 visits to groceries and markets in Havana, Pinar del Río, and other Cuban cities, we were struck by the scarcity of foods available and the lack of variety.

Yet, the statistics in tables 2 and 3 are averages and, as such, offer a limited and distorted view of reality. They mask the great inequalities in the diets of Cubans of differing social classes before 1959. The prerevolutionary average consumption figures were obviously bolstered by a large urban middle class and many skilled workers who could afford adequate quantities of beef, milk, and eggs. But, as we noted earlier, these foods rarely graced the dinner tables of agricultural workers or other lower-class Cubans. Ricardo Leyva notes in an article on Cuban health, "In the 1950s no rich man ever suffered from food shortages, but the poor were extremely lucky to escape it."[49]

How far have revolutionary policies gone toward reducing previous inequities in food consumption? A recent study of Cuba's "basic needs" programs indicates that significant variations still exist in the level of food consumed in different areas of the country. Using government statistics, Claes Brundenius maintains that food consumption in Havana is perhaps 33 percent higher than the national norm. Even greater gaps exist between the capital and the most underdeveloped regions of the nation such as Guantánamo province.[50] Such regional inequalities may be related to differences in the quantity of food available through the ration cards; allocations in some

Table 3. Monthly Quotas of Selected Food Items: 1958–80 (pounds/person)

Items	1958[a]	1963	1969	1972	1978	1980	1980 price per lb.
Rice	10.2	6	3–4	6	5	5	(20¢)
Dry Beans	2.1	1.5	1.5	1.5–3.0	1¼	1¼	(32¢)
Cooking Fat	2.9	2.0	2.0	2.0	1¼	1.0	(24¢)
Beef	9	3	3	3	1⅔	1¼	(38¢)
Eggs (units)	7	2	15–24	15–24	free[c]	free[c]	(10¢ pu)[d]
Fish	2.2	1	2	free[c]	free[c]	free[c]	(45–70¢)
Fresh Milk	14	[b]	[b]	[b]	[b]	[b]	(20¢/qt.)
Bread	—	free[c]	15	—	15	15	
Canned Milk	—	3	3	3	3	3	(21¢ pu)[d]

Sources: 1958–69: Leyva, "Health and Revolution in Cuba," p. 462; 1958–72: Sergio Roca, "Distributional Effects of the Cuban Revolution: Urban Versus Rural Allocation" (Paper delivered at the 88th Annual Meeting of the American Economic Association, Dallas, 1975), table 12; 1978 and 1980: data collected by Nancy Forster and Howard Handelman; selected data for 1972 from unpublished data collected by Carmelo Mesa-Lago.

[a]Average (unrationed) consumption.   [b]Children under eight years of age receive one liter of milk daily, as do elderly, ill, and pregnant adults.   [c]"Free" means unrationed.   [d]Price per unit.

areas of Cuba may be smaller than the quantities indicated in table 3 (which uses 1980 figures from Havana, Pinar del Río, and other large cities). In the past, libretas in various areas have assigned differing quantities of food. While the localities that we studied had almost identical ration book allocations in 1980, this may not be so in remote regions that we did not visit. It may also be that certain areas do not receive the quantities of food to which the libreta technically entitles them (that was true of the beef ration even in Havana). Finally, foods sold in unrationed quantities (eggs and fish) or sold on the black market or peasant free market are undoubtedly more available in Havana than in the less-developed areas of the country.

According to 1979 survey data collected by the Cuban government, food purchased through the ration book could, by itself, provide an average of 2,100 calories daily.[51] Despite the regional differences just noted, it appears that most Cubans can afford to buy and do consume close to that norm through their libreta. For the poorest strata of the population, that quantity of calories alone constitutes an improvement over prerevolutionary consumption levels. To the extent that inequities in the ration book allocations exist, these do not differentiate among classes within a particular geographical area. Indeed, it is probably Havana's middle class and skilled workers whose diets have deteriorated relative to the prerevolutionary era.

Beyond the quotas available through the libreta, Cubans may obtain food in a variety of ways: through purchases of items that are not rationed (the list of unrationed goods is growing—eggs, fish, and yogurt are important foods currently sold in unlimited quantities); consumption by smallholders of food grown on their own farms; meal programs for school children, including all meals for the many secondary students attending boarding schools; low-priced lunches in worker cafeterias located throughout urban areas; and consumption in restaurants (though this is quite expensive and not a major dietary supplement). These various sources account for the remaining 600–700 calories (beyond ration book allowances) in the average Cuban's diet. Of these supplementary sources of food, only purchases of unrationed foods and restaurant meals are related to income. Consequently, even among the poorest Cubans today, few probably consume fewer than 2,400 calories daily. At the same time, because of rationing and the high cost of black market or peasant free market foods, few better-paid Cubans are likely to eat more than 3,200 calories.

In short, while the Cuban Revolution has failed to raise average consumption (indeed the norm fell in the 1960s), it has virtually eradicated malnutrition by dispensing the nation's available stock of food more equitably. This redistribution has been accomplished by raising the purchasing power of the lower classes and by rationing foods when supply does not meet consumer demand.

To be sure, many problems remain. Having become accustomed to a guaranteed base level of nutrition, many urban Cubans now yearn for a more varied diet. Using survey information collected by the Institute of Internal Demand, government nutritionists calculated that in 1979 the average Cuban consumed slightly above the nutritionally desirable level of cereals (104 percent), and nearly the target level of fats (85 percent), black beans (85 percent), and eggs (83 percent). However, average consumption of milk and dairy goods was only 71 percent of the "optimal" rate, meat only 57 percent, fish 57 percent, fruits 50 percent, and vegetables 36 percent of the government standard. Poor government planning and inadequate price incentives for smallholders have resulted in unnecessary shortages of items such as black beans. In general, the government has accomplished as much as possible through redistributive policies and must now find agrarian policies that will more successfully stimulate increased food production.

For now, however, the results of more equitable food distribution have been impressive. The 1979 data showed that 44 percent of all Cuban families were eating fish at least once a week, with an additional 43 percent having it at least twice monthly. Ninety-six percent of all Cubans in 1979 ate eggs at least once weekly, including 33 percent who consumed them daily and 50 percent who ate eggs two or three times per week. When we consider that in the mid-1950s only 2.2 percent of the nation's rural population ate eggs even once weekly, it becomes apparent how far Cuba has come in eradicating malnutrition associated with poverty. Earlier we cited a 1950 study by the International Bank for Reconstruction and Development that indicated that 30–40 percent of Cuba's population and over 60 percent of its rural populace were undernourished at that time. By 1979, spokespersons for Cuba's Institute of Nutrition claimed that, for the country as a whole, malnutrition had been lowered to 5 percent. Virtually no other Latin American nation—including those with higher average food consumption levels—can match that record of accomplishment.[52]

Notes

1. Research for this chapter was supported by the American Universities Field Staff and the Latin American Center of the University of Wisconsin-Milwaukee. Portions of the material included in this chapter have previously appeared in Nancy Forster, *The Revolutionary Transformation of the Cuban Countryside* (Hanover, N.H.: Universities Field Staff International, 1982), and Howard Handelman, "Cuban Food Policy and Popular Nutritional Levels," *Cuban Studies* 11, no. 2/12, no. 1 (1981–82): 127–46.

2. Leon G. Mears, "The Food Situation in Cuba—Where Food Shortages Plague the Castro Government," *Foreign Agriculture* (May 1962), pp. 7–8.

3. "Feeding the People," *Cuba Review* (Dec. 1976), p. 18.

4. Wyatt MacGaffey and Clifford P. Barnett, *Twentieth-Century Cuba* (Garden City, N.Y.: Doubleday, 1962), pp. 82, 404; on prerevolutionary rural Cuba, also see Lowry Nelson, *Rural Cuba* (Minneapolis: University of Minnesota Press, 1950).

5. Antonio Núñez Jiménez, *Geografía de Cuba* (Havana: Editorial Lex, 1959), p. 322.

6. Andrés Bianchi, "Agriculture," in *Cuba: The Economic and Social Revolution,* ed. Dudley Seers (Chapel Hill: University of North Carolina Press, 1964), p. 74.

7. Jorge I. Domínguez, *Cuba: Order and Revolution* (Cambridge: Belknap Press, Harvard University Press, 1978), pp. 423–33; Juan Martínez-Alier, *Haciendas, Plan-*

tations and Collective Farms: Agrarian Class Societies—Cuba and Peru (London: Frank Cass, 1977).

8. Bianchi, "Agriculture," pp. 90–95.

9. Jacques Chonchol, "Análisis crítico de la reforma agraria cubana," El Trimestre Económico 117 (1963): 72. The tripling of irrigated area took place during the 1950s largely in rice plantations.

10. Bianchi, "Agriculture," pp. 90–94.

11. Ricardo Leyva, "Health and Revolution in Cuba," in Cuba in Revolution, eds. Rolando E. Bonchea and Nelson P. Valdés (New York: Anchor, 1972), p. 463.

12. Melchor Gastón et al., ¿Por qué reforma agraria? (Havana: Agrupación Católica Universitaria, 1957).

13. Martínez-Alier, Haciendas, p. 13. Estimates of the number of landless agricultural workers in Cuba during the 1950s varied widely from 350,000 to 500,000.

14. Gastón et al., Reforma agraria, pp. 20–24.

15. "Nutritional Status of Cuban Children," Nutritional Review 16, no. 9 (Sept. 1958): 271–73.

16. Quoted in MacGaffey and Barnett, Twentieth-Century Cuba, p. 196.

17. Seers, Cuba, p. 18.

18. Gastón et al., Reforma agraria, p. 60.

19. From 1934 to 1956 average rural salaries had grown by 194 percent, but food prices rose by an average of 228 percent in the same period (Leyva, "Health and Revolution in Cuba," p. 458).

20. Initially large estates whose productivity was more than 50 percent above the national average could maintain up to 100 caballerías (1,342 hectares) of land. That exemption, however, was soon removed. See Arthur MacEwan, Revolution and Economic Development in Cuba (New York: St. Martin's Press, 1980).

21. Former tenants were entitled to two caballerías (26.84 hectares) with an option to buy more. Many ex-tenants also spontaneously stopped paying rent even on unexpropriated land. See Martínez-Alier, Haciendas, p. 129.

22. INRA was not happy with the performance of the sugar and rice cooperatives and asked the workers to vote a change from cooperative to state farm status. Since state farm workers at that time were apparently receiving higher incomes than most co-op members and were being pampered by the state, there is no reason to believe that the vote to dissolve was done under duress.

23. Domínguez, Cuba: Order and Revolution, p. 440; Martínez-Alier, Haciendas, pp. 137–39.

24. René Dumont, Cuba: Socialism and Development, trans. Helen R. Lane (New York: Grove Press, 1970), pp. 80–83.

25. Archibald R. M. Ritter, The Economic Development of Revolutionary Cuba: Strategy and Performance (New York: Praeger, 1974), p. 235.

26. Bianchi, "Agriculture," pp. 138–39.

27. Ibid., pp. 137–38.

28. Martínez-Alier, Haciendas, p. 140.

29. Domínguez, *Cuba: Order and Revolution*, p. 443.

30. Dumont, *Cuba: Socialism and Development*, p. 94.

31. Domínguez, *Cuba: Order and Revolution*, p. 445.

32. Carmelo Mesa-Lago, "Economic Policies and Growth" in *Revolutionary Change in Cuba*, ed. Carmelo Mesa-Lago (Pittsburgh: University of Pittsburgh Press, 1971), p. 359.

33. Bianchi, "Agriculture," p. 148.

34. For a full discussion of the Guevara-Rodríguez debate (which dealt with far more than agricultural policy and was designed to clarify the underlying ethos of the revolution and its economic program) see Bertram Silverman, ed., *Man and Socialism in Cuba: The Great Debate* (New York: Atheneum, 1971). On "material" versus "moral" incentives see: Terry Karl, "Work Incentives in Cuba," *Latin American Perspectives* 2, no. 4 (Supplement, 1975): 21–42; Arthur MacEwan, "Incentives, Equality and Power in Revolutionary Cuba," in *The New Cuba: Paradoxes and Potentials*, ed. Ronald Radosh (New York: William Morrow, 1975).

35. Mesa-Lago, "Economic Policies and Growth," p. 286.

36. Ritter, *Revolutionary Cuba*, pp. 282–83.

37. Ibid., p. 176.

38. Karl, "Work Incentives in Cuba."

39. Mesa-Lago, "Economic Policies and Growth," p. 311, and Ritter, *Revolutionary Cuba*, p. 176.

40. Ritter, ibid., p. 237. At that time, not only private individuals, but also the armed forces, state farm cafeterias, the Ministry of Construction, etc., were purchasing privately produced commodities. See Domínguez, *Cuba: Order and Revolution*, pp. 451–52.

41. Domínguez, ibid.

42. Nelson Amaro and Carmelo Mesa-Lago, "Inequality and Classes," in *Revolutionary Change in Cuba*, ed. Carmelo Mesa-Lago (Pittsburgh: University of Pittsburgh Press, 1971), p. 359.

43. National Bank of Cuba and the Bureau of Statistics of the Central Planning Board, ed. Pedro Alvarez Tabío, *Development and Prospects of the Cuban Economy* (Havana: Cuban Book Institute, 1975). The proportion of state farm land devoted to cane cultivation and to pasture has probably not changed significantly since that time.

44. Extrapolated from Comite Estatal de Estadísticas, *Anuario estadístico de Cuba* (Havana), 1972–76 issues.

45. Domínguez, *Cuba: Order and Revolution*, p. 452; and data furnished the authors by spokespersons for ANAP.

46. *Latin America: Weekly Report*, July 18, 1980, p. 7.

47. Nancy Forster, "Cuban Agricultural Productivity: A Comparison of State and Private Farm Sectors," *Cuban Studies*, 11, no. 2/12, no. 1 (Jan. 1981–82): 105–25.

48. Unfortunately, the most recent comparative figures on Latin American nutrition that we were able to secure (published by the Inter-American Development Bank)

covered only the period 1971–73. At that time, Argentina and Uruguay had per capita calorie consumptions of 3,000–3,200 daily, while Chile, Brazil, and Mexico ranged from 2,657 to 2,781. Since then, average calorie consumption has probably risen slightly for Brazil and Mexico and has fallen sharply for Argentina, Chile, and Uruguay. Moreover, Brazil and Mexico (and, more recently, Chile) have wide disparities in dietary levels that are not revealed by the national averages. For data on average consumption see, *Nutrition and Socio-Economic Development in Latin America* (Washington: Inter-American Development Bank, 1979), p. 18.

49. Leyva, "Health and Revolution in Cuba," p. 463.

50. Claes Brundenius, *Economic Growth, Basic Needs, and Income Distribution in Revolutionary Cuba* (Malmo, Sweden: Research Policy Institute of the University of Lund, 1982).

51. All of the nutritional statistics in the succeeding pages that deal with Cuban nutritional levels since 1975 are unpublished figures provided to us by Cuba's Institute of Internal Demand.

52. As of 1979, Cuba's child mortality rate of 21.0 per 1,000 and its life expectancy of 70.4 years were the best in Latin America. Infant mortality is a prime indirect indicator of popular nutritional levels. The Cuban data on infant mortality and life expectancy are drawn from *Gramma* (Havana), June 22, 1980.

Rose J. Spalding

Food Politics and Agricultural Change in Revolutionary Nicaragua, 1979–82

In recent years, several Latin American nations have experienced recurring food deficits.[1] This decline in food self-sufficiency has been associated with a number of political and economic problems. Increased dependence, vulnerability to foreign staples markets, and the increasing costs of food imports (while the terms of trade for traditional exports decline) have been results of the deficit. Difficulties in distributing imported foods in the internal market and a high incidence of malnutrition in marginal areas are also linked to inadequate food production.

Recognizing these problems, a few Latin American governments have drafted new agricultural policies emphasizing increased staples production. Some of these programs reflect "Green Revolutionism," focusing on narrow technological improvements, and have had only limited success. Others involve a broader approach that addresses the problems at a more fundamental level. The latter programs consider not only the problem of technology diffusion but also the issues of ownership, income, credit, marketing, and consumption.

The agricultural policies of the new revolutionary government of Nicaragua fall primarily into the second category. This study examines the ways in which Nicaragua's new agricultural policy is attempting to change the food production sector. The first section focuses on the agricultural legacy of the Somoza period (1936–79). The second analyzes the agricultural programs developed during the first three and a half years of the reconstruction process (1979–82). In the third section, the short-term consequences of these programs are described and assessed. The conclusion proposes four development models that the country could adopt and discusses the next round of decisions that the new state must make.

Somoza's Agricultural Legacy

Under the Somoza dynasty (1936–79), Nicaragua followed an agro-export development model. Although production tended to increase throughout the agricultural sector, growth was less dynamic and consistent in staples production than in the production of export-oriented crops. Dependence on imports to supply the domestic food market became substantial during this period. In the 1960s, imports regularly accounted for over 10 percent of the nation's cereal consumption; between 1971 and 1980, there were five years in which that figure rose to around 20 percent.[2] Staples production was prone to sharp fluctuations throughout the 1970s.

The causes of this development are numerous and varied. One approach that has received substantial attention emphasizes the interplay between the expanding agro-export sector and uneven staples production. While the export sector grew, claiming more and more of the nation's productive resources, producers of traditional staples crops were displaced. The origins of this process predate the dynasty, beginning in the 1880s with the dramatic growth of the coffee sector.[3] But the process deepened during the 1940s and 1950s with the rise of cotton production in the country's most productive regions.

Responding to post–World War II increases in the world market price for cotton, Nicaraguan producers began expanding their cultivation of this crop, concentrating particularly in the fertile flatland of the Pacific Coast region. By the 1950s the impact of "King Cotton" on landholding patterns was becoming marked; as the number of farms in the region decreased and their average size increased, the pattern of extreme land concentration became quite visible.[4] Small and medium-sized producers declined; sharecroppers, those with accumulated debts, and those whose land titles were challenged were ousted from their land. The growth of the cotton sector reflected the rise of a new entrepreneurial producer who employed modern technology and experimental techniques and developed close ties to the international marketing network. These cotton growers forged bonds with the emerging Banco Nicaragüense economic group and arrived at a working relationship with the Somozas.[5]

The economic preeminence of cotton did not preclude the growth of other export sectors. By the latter part of the 1960s, the livestock industry was flourishing.[6] Under the impetus of growing beef consumption in the United States, the Nicaraguan cattle sector expanded markedly. With United States congressional approval of beef quotas and USDA assistance in disease prevention and quality control, this sector prospered (table 1). While the land

Table 1. Changes in Production of Nicaragua's Major
Agricultural Products, 1960–76 (thousand quintales)[a]

Export Products	1960–61	1965–66	1970–71	1975–76	% Change 1960–76
Coffee	571	698	857	1,068	+ 87%
Sugarcane	16,897	20,108	42,174	56,603	+235
Cotton	2,139	7,071	5,210	7,190	+236
Beef Slaughter (thousand heads)	133	181	310	325	+144
Tobacco	—	—	17,713	31,200	—
Internal Market					
Corn	2,588	3,723	4,136	4,176	+ 61%
Beans	605	1,075	790	962	+ 59
Sorghum	847	1,075	977	1,366	+ 61
Rice	462	727	1,151	1,224	+165

Source: FIDA, *Informe de la Misión Especial de Programación a Nicaragua* (Managua, MIDINRA, 1981), pp. 11, 40.

[a]A quintal equals 100 pounds.

under cultivation increased by over 70 percent between 1960 and 1978 (from 411,000 hectares to 702,000 hectares), pastureland expanded by 166 percent (from 1,077,000 hectares to 2,864,000 hectares).[7]

As traditional peasants and small producers lost their land, some migrated to the urban areas. The country's weak industrial sector proved incapable of absorbing them, and underemployment increased. Some moved across the country to the relatively uninhabited agricultural frontier, clearing forests and squatting on unused lands. Others remained, cultivating subsistence crops on steadily shrinking parcels of land for part of the year and serving as a seasonal labor force for the agro-export sector as industry needs dictated.

These transformations ultimately undermined the traditional staples producers. By the mid-1960s the government appeared to recognize that a problem was emerging. This realization, combined with pressures from the United States under the Alliance for Progress and the growing number of peasant land invasions in the more heavily populated Pacific Coast region, led the dynasty to launch a land reform program. In 1964 the Instituto Agrario de Nicaragua was established to oversee the colonization of the agricultural frontier. Sixteen thousand, five hundred peasants who had migrated to this region received legal title to their land, and colonization projects for 2,651 additional peasant families were set up. This expanded and stabilized peasant production in the interior of the country.[8]

While these efforts enabled the food supply to continue expanding, the staples sector lost much of its vigor, as production increases were lower than in other economic sectors (table 1). Production of cotton, sugar, and livestock increased by 236 percent, 235 percent, and 144 percent respectively between 1960 and 1976. Production of basic foods like corn and beans, on the other hand, increased only around 60 percent. Most of this staples expansion occurred during the 1960s. In the first part of the 1970s, corn, bean, and rice production dropped dramatically, barely regaining 1970 levels by the middle of the decade and fluctuating sharply in the years that followed.[9]

Staples production was increasingly confined to the smaller farms, while the large units concentrated on the more lucrative export products. In 1971, 58 percent of bean production and 62 percent of corn production took place on farms of less than 35 hectares. For sugar cane, on the other hand, 75 percent of the crop was produced on estates larger than 350 hectares, and close to 40 percent of the vital cotton crop was also produced on these large estates.[10]

In addition to being associated with small units (frequently *minifundios*), staples production was increasingly located in the agricultural frontier. This shift entailed the use of less fertile land that was prone to rapid exhaustion. It also meant increased distribution problems because of the area's underdeveloped transportation system. Further undermining this sector's ability to generate an adequate and stable food supply was its continued reliance on traditional production techniques and its lack of technical assistance.

As the information in table 2 demonstrates, agricultural credit went disproportionately to the export sector. While over half of the land cultivated in 1976 was used for the internal market, only one-fourth of the area that received bank credit was producing basic staples, and less than 10 percent of the money allocated by the banks for agriculture went to staples producers. One critical analysis of the credit system concluded that even the Instituto de Bienestar Campesino, a special program nominally devised to assist the peasant sector, distributed credit disproportionately to the larger units.[11] Without access to credit and improved technologies, small producers could hardly expand food output rapidly. They remained vulnerable to drought and flooding and had a routinely low yield.

Table 2. Bank Credit Distribution by Sector (1976)

	Hectares Cultivated (thousands)	% of Total	Hectares Financed (thousands)	% of Total	Credit Allocated (million córdobas)	% of Total
Agro-export Products	333	47.2%	200	75.1%	510.3	90.3%
Domestic Market Products	372	52.8%	66	24.9%	54.4	9.7%
Total	705	100 %	266	100 %	564.7	100 %

Source: FIDA, Informe de la Misión Especial de Programación a Nicaragua (Managua: MIDINRA, 1981), p. 44.

This pattern of uneven performance in the staples production sector and substantial dependence on imports had important nutritional consequences. On a per capita basis, the average caloric intake in Nicaragua did meet minimal nutritional standards throughout most of the 1960s and 1970s (table 3). But inequality in the distribution of wealth meant that more than half of the population received less than the minimal amount.[12] A United States Agency for International Development study indicated in 1976 that 57 percent of the children aged 0–4 and 57 percent of the rural population suffered from some degree of malnutrition.[13] And the problem was not diminishing. Average caloric and protein consumption reached a peak in the middle to late 1960s and then tended to drop (table 3). The rate of decline is particularly striking for calories and proteins obtained from vegetable products. Since the diets of the lower income groups have traditionally depended heavily on these products, the steady decrease indicated a serious deterioration in the food supply of the poor. In contrast, the consumption of animal products increased at a regular rate throughout this period. Diets of more prosperous sectors, where animal products were regularly consumed, were substantially improved. This reflected a steady, income-based polarization in the food supply and had a particularly deleterious effect on the lower income groups, leading in the worst cases to malnutrition, reduced intellectual and productive capabilities, higher infant mortality, and a host of social ills.

New Directions in the Agricultural Economy, 1979–82

Our strategy differs from other models of economic development whose first priority is to establish a model of accumulation. Our first objective is to satisfy the basic needs of the majority of the population. This creates a new logic which we call the "logic of the majority," i.e. the logic of the poor. Instead of organizing the economy from the perspective and interest of the top 5 percent, as was done during the Somoza dynasty, we are trying to organize the economy from the perspective of the majority.

Xabier Gorostiaga, S.J., Director
Instituto de Investigaciones
Económicas y Sociales

The Sandinista government had a special commitment to redistributing resources and raising the standard of living of the rural poor. Because it operated with scarce resources and within the confines of a mixed economy, its options were limited. Nonetheless, it developed a number of programs that reflected these concerns.

One of the more interesting is the Programa Alimentario Nacional (PAN), a food program inaugurated in the spring of 1981. This ambitious program

Table 3. Evolution of the Nicaraguan Food Supply, 1961–79

	Average calories per capita per day[a]			Average grams of protein per capita per day		
	Total	From Vegetable Products	From Animal Products	Total	From Vegetable Products	From Animal Products
1961–63	2185	1840	345	64.1	40.2	23.9
1964–66	2348	1982	366	68.3	44.3	24.0
1966–68	2517	2130	387	71.8	47.4	24.4
1969–71	2464	2038	426	72.7	45.9	26.8
1972–74	2379	1969	410	68.7	43.5	25.2
1974–76	2404	1973	431	67.1	40.5	26.6
1977–79	2368	1913	455	66.0	37.8	28.2

Source: FAO, Production Yearbook, 1977 and 1978

[a]FAO estimates an average of 2,300 calories per capita per day as a minimum requirement.

was committed to enhanced production, an improved standard of living, and redistribution of agricultural resources. It encouraged small and medium-sized producers to increase their cultivation of crops like corn and beans, improve storage and marketing of these products, and make them more accessible to economically marginal urban consumers.

Several aspects of the country's agricultural policy were affected by these new objectives. First, a process of land redistribution was inaugurated, gradually expanding peasant agriculture. Second, under the newly nationalized banking system, the pattern of credit allocation was adjusted in favor of small producers. And finally, the nation's marketing structure was recast to correspond to new, revolutionary priorities. Each of these developments warrants analysis.

Land Redistribution

Earlier I noted a pattern of increased land concentration that centered around the growth of export crops and cattle. The new government began deconcentrating and redistributing some of this land through a number of changes in property laws.

Within 24 hours after the new government was established, the first of these laws was decreed. Decree No. 3 confiscated all the land and other holdings that had been amassed by the Somoza family and their close political allies. When the dust settled, a final inventory determined that approximately 20 percent of the country's agricultural land fell into this category. According to Vice-Minister of Agrarian Reform Salvador Mayorga, approximately one million hectares of land were expropriated under this decree. Most of this was from large, relatively modern and productive farms, which were generally reorganized as state farms. But approximately one-fifth of this land was to be redistributed to small or landless peasants.[14] Smaller farms owned by National Guardsmen and unused land on the larger estates were pegged for redistribution, beginning the process of deconcentrating land ownership.

A second, larger step in this direction came with the passage of the Agrarian Reform Law in August 1981. In the year before this law was promulgated, the number of land invasions (both spontaneous and state-sponsored) escalated, creating momentum for a new agrarian reform program. This new law allowed expropriation of any abandoned land (without compensation), of rented or sharecropped land on farms larger than 35 hectares (70 hectares outside the more densely populated Pacific coast), and of idle or underused land on farms larger than 350 hectares (700 hectares outside the

Pacific coast region). [15] Decapitalization (selling farm implements or live-stock, sharply reducing land under cultivation, misusing government agricultural loans, and the like) could constitute "technical abandonment" and also lead to confiscation.

It was estimated that at least 800,000 hectares of land were susceptible to redistribution under this law. [16] Some of this land was expected to be incorporated into the state farm sector when breaking up an estate jeopardized production and threatened to reduce efficiency. But most of the land taken under this provision was to be redistributed to peasant producers.

In the first year following the passage of this law, the pace of confiscations and redistribution was fairly slow. Only around 160,000 hectares (perhaps one-fifth of the land susceptible to confiscation) were expropriated during the first nine months. [17] And after almost one year of agrarian reform, only 60,000 hectares had been retitled to peasant producers. [18] Thus only a small portion of the available land had been taken, and less than 40 percent of that had been redistributed.

This cautious approach to agrarian reform was explained on the one hand by the need to avoid precipitating further decapitalization by a skittish and insecure landed class, and on the other by the need to select carefully the recipients of expropriated land. Widespread land expropriation would have provoked panic within the agricultural bourgeoisie, threatened the foundations of the "mixed economy," and stretched the managerial capacity of the bureaucracy and the agrarian reform tribunals beyond the breaking point. Quick redistribution of that land would have increased the probability of production failures and decreased government leverage over the newly landed peasantry. In order to assure improved production, the use of better technologies, cooperation in marketing, and enthusiastic integration into the revolution, officials of the Ministerio de Desarrollo Agropecuario y Reforma Agraria (MIDINRA) generally withheld title to reformed land until smoothly functioning peasant cooperatives had been established. [19]

The government expected that 40 percent of the land would ultimately be held by peasant cooperatives and credit associations (table 4). Movement in the direction of substantially reducing land held in large estates was underway by mid-1982. As table 4 indicates, 66 percent of the land was still held by private agribusiness or middle-sized farms larger than 35 hectares. This was much larger than the objective of 30 percent but far less than the 92 percent of the land controlled by these units in 1978. The numbers of both state farms and small individual holdings were close to their ultimate targets by 1982. Peasant cooperatives and credit associations, however, had only begun to develop. The stepped-up pace of land redistribution in 1983, however,

Table 4. Changes in Land Distribution (Percentage)

	1978	1982	1992 (projected)
Medium and large producers (over 35 hectares)	92%	66%	30%
Peasant producers (7–35 hectares)	7	4	5
Minifundistas (0–7 hectares)	1	2	—
State farms	—	22	25
Cooperatives	—	6	40
Total	100%	100%	100%

Source: CIERA, *Impacto del crédito rural sobre el nivel de vida del campesinado* (Managua, 1982), table 14, p. 227.

began bringing land distribution patterns more into line with the long-term plan.[20]

Agricultural Credit

As noted above, small producers, particularly staples producers, historically had very limited access to bank credit. Even in the credit program nominally designed to serve them, underfinancing and high interest rates were the norm. Consequently, most peasants functioned without access to state-sponsored credit. They borrowed from larger landowners or used savings from seasonal harvest labor to start up cultivation each year. Without the access to improved seeds or technology that credit can provide, staples output in Nicaragua was notoriously low, even for an undercapitalized third world nation.

The government inaugurated a credit program that was designed to stimulate production and promote a better standard of living for the peasantry. This was directed by the newly expropriated and reconstituted national banking system. At the end of the war against Somoza, almost all of Nicaragua's financial institutions were bankrupt. The Sandinistas quickly nationalized this sector and assumed responsibility for its debts. The banks were then reorganized and placed under state management. The new Sistema Financiero Nacional was assigned a dual role of making profitable loans to capitalist producers and the developed state sector, while providing developmental loans to peasant producers.

The credit channeled to the country's peasantry increased dramatically under the Sandinista government (table 5). The Rural Credit Program, which was targeted to small producers, underwent a remarkable expansion between 1979 and 1981, with its credit allocation growing from 153 to 975 million cordobas.[21] The more conventional bank credit system also expanded, but much more slowly (at roughly the rate of inflation), and its credit allocation in 1981 actually dropped below the 1980 level. While medium and large agricultural capitalists still received more funds through regular bank loans than did smallholders through the Rural Credit Program, the gap was narrowed consistently.

Increased credit for small producers generally meant increased credit for staples production (table 6). In 1977–78, two-thirds of the accredited land was used for the production of exports and only one-third for production of the domestic supplies. In 1980, this pattern was reversed, with more land dedicated to production for the domestic market than for export crops. By 1981, as the system began to stabilize, accreditation was about equally divided between export and internally oriented production. Given the bias of the prerevolutionary system toward the more lucrative agro-export market, this shift was significant. Again, the new programs did not eradicate all vestiges of the past, but rather shifted the direction of economic development.

Implementation of the new credit orientation, however, was not free of tension or division. Many of the credit distribution decisions of 1980, for example, were criticized for their lack of focus and for their inefficiency.[22] From the standpoint of increased production, the policy of "spilling credit" had limited success. While distributing credit in isolated areas by airplane may temporarily improve the standard of living of some marginal peasants, it does little to increase staples production and even less to provide urban consumers with needed foodstuffs. After a year of credit euphoria, stricter controls were placed on credit distribution, and in 1981–82 the area financed was sharply contracted (table 6). By most indicators, however, credit was still much more readily available in 1981 than it had been before the revolution, particularly for small producers. In 1978, only 26 percent of the land cultivated by peasant producers had received credit from Somoza's peasant credit program. In 1981 (even after the contraction in the program), two-thirds of smallholders received some financing. Producers of staples like corn and beans experienced almost a doubling of the accredited portion of their land. Since approximately two-thirds of the land cultivated by small

Table 5. Distribution of Agricultural Credit, 1977–81 (million cordobas)

	Rural Credit Program		Bank Credit	
	Amount	% of Total	Amount	% of Total
1977	112	5%	2083	95%
1978	91	4	2202	96
1979	153	6	2343	94
1980	950	18	4260	82
1981	975	23	3334	77

Source: CIERA, *Impacto del crédito rural sobre el nivel de vida del campesinado* (Managua, 1982), from data presented in table 7, p. 49.

producers was used to produce beans and corn, the expansion of loans in this sector sharply increased the peasantry's participation in the credit system.[23]

Not only was credit more readily available, but the terms for contracting it were also more flexible. Interest rates favored the peasant sector. As with land redistribution, the credit system was used to encourage the formation of cooperatives. For the 53 percent of Rural Credit beneficiaries who formed service cooperatives (Cooperativas de Crédito y Servicio) to share technical assistance and marketing facilities, the interest rate was 10 percent. For that 7 percent who formed more fully collectivized units (Cooperativas Agrarias Sandinistas), the interest rate was reduced to 8 percent. This contrasted with the 13 percent interest rate charged the 40 percent of small producers who had not joined the cooperative movement and the even higher 17 percent rate paid by larger commercial farmers.[24] Since the inflation rate was consistently above 20 percent, even the highest interest rate constituted a state subsidy to growers. Still, large capital obviously received a smaller boost than the peasant producers.

Marketing Structures

Innovations in the market structure were also designed to stimulate small producers. The Nicaraguan government had long been involved in marketing crops produced for the domestic market, but historically its role undermined the economic position of staples producers. The Somoza government developed the Instituto Nacional de Comercio Exterior y Interior

Table 6. Area Financed by the National Financial System

	1977–78		1980–81		1981–82	
	(1000 hectares)	% of Total	(1000 hectares)	% of Total	(1000 hectares)	% of Total
Export Agriculture	161	67%	233	42%	159	50%
Internal Market Agriculture	78	33%	318	58%	161	50%
Total	239	100%	551	100%	320	100%

Source: MIDINRA, *Tres años de reforma agraria* (Managua: CIERA, Aug. 1982), table 3, p. 38.

(INCEI) to buy basic grains from producers and sell them directly to consumers. One of the main purposes of this organization was to hold down the prices of basic foods by releasing large quantities of stored grains as domestic prices began to rise. Thus the state restrained price increases in the staples sector, forcing economically disadvantaged peasant producers to subsidize the rest of the economy.[25] This strategy also compelled economically marginal peasants to join the harvest labor force in the agro-export sector in order to supplement their meager incomes.

As in other areas, the revolutionary government took an established institution, restructured it, and gave it new objectives. INCEI was replaced by the Empresa Nicaragüense de Alimentos Básicos (ENABAS), which provided basic commodities at low prices and raised prices paid to producers (table 7). In its first year of operation, this agency charged consumers a modest amount more than the price it paid producers. In agricultural year 1981–82, ENABAS began directly subsidizing the marketing process. Government policy helped staples producers keep up with the rate of inflation and, some cases, even gain modestly.

While prices paid to producers generally rose, those paid by consumers were held constant or even lowered in spite of inflation. In the case of corn, consumers paid less than two-thirds of the price guaranteed to producers in 1982. After including costs of storage, transportation, distribution, and administration, the amount of the subsidy was substantial. A study by the Centro de Investigaciones y Estudios de la Reforma Agraria (CIERA) estimates the total subsidy for 1980–82 at over one billion cordobas ($100 million at the official exchange rate), almost half of which was spent in 1982 alone.[26] The financial burden this placed on the state in time of fiscal austerity and the vulnerability of the program to abuse created pressures to cut ENABAS back.[27] But the commitment to increase peasant incomes, stimulate staples production, and stretch the buying power of urban marginals while retarding inflation kept the program growing throughout the 1979–82 period.

In 1981 the government planned to absorb 40 percent of the domestic grains market, leaving the remainder in private hands.[28] This level of intervention was thought necessary in order to undermine exploitive purchasing practices of market intermediaries, redistribute resources toward peasant producers, expand the market into isolated areas, and cover the needs of low income urban consumers. Initially ENABAS had difficulty securing that degree of control over the internal market, particularly over domestic corn production. In 1980 only 12 percent of the domestic corn output was captured by ENABAS; in 1982 this had risen only to 18 percent.[29] With crops like rice, however, where state farms contributed heavily to produc-

Table 7. ENABAS Producer and Consumer Prices 1978–82. (cordobas/quintal)

Product	1978		1979–80		1980 (August)		1981–82		1982–83	
	Producer Price	Consumer Price	Producer Price	Consumer Price	Producer Price	Consumer Price	Producer Price	Consumer Price	Producer Price	Consumer Price
Corn	50	—	60	—	80	90	100	90	130	80[a]
Rice	110	—	140	—	205	220	323	270	323	270
Beans	143	—	180	—	220	260	320	260	350	260
Sorghum	46	—	55	—	—	—	85	80	85	80

Source: CIERA, *Impacto del crédito rural sobre el nivel de vida del campesinado* (Managua, 1982), table 2a, p. 135.

[a] Elsewhere CIERA gives 90 cordobas/quintal as the 1982–83 consumer price for corn (*Distribución y consumo popular de alimentos en Managua* [Managua, 1983], p. 69).

tion and agreements were reached with larger private producers, ENABAS acquired over 75 percent of production in 1982. In all, this agency marketed over 45 percent of domestic grains by the end of 1982. Through its monopoly control over staples imports, ENABAS' total participation in the staples market rose to approximately 50 percent at the end of this period.[30]

Consequences of the New Agricultural Policies

In adopting this new approach to agriculture, the government had a number of objectives. Its policies were designed to decrease unemployment, retard inflation, reduce vulnerability to foreign influences, slow urban migration, build internal political support, and give shape and purpose to the revolution. Perhaps the most important objectives of the program, however, were the systematic redistribution of resources, an increase in national productivity, and the elimination of a food deficit.

Given the brief time since these policies went into effect, the rudimentary quality of much of the statistical information on the Nicaraguan economy, and the problems introduced by the steady military pressure on the new government, precise analysis of the impact of these programs is not possible. It may be ten years or more before a clear picture of their consequences can be presented. At this stage, however, some tentative conclusions can be drawn.

Seasonal, landless agricultural laborers, one of the most economically disadvantaged sectors of the population, experienced only limited gains from the new approach. Without access to land, they were not able to take advantage of the increased credit or the higher prices paid to producers. They gained, of course, from the initial increases in agricultural wages and from the low cost of basic foods. They also benefited from the literacy campaign, an improved health care system, a better transportation network, and other social programs. Because their gains were in many ways more modest than those of producers with access to land, however, the gap between the poor and the poorest may have actually widened during this phase of the reconstruction.

Those with access to land, even small parcels, derived fuller benefits. A recent CIERA survey concluded that between 1978 and 1982 the average annual income increase for small producers (0–7 hectares) was 25 percent more than the increase for medium-sized producers (7–35 hectares). Furthermore, in 1981 the smallest producers (less than 3.5 hectares) received over one-third more credit per unit worked than those with 7–35 hectares and three-fifths more credit per unit than those with more than 35 hectares.[31] This again reflects the special effort made to support small producers and reduce the income differential among categories of producers. As the land redistribution program expands and more landless workers are incorporated into cooperatives and given title to land, these income benefits could be distributed more widely across the rural population. Under those circumstances, the redistributive thrust of these programs could be made clearer and more uniform.

The government's approach apparently had positive results in certain areas of production. In 1980, agricultural output surpassed the targets set by the Ministry of Planning, even though the amount of land in cultivation generally fell short of the targeted goals.[32] Expanded production was particularly strong in the politically favored domestic staples sector. The output of rice increased by 80 percent between 1977 and 1982, and bean production rose by almost 50 percent (table 8).

Production of export crops, on the other hand, increased much less. By 1981, most exports had returned to around 1977 levels, but some, such as cotton, remained at low levels. In 1982, cotton production dropped yet again, barely reaching half the 1977 levels (table 8). There are a number of reasons why the cotton sector was not resuscitated. One was the government's decision to replace cotton cultivation on marginal land with staples production.[33] Hostility among cotton growers (due to increasing expropriations, restrictions on profit margins, government monopolization of export trade, uncertainty about the legal status of rented land, and difficulties in obtaining productive imports) also caused cutbacks in production. Some government actions, therefore, may have had a negative impact on production, particularly among large producers in the historically privileged agroexport area.

Even in domestic market crops, production sometimes failed to live up to expectations. As MIDINRA secretary Jaime Wheelock noted early in 1983, Nicaragua was investing ten times as much in the production of basic grains as it did in the prerevolutionary period, while only attaining an overall 50 percent increase in staples output.[34] The corn sector was an area of particular concern. By 1980 it was successfully reactivated to the 1977 level, but its expansion rate in 1981 lagged behind that of other key staples. In 1982, corn production dropped back to pre-1977 levels. Given the centrality of corn in the Nicaraguan diet and the degree of effort expended to increase its output, the performance of this sector was disappointing.

Studies conducted by PAN and CIERA illustrate the difficulty of stimulating greater corn production. A generous allocation of credit to peasant producers, ironically, may result in a drop in yield, as families use loans to

Table 8. Production Changes of Major Agricultural Products 1977–82.
(Index: 1977 = 100)

	1977	1980	1981	1982[a]
Export Products				
Raw Cotton	100	30	61	52
Sesame	100	204	158	107
Bananas	100	76	95	87
Coffee	100	101	106	111
Sugarcane	100	90	100	113
Tobacco (Havana)	100	135	92	142
Domestic Products				
Rice	100	123	165	180
Beans	100	95	135	148
Corn	100	109	111	99
Sorghum	100	205	188	136

Sources: CEPAL, Notas para el estudio económico de América Latina, 1980: Nicaragua (Mexico City, 1981); CEPAL, Notas para el estudio económico de América Latina, 1982: Nicaragua (1983).

[a]Preliminary data.

purchase basic necessities instead of expanding cultivation. Even price increases may not bring about a larger output. Among the traditional peasantry, corn production does not respond closely to the logic of the market. It serves to guarantee subsistence for the family/community and is used only secondarily for commercial purposes. Given this situation, price increases do not necessarily correlate highly with increased production or sales, particularly when those price increases are as modest as they were in Nicaragua.[35] Even when a price change does trigger increased planting, the rudimentary technology available cannot ensure increased output. Consequently, the government's program for stimulating production had only limited success.

Overall, however, the new approach has augmented production in some sectors, and it may have more impact on others in the future. As the cooperative movement expands within the peasantry, facilitating improvements in technology, increased yield, and better integration into the marketing system, these programs may have a more positive impact on production. It may be, however, that further adjustments will have to be made in credit and price mechanisms in order to elicit a stronger productive response.

Production increases have reduced some of the deficit in basic grains production. As table 9 indicates, imports of staples soared during 1980 in the immediate aftermath of the war against Somoza. But in 1981, grain imports began to drop and were largely eliminated for rice and beans at the end of this period. Flooding and drought exacerbated production problems in the corn sector, however, and necessitated increased corn imports in 1982. Thus self-sufficiency remained beyond reach.

The long-term eradication of a food deficit was made more challenging by rising expectations following the insurrection. The Sandinist government has committed itself to overcoming the widespread malnutrition and making an adequate diet accessible to the full population. As expectations and family incomes rose, the demand for food rose accordingly, and pressure on the government to increase production has intensified. Production at previous levels was no longer adequate to meet national demand. The effort to eliminate the deficit still continues.

In the 1979–82 period, the new government began work on a number of critical tasks. Its success in achieving structural reform was only partial, but it built a foundation for a major economic reorientation. If land redistribution proceeds, infrastuctural reform continues and price and subsidy mechanisms are refined, positive consequences of the new approach should be felt more forcefully.

Future Directions

This study would not be complete without some discussion of the future directions Nicaragua's agricultural economy may take. Projection into the future, however, is a difficult task. The almost daily military attacks led by ex-members of Somoza's National Guard and by Indian separatists have diverted time, energy, and scarce resources away from the discussion of future economic development. Both research and planning have been impeded. Nonetheless, there has been some on-going discussion within the country over the kind of development strategy that should be employed.

A number of different positions can be taken on the issue (table 10). The government might continue to emphasize a "food first" approach. On the other hand, more attention might be given to agro-exports, returning to a more traditional model. Alternatively, an export-oriented approach that centers on food exports could be devised. Or finally, a plan that emphasizes

Table 9. Imports[a] and Exports of Basic Grains (thousand quintales)

Product	1975	1979	1980	1981	1982
Corn	3	(29)	1260	652	1109[c]
Beans	(8)[b]	(64)	350	262	42[c]
Rice	(15)	223	763	436	0
Sorghum	(304)	8	0	(433)	(200)[d]

Sources: CIERA, *El impacto del crédito rural sobre el nivel de vida del campesinado* (Managua, 1982), table 33, p. 259; and CIERA, *Informe del primer seminario sobre estrategía alimentaria* (Managua, 1983), table 4, p. 20.

[a]Imports include donations.   [b]Figures in parentheses are exports.

[c]Estimations.   [d]Projection.

domestic processing of agricultural products could receive more attention.

A strong argument has already been advanced in favor of an emphasis on *food self-sufficiency*. This approach would enable the economy to achieve several objectives simultaneously. As we have seen, funneling additional resources to staples producers helps to revive and support the peasant economy. It can promote a more equitable distribution of food, especially in rural areas where isolation and poverty impede access to imported products. This strategy enables the government to cut spending on food imports, saving scarce foreign exchange for payment on products like petroleum that Nicaragua cannot produce itself. And finally, this approach reduces the vulnerability of the nation to a food cutoff or boycott. One incentive for adoption of the PAN was the Reagan administration's abrupt cancellation in April 1981 of a $9.8 million loan to purchase United States wheat. This move vividly demonstrated the country's vulnerability to food sabotage. The achievement of a greater degree of food self-sufficiency is expected to enable the nation to avoid such political manipulation. The difficult question is: what role should the other strategies play? Should some non-food crops be given equal (or even greater) importance? And what direction should the nation take once food self-sufficiency has been attained?

There is much to support continued use of the *agro-export model*. Exports of cotton and coffee, supplemented with sugar, beef, and bananas, have traditionally generated substantial amounts of foreign exchange. In the last two years, as loans and credits from supportive countries have begun to contract, foreign exchange has become increasingly scarce. Simulta-

Table 10. Alternative Development Strategies

Commodity Emphasis	Market Focus	
	Domestic Market	*Export Market*
Basic Foods	Food self-sufficiency model	Staples export model
Raw Materials	Agro-industry model	Traditional agro-export model

neously, the country's foreign obligations have expanded. In 1982 payments for petroleum imports alone consumed forty cents for each dollar earned by exports, and payments on the foreign debt consumed another forty-one cents.[36] This obligation will grow still more burdensome after 1985, when Nicaragua is scheduled to resume payment on the principal of its foreign debt. Given these realities, increased production of crops that generate foreign exchange seems almost imperative.

There are, of course, other ways to generate these resources, but the traditional approach has certain advantages. The Nicaraguan export economy is already somewhat diversified, with both coffee and cotton playing major roles. Producers of these commodities have long experience with these crops and understand their international market characteristics. The national economy is already organized around these products and has a major infrastructural investment in their continued production. Any shift away from this approach would be risky and costly.

The Sandinist government apparently has decided to avoid breaking with this model. It has, as indicated earlier, contributed to a cutback in cotton cultivation in ecologically marginal zones. But it is making major investments in the expansion of the sugar sector, building a new sugar mill that is expected to increase exports by 10 percent annually beginning in 1984.[37] Furthermore, the foreign exchange needed for production inputs (fertilizers, pesticides, etc.) for export crops has been allocated on a first priority basis. The recurring labor shortages that have emerged during export crop harvests have been regularly filled only by the government's policy of closing schools and offices and organizing voluntary brigades and militia units to work in the harvest. Export crops are seen as a vital feature of the economy, and the government has made little movement to alter this.

Some have argued that the state should shift its approach and emphasize the development of an *export-oriented food sector* instead. Nicaragua's traditional exports are vulnerable to sharp price fluctuations. The problems this produces have been particularly apparent in the last few years, as a simultaneous decline in the prices of several key exports has caused a sharp drop in export earnings. Between 1980 and 1982, the export price for Nicaragua's coffee dropped from $166 to $123 per quintal, and the beef price fell from $1.30 to $1.08 per pound.[38] Decreases in cotton and sugar prices in 1982 further compounded the problem. Total export earnings for 1982 were 14 percent lower than they had been in 1981.[39]

The terms of trade for traditional agricultural exports have tended to deteriorate vis à vis those for manufactured or processed goods. Between 1980 and 1981, the volume of Nicaragua's exports increased 15 percent while their value increased only 11 percent. Conversely, the volume of the country's imports increased by 4 percent, while their value increased almost 12 percent.[40] Recognition of this pattern has caused several analysts to argue that the nation would be better off shifting away from traditional exports toward new kinds of products.

MIDINRA Vice-Minister Salvador Mayorga has argued on behalf of a staples export emphasis.[41] Such a policy could address two needs at once. The push for increased staples production could help ensure that the country's internal food needs are fully met through an abundant output of basic foods. And marketing the surplus of staples would help provide the country with an export whose price is not prone to sharp fluctuations and for which the terms of trade are generally good. This kind of product could function as ballast for the Nicaraguan economy, bringing greater stability to its market position.

Yet this model also presents certain problems. Because of the low level of technology employed by most staples producers, Nicaraguan crop yield is low. It would take a major restructuring of the staples production process for this sector to become a real competitor with the traditional exports in foreign exchange earnings. If this were accomplished, Nicaragua would then have to compete in the export market against the United States, the world's major grain exporter. The oligopolistic nature of the international grains market would complicate the task of developing a new market and would create new kinds of trade vulnerabilities. Finally, for a government committed to social revolution, this new role would pose special problems. It would be difficult to withhold cheap food from nations where inadequate food production threatened to exacerbate malnutrition and hunger. These dilemmas do not invalidate this model, but they do illustrate the kinds of difficulties it presents.

Finally, the country could focus on increasing the level of processing and transformation of agricultural products within Nicaragua itself, expanding the *agro-industry sector.* Currently, little processing of Nicaragua's raw material takes place in the country. Some oil is extracted from cottonseed, beef is deboned, and coffee beans are extracted, but most of the processing, mixing, and packaging of these products is done outside the country. The government could encourage domestic processing by using tariffs, subsidies, and other import-substituting industrialization strategies. It could promote second-stage processing of cotton, expand the textile sector, and develop a garment industry. A food processing industry might also be elaborated using some of the products that are relatively abundant (beef, sugar, juices, oils, and perhaps eggs and seafood).

This developmental approach has a number of advantages. The growth of new industry could help forestall the impending collapse of the industrial sector, halt the rise in unemployment, and stimulate the GNP growth rate. It would foster better integration of the agricultural and industrial sectors of the economy, facilitating more coherent national planning. Expanded production of certain industrial products could also make them more readily available in the internal market, augmenting the array of goods to which Nicaraguan consumers have access.

Yet this strategy too would present various difficulties. Nicaragua's small internal market would quickly be saturated. In order for agro-industry to develop, export markets would soon have to be identified. Traditionally most of Nicaragua's industrial products have been sold to other Central American nations through the Central American Common Market. Given the collapse of most of the economies of Central American nations and the palpable tensions that have developed between Nicaragua and most of her neighbors, high levels of exports within that regional framework are improbable.

Exporting outside that area is a possibility, but it would entail breaking into a highly competitive international market that is in the middle of a global recession. The difficulty of succeeding in this venture is obvious. The task would be more feasible if conducted by well-established transnational corporations, but the political and economic costs of allowing global corporations to develop the agro-industry sector are probably too high to make this option attractive to the revolutionary government.[42] While this strategy could, under the right circumstances, generate substantial foreign exchange and promote more favorable terms of trade, it would be a very uncertain operation.

The experience of other Latin American nations that have gone through the process of import-substituting industrialization illustrates the common pitfalls associated with this strategy. Both Mexico and Brazil demonstrate that the high cost of importing capital goods for industrial processing soon eats into foreign exchange and exacerbates balance of payments problems. The foreign loans typically used to finance these ventures can lead to heavy interest payments and further exchange shortages. While the careful selection of appropriate technology, heavy use of domestic raw materials, and the simultaneous development of a foreign exchange–generating export market can eliminate some of these problems, this strategy too presents a host of difficulties.

The development strategies discussed in this section are not mutually exclusive. Indeed, in varying degrees all four of these approaches are now being employed in Nicaragua. But in times of resource scarcity, it is impossible to pursue all angles simultaneously. In the short run, the Sandinist government has given special emphasis to food self-sufficiency, both to fulfill revolutionary commitments and to address certain internal development problems. In the medium run, expanding (or at least preserving) the traditional agro-export sector appears to be an important priority for this government. As the debate about directions continues, in the long run perhaps one of the other two models will be given a more prominent role. The ultimate direction of the Sandinist revolution depends on many factors that are not within the control of the revolutionary government (such as international recession, insurrections in Central America, superpower stances, etc.). Recent military developments make it increasingly difficult for the government to consciously select a development strategy, or even, for that matter, to sustain the advances of the first three years. But the discussion about alternative models continues and may eventually allow the country to chart a strong development path.[43]

Notes

Abbreviations

CEPAL	Comisión Económica para América Latina
CIERA	Centro de Investigaciones y Estudios de la Reforma Agraria
ENABAS	Empresa Nicaragüense de Alimentos Básicos
FAO	Food and Agriculture Organization of the United Nations
FIDA	Fondo Internacional de Desarrollo Agrícola
MIDINRA	Ministerio de Desarrollo Agropecuario y Reforma Agraria
MIPLAN	Ministerio de Planificación

Acknowledgment

Field research for this study was conducted with support from the National Endowment for the Humanities.

1. For discussion of the food problem, see William W. Murdoch, *The Poverty of Nations: The Political Economy of Hunger and Population* (Baltimore: Johns Hopkins University Press, 1980), pp. 93–166; Alberto Valdés, ed., *Food Security for Developing Countries* (Boulder, Colo.: Westview Press, 1981), pp. 1–10; Alain de Janvry, *The Agrarian Question and Reformism in Latin America* (Baltimore: Johns Hopkins University Press, 1981), pp. 141–81; and Frances Moore Lappé and Joseph Collins, *Food First* (Boston: Houghton Mifflin, 1977).

2. Cereal imports as a percent of consumption (production + imports − exports) totaled 21 percent in 1972, 22 percent in 1973, 19 percent in 1977, 19 percent in 1978, and 24 percent in 1980 (FAO, *Production Yearbook* [Rome], various years, and FAO, *Trade Yearbook* [Rome], various years). A number of developments contributed to this important dependence. Although wheat production is not ecologically suited to the nation, many Nicaraguan consumers had developed a taste for this product. Wheat was, therefore, a chronic and growing import. Corn production fluctuated strikingly; it dropped dramatically in the early 1970s and did not fully recuperate for six years. At the end of the decade, rice production also dropped sharply. The overall pattern, therefore, reflected a substantial and recurring (though not systematically deepening) food deficit.

3. Jaime Wheelock, *Nicaragua: Imperialismo y dictadura* (Havana: Editorial de Ciencias Sociales, 1980), p. 49–83.

4. Pedro Belli, "An Inquiry Concerning the Growth of Cotton Farming in Nicaragua" (Ph.D. diss., University of California, Berkeley, 1968), p. 91.

5. See the discussion in Wheelock, *Nicaragua*, pp. 148–50; and Orlando Núñez Soto, *El somocismo y el modelo capitalista agroexportador* (Managua: Universidad Nacional Autónoma de Nicaragua, 1981), pp. 5–30.

6. Philip F. Warnken, *The Agricultural Development of Nicaragua: An Analysis of the Production Sector* (Columbia: Agricultural Experiment Section, University of Missouri, July 1975), pp. 16–19.

7. FIDA, *Informe de la Misión Especial de Programación a Nicaragua* (Managua: MIDINRA, 1981), p. 1.

8. It should be noted that thousands of squatters did not have their land ownership legally recognized and that even those who did were not always fully protected from land takeovers. It has also been argued that the colonization scheme of the Instituto Agrario de Nicaragua was designed to shift a large peasant population to the interior, where it could be more easily tapped for seasonal labor by agribusiness developing in that region. See the critical analyses in Núñez Soto, *Somocismo*, p. 77, and FIDA, *Informe*, pp. 41–44.

9. Production of all three of these crops remained lower in 1975 than it had been in 1970 (FAO, *Production Yearbook,* various years).

10. FIDA, *Informe,* p. 40.

11. Centro de Investigación de la Realidad Nacional, "Invierno: Un programa integral de desarrollo en conflicto con las estructuras de agro," *Nicaragua: Reforma o revolución* (Dec. 1978), 1:78.

12. According to a FAO study conducted in 1970, the bottom 50 percent of the income strata consumed only about one-fourth of the animal protein that was consumed by the top 5 percent, and only a little more than half of the vegetable protein (cited in FIDA, *Informe,* pp. 57–58).

13. AID, *Nutrition Sector Assessment for Nicaragua 1976,* cited in CIERA, *El hambre en los países del tercer mundo* (Managua, 1983), p. 37.

14. Interview with Salvador Mayorga, *La Prensa* (Managua), March 7, 1982. For more information about the first phase of the land reform, see Carmen Diana Deere, "Nicaraguan Agricultural Policy: 1979–81," *Cambridge Journal of Economics* 5 (June 1981): 195–200; and David Kaimowitz and Joseph R. Thome, "Nicaragua's Agrarian Reform: The First Year (1979–80)," in *Nicaragua in Revolution,* ed. Thomas W. Walker (New York: Praeger, 1982): 223–40.

15. Land is considered "idle" if it has not been put into production for two or more years. "Underused" land is that with less than 75 percent of cultivable land being farmed or with less than one head of cattle per 1.4 hectares (2 hectares in the interior) located on pasture land. See Joseph Collins, *What Difference Could a Revolution Make? Food and Farming in the New Nicaragua* (San Francisco: Institute for Food and Development Policy, 1982), pp. 87–96.

Compensation provisions vary depending on the circumstances surrounding confiscation. Those who have abandoned the country receive no compensation. Payment can be provided for idle or underutilized land depending on the degree of damage the former owners have done to the estate. Landowners may receive bonds (based on the assessed value) at up to 4 percent interest, payable within 15 years. In the hardest-pressed cases, owners may even receive an immediate pension of up to 1,000 cordobas per month.

16. Interview, MIDINRA vice-minister, Aug. 5, 1982. See also Agencia Nueva Nicaragua, "Sandino's Dream was Somoza's Nightmare and Our Hope," (March 1982, press release), p. 42. Collins mentions 1.6 million hectares in his study (*Difference,* p. 89). Presumably this figure includes more land from the Atlantic coast and from rented/sharecropped parcels.

17. CIERA, *Impacto del crédito rural sobre el nivel de vida del campesinado* (Managua, 1982), p. 126.

18. *Nuevo Diario* (Managua), July 18, 1982.

19. Interview with MIDINRA vice-minister, Aug. 5, 1982; see also Collins, *Difference,* p. 96.

20. In January 1983, MIDINRA secretary Jaime Wheelock announced the launching of a new phase of the land reform program, in which 344,000 hectares of idle land

would be redistributed to peasant cooperatives (*Barricada international* [Managua], Jan. 24, 1983). In July 1983, MIDINRA announced that 153,000 hectares of land had been retitled in the previous year, more than double the amount legally redistributed the year before (*Nuevo Diario,* July 19, 1983).

Expropriations affected 160,000 hectares in the first nine months of the agrarian reform law. In January 1983, Wheelock announced that 138,000 hectares would be expropriated under this law in 1983 (*Barricada international,* Jan. 24, 1983), indicating a slower rate of expropriation.

21. There was a lack of consensus on the operational definition of a "small producer," but the Banco Nacional de Desarrollo (which oversees the allocation of most agricultural credit) used the following definitions:

Small producers are those who possess up to 10.5 hectares in basic grains, 7 hectares in coffee or cacao, 2 hectares in vegetables, 14 hectares in cotton, or 7 hectares in other perennial crops.

Medium producers are those with 10.5–52.5 hectares in basic grains, 7–21 hectares in coffee or cacao, 14–70 hectares in cotton, or 7–14 hectares in other perennial crops.

Large producers are those with more land in any of these categories.

See MIDINRA, *Plan operativo de granos básicos: Ciclo agrícola 1982/83* (Managua, May 1982), p. 172.

22. See Collins, *Difference,* pp. 51–57; MIDINRA, *Plan operativo;* and Banco Nacional de Desarrollo, *Crédito rural en Nicaragua* (Managua, 1982, Mimeographed).

23. In 1978, 27 percent of the land producing corn and 38 percent of that producing beans for small producers received financing. In 1981 this had risen to 51 percent and 73 percent respectively. Curiously, credit was even more available to the handful of small producers cultivating export-oriented crops like cotton and sesame, where 100 percent of the land received financing. Perhaps this is because local bank officials retained a prerevolutionary approach to lending, emphasizing "collateral" and "probable repayment." The higher production costs of export agriculture may also necessitate some access to credit, and so the greater demand within this sector may lead to a greater response.

The new government also has a commitment to increase the protein content in the diet of the average citizen. To do this, special emphasis has been placed on increased production of chickens and eggs. To sustain a rapidly growing poultry sector, the government has encouraged the increased production of sorghum, which is used in chicken feed. This may explain why credit among small sorghum producers also covered 100 percent of the land so employed. See CIERA, *Impacto,* p. 51.

24. Interview with Sistema Financiero Nacional official, Aug. 14, 1982; and CIERA, *Impacto,* p. 35.

25. For FIDA's critique of this policy, see its *Informe,* pp. 50–52. This pattern has also been found in Mexico, where the commitment to rapid industrial expansion and labor pacification led to a cheap food policy that drastically undermined the economic

position of staples producers. See Carlos Montáñez and Horacio Aburto, *Maíz: Política institucional y crisis agrícola* (Mexico City: Editorial Nueva Imagen, 1979).

26. This includes a hefty subsidy (220 million cordobas in 1982) for sugar consumption. See CIERA, *Informe del primer seminario sobre estrategía alimentaria* (Managua, 1983), p. 26.

27. A wide gap between producer and consumer prices gives buyers an incentive to purchase staples at the low price and recycle them into the countryside for resale at the higher price. Low consumer prices may also encourage illegal staples exporting to neighboring countries where food prices are much higher. For a discussion of some of these problems, see MIDINRA, *Plan operativo*.

28. MIPLAN, *Programa económico de austeridad y eficiencia, 1981* (Managua, 1981), p. 71.

29. See CIERA, *Informe*, p. 23. Originally ENABAS' price offering was too low to enable it to compete successfully with private intermediaries. Even after price adjustments were made, the infrastructure of the agency (storage, transportation, etc.) proved inadequate to the task, and the bureaucratic elements of the program (such as payment in checks and complicated quality controls) made it a less attractive purchaser than many of the traditional middlemen.

30. Ibid., pp. 23–24. CIERA reports that in 1982 ENABAS sold 34 percent of all the corn that was marketed, 44 percent of all beans, 84 percent of all rice, and 64 percent of all sorghum, for a total participation of 49 percent in the grains market. Because official data do not completely cover the parallel market, these figures may overstate ENABAS' role.

31. CIERA, *Impacto*, pp. 216, 243.

32. MIPLAN, *Programa, 1981*, p. 31.

33. Interview with MIDINRA vice-minister, Aug. 5, 1982.

34. *Barricada internacional*, Feb. 28, 1983.

35. ENABAS' price increases for corn producers barely kept up with inflation between 1979 and 1982. The role played by the Nicaraguan state has not been uniformly supportive of high producer prices. When uncertainty and slow recuperation caused staples prices to soar in 1980, the government's purchase of imports to cover demand led producer prices to drop sharply. The commitment to improve peasant incomes has been balanced both against the need to provide adequately and cheaply for urban marginals and against the realities of sharp budgetary limits.

36. CEPAL, *Notas para el estudio económico de América Latina, 1982: Nicaragua* (Mexico City, 1983), pp. 25, 28.

37. *Nuevo Diario*, July 31, 1982; *La Prensa*, Aug. 1, 1982.

38. Ministerio de Comercio Exterior, *Nicaragua: Boletín estadístico: Comercio exterior 1980–1982* (Managua: 1983): 10.

39. CEPAL, *Notas*, p. 21. This was due partly to an 8 percent decline in export volume associated with the declining prices.

40. Ibid., pp. 25–27.

41. Salvador Mayorga, "La experiencia agraria de la revolución nicaragüense,"

Reforma agraria y revolución popular en América Latina 12 (Managua: CIERA, 1982), pp. 91–120. See also Collins, *Difference,* pp. 110–11.

42. The new government has, however, recently developed a law that encourages foreign investment to take place and puts very few restrictions on investment activities or the repatriation of capital. See the *New York Times,* Dec. 22, 1982, section 4, p. 1.

43. See the discussion in CIERA, *Informe,* pp. 6–14, 43–51.

Ivan Sergio Freire de Sousa, Edward Gerald Singer, and William L. Flinn

Sociopolitical Forces and Technology: Critical Reflections on the Green Revolution

The "Green Revolution" was an international campaign launched in the 1940s to increase the productivity of land, especially in the poorer countries of the world, through the introduction of new plant varieties and other advanced agricultural technologies.[1] Prior attempts to raise crop yields had failed because varieties of corn developed in Iowa, rice from Japan, and wheat from the midwestern United States were not suitable to local cultivation, climatic condition, or consumer taste. Local varieties of wheat and rice, in response to heavy fertilizer applications, were usually unsuccessful too; they grew tall but lodged easily.

Norman Borlaug, director of the Rockefeller Foundation and father of the Green Revolution, began a wheat-breeding program in Mexico to develop a high-yielding dwarf wheat variety that was highly responsive to fertilizer and matured quickly. His success with wheat was followed by similar successes with rice varieties at the International Rice Research Institute in the Philippines. The introduction of the "miracle" varieties of wheat and rice as well as advances in breeding of corn and sugar cane brought a doubling and in some cases tripling of yields in parts of the world.

Despite these fantastic gains achieved in the 1940s and 1950s, prospects for solving the world food problem in the short term have diminished. Continuing high rates of population growth and the difficulty of developing "miracle" strains in genetically complex food crops, such as vegetables, are partially responsible for restricting the success of the Green Revolution. A more basic limiting factor, however, is the nature of the Green Revolution approach itself. High-yielding varieties demand a package of inputs including fertilizers, pesticides, fairly sophisticated farm management techniques, and (for some crops) irrigation controls that must constantly be modified and adapted to varying local conditions.[2] Without these materials and techniques, Green Revolution varieties may actually yield less than local varieties.

This technological package was developed in an era of cheap energy. Because the production of nitrogen fertilizer depends on natural gas, irrigation pumps run on gasoline, and pesticides are made from petroleum products, the cost of equipment has escalated rapidly. Accordingly, recent discussion of the Green Revolution has centered on the second or "coming" wave of techniques in which high-yielding varieties, bred for disease and insect resistance, will fix their own nitrogen.[3]

Yet even this prospective change from energy-intensive to energy-extensive varieties does not address a main criticism of the Green Revolution—its failure in most cases to reach small farmers and the "poorest of the poor."[4] The problem exists because most of the world's poor countries are energy-deficient and because the majority of farmers in these countries have little or no access to credit for the acquisition of necessary inputs. Small farmers can theoretically adopt most or all of the techniques of the Green Revolution, but in practice large farmers can more readily embrace the Green Revolution because of better access to land, credit, and farm management methods.[5] The result may be that even when more food is produced, small farmers do not share in the economic or nutritional benefits, and social problems in the countryside may be compounded. Attempts are being made to mitigate these limiting characteristics of the Green Revolution with appropriate intermediate and alternative technologies as well as through programs in farming systems and integrated rural development.

Although knowledge of the consequences of technologies is important, there remains an implicit and unchallenged assumption that *if* researchers knew the most socially desirable technologies, they would respond accordingly. In agriculture, the test of this will come in the application of lessons from the first Green Revolution to the conception and implementation of the second wave of new technologies. We maintain, however, that the search for understanding the "mistakes" of the Green Revolution should focus on the sociopolitical forces that create and mold the work of research institutions. These forces, more than explicit prior knowledge of social consequences of technological change, guide the creation and application of new technologies such as that of the Green Revolution.

Until recently, the sociopolitical forces behind technological change had been virtually ignored.[6] Some argue that powerful interests seeking to maintain or acquire economic or political advantage consciously or unconsciously have defused attempts at analyzing these forces.[7] Also, frequently held notions about the creation of technologies may be based in systems of thought that conceal a broader picture of how and why technologies are developed. Such unexamined assumptions direct the concerns of many well-intentioned people who do occupy powerful positions away from sociopolitical forces. From three broadly defined disciplines—psychology, economics, and sociology—commonly held systems of thought on the creation of technologies are here examined. Next, a broader view of technological change is employed to show the decisive role of sociopolitical forces in the Green Revolution. We conclude by identifying some emergent sociopolitical constraints on researchers and research organizations.

Current Interpretations of Technological Change

Although not directly employing the psychologist's conceptual tools, observers of the Green Revolution (according to the traditional diffusion model) have adopted certain assumptions of this approach.[8] Much of the psychological literature focuses on what constitutes a creative individual, but its logic and assumptions are easily transferred to a typical "problem" of the Green Revolution: What constitutes an innovative person?

Conferences on scientific creativity at the University of Utah have identified three dimensions in the study of creativity: the *person* (who the creative individual is), the *product* (what a creative person does that can be called creative), and the *process* (how the creative person does what he does).[9] From these meetings came an outline of variables potentially involved in creativity, suggestions for research on the problem, and implications involved in measurement of creativity. For example, if the product of creative thinking is being considered, measurements should take into account two elements: kinds (ideas, patents, etc.) and aspects (value, novelty, etc.). In the case of creative individuals, it was suggested that researchers should identify creative people in terms of their products, their eminence, their training, and their psychological traits as well as defining organizational responsibility.

In terms of process, it was suggested that research should be able to analyze and compare the productive processes involved in divergent and convergent thinking as well as the methods utilized by creative people (such as flexibility, perserverance, and planning).

The limitations of the individualistic or psychological model of creativity and the diffusion of innovations have been argued elsewhere by scholars of several theoretical persuasions and need not be repeated here.[10] It is sufficient to point out that in this model, the "fault" for not creating lies with the individual. Neoclassical economics provides one of the alternatives to an individualistic approach.

Like its psychological counterpart, the economic perspective on creativity is not a uniform one. Economics does not yet have a complete technological model of the research process.[11] Economists' contributions to understanding creativity come indirectly from studies on inventions and from studies of resource allocation and the rate of return on agricultural research investments.[12]

Among neoclassical economists at least, a basic concern for economic growth has led technology to be classified as: (1) an autonomous factor that occurs independently of socioeconomic events[13] or (2) a dependent factor that responds to economic pressures.[14] Under either of these two views of technology, however, the process by which innovations are generated has seldom received explicit attention, although modern exceptions include studies by Yujiro Hayami, Vernon W. Ruttan, and Robert E. Evenson.[15]

For Joseph A. Schumpeter technology reflects economic necessity.[16] An innovation is what is created under economic pressure and, once in production, affects the economy. Schumpeter, however, does not offer a theory of innovation as such. J. R. Hicks provides the basis for such a theory. For individual firms, he shows that a change in the relative prices of the factors of production leads to "biased technological progress" in which the generation of technology economizes the use of the most expensive factor(s).[17]

Hayami and Ruttan's approach goes beyond Hicks' microconsiderations of the firm and permits analysis of technological change throughout a society.[18] Their model asserts that technological change is an endogenous variable in the development process, that it depends on economic forces, that there are multiple paths to technological development, that technology is not neutral in its resource-saving characteristics, and that technical change has the role of facilitating the substitution of one resource for another.[19]

With few exceptions, Hayami and Ruttan's hypotheses have received little extensive critique from economists or others.[20] However, they have exerted a major influence on economists and policymakers involved with agricultural development in the United States as well as in developing countries. We see three major shortcomings in the Hayami and Ruttan model. The first results from their focusing exclusively on the market at the expense of other factors in technological development. Assumptions of a "free market" (i.e., a system of prices that reflects resource scarcity) fail to consider the overwhelming reality of governmental involvement in most economies, including that of the United States.[21] "Monetarists" such as Theodore W. Schultz and H. G. Johnson, however, do call attention to the distortions resulting from public interventions in the free operation of market forces.[22]

Secondly, Hayami and Ruttan retain the Schumpeterian assumption that innovation is the central force and determinant element in the economy. This form of technological determinism emphasizes economic development's supply side, where the solutions for agricultural stagnation are: (1) technological development (new technologies) and (2) the provision of extension services and credit programs. The third shortcoming is their use of a concept of "society" that conceals possible divisions that must be recognized when decisions about "society's needs" or "benefits to society" are at stake.

In sum, the initial impact of the induced innovation model was for economists to tie technological change to economic forces rather than to either general sociocultural mechanisms (e.g., inventions evolving from existing knowledge in the culture) or personality attributes. The economic studies reviewed above do not really touch upon sociopolitical aspects of the problem, but they do help raise and clarify the issues in the process of creating technology. The neoclassical tradition has shown what the psychological approach could not even address—that above and beyond internal dynamics of the individual, the form and pace of technological development are tied to market forces. Induced innovation theory, with further refinements but nagging problems, has shown the necessity of introducing social institutions into a model of technological change.

Sociology has taken at least three broad directions in pursuit of a systematic theory of the production of science and technology, but none of these has succeeded in resolving the many and diverse issues of technological change. One of these directions—the most traditional and perhaps the least satisfactory—is concerned with how far a given cultural base determines a particular invention, assuming a constant level of mental ability.[23]

The sociocultural account offers a refreshing challenge to psychological reductionism and poses the problem of the social determinants of technological change. The approach, however, falls short of specifying the mechanisms of technological change. Assuming that "creative minds" are socially determined, what are the cultural factors or traits that produce a specific technological form or content? The question has not received a consistent answer. Moreover, in defense of the induced innovation model, Jacob Schmookler has demonstrated that the availability of knowledge is less likely than the action of market forces to trigger inventions.[24]

Another sociological direction, largely credited to Robert K. Merton, asks, "Why it is that most individuals, most of the time, come to 'want' to do what it is that society 'needs them to do'?"[25] Although more convincing, this approach has nevertheless "become more and more bound up with the internal workings of the social system of science, and less and less directly interested in the relations that exist between science and the social and political environment in which it takes place."[26] Despite this criticism the Mertonian approach has provided useful theories on an "interactional tendency" (concerned with the relationships among individual scientists) and an "institutional tendency" (concerned with macroinfluences on scientific organization and the role of the scientist in society).

Radical sociology offers a third sociological approach.[27] It is distinguished by a focus on the social determination of the substance (e.g., "capitalist vs. proletarian") of science and technology. Luke Hodgkin claims that scientists are social beings, not only because of their relationships outside their work but also because of the relationships involved in their scientific practice; in fact, he says, "this work in some sense determines all the rest."[28] Both the process of production of science (scientific practice) and its product (scientific knowledge) are social: "I don't mean science is wrong, distorted or serves ruling-class interests automatically . . . scientific work, like any other work, takes place within the framework of an 'ideology of practice' . . . and this ideology—shared to a greater or lesser extent among a number of scientists—is socially determined, and in its turn determines the choices and orientations for a scientist's practice, and so for the kind of knowledge he produces."[29] Social determination includes both economic and political dimensions of social reality. Two very different views about technology in social development hinge on whether primacy is given to the forces of production (any facility or instrument that purposely contributes to production, e.g., G. A. Cohen) or to the relations of production (those sociopolitical relations through which the surplus product is drawn from the direct producer, e.g., Michael Burawoy).[30]

Both the Mertonian and radical sociology views of science do begin to specify several relevant social dimensions of technological change. Recent works have been guided by at least three basic inquiries: (1) What determines the nature of the questions scientists pursue? (2) Do technologies have a social character over and above any inherent physical properties and economic rationality? and (3) By what processes and through what mechanisms is the social character of technology transformed?

Issues pertaining to the social system of science include relations among scientists, relations among organizations, and the impact of organizations on scientists' work.[31] Many studies of the social system of science have assumed the independence of scientific institutions from their sociopolitical environment (e.g. Robert K. Merton, Harriet Zuckerman).[32] This assumption underscores the importance of the internal structure of scientific institutions to scientific production. Sociologists studying the relationship between science and the sociopolitical environment have focused on problem choice in the research establishment, on agricultural labor supply and control, on the economic organization of agriculture and the economic power of farms, on the role of the state, and on structured determinations.[33]

Advances in genetic engineering (currently led by the private sector in the United States) are rearranging institutional relationships and forging new ties between social institutions and science. The very high capital requirements of this research, as well as the great social implications of the control and use of the new technologies, have begun to attract the attention of sociologists.[34] The promise of technical advances in genetic engineering, such as nitrogen fixation in nonleguminous crops, increased photosynthetic efficiency, pest and disease resistance, and salt, heat, and drought tolerance, has major implications for developing countries.[35]

A survey of widely differing approaches—psychological, economic, and sociological—to the question of why and how technology changes shows the lack of conceptual tools for recognizing the importance of sociopolitical forces and for studying their role in the Green Revolution. Without pretending to advance a new theory, we borrow from the new initiatives of the sociological approach to underscore the importance of sociopolitical forces in the success of Green Revolution technologies.

Toward a Broader View of Technological Change

Colin Norman echoes a growing appeal for a broader view of technology in society when he writes that "technology has a pervasive impact on society. Less obvious is the influence of society on technology. . . . Technological systems underpin economic and social systems, and social and political values and institutions in turn shape both the development and application of technology."[36] Others have addressed the Green Revolution in general contexts such as "decision making" and "dependency" or have urged "structural changes" necessary to the Green Revolution's success.[37] We attempt a further specification of sociopolitical forces by drawing on three broad categories of sociopolitical structures hypothesized to have had a decisive influence on the Green Revolution: (1) socioeconomic structures, (2) political institutions, and (3) the organizational character of the research institutions themselves.

Market forces join with production structures and political factors to create interest in specific technologies. By isolating market forces, the induced innovation model of neoclassical economics provides the basic rationale for the Green Revolution. Relative factor prices were believed to reflect the resource endowments of different countries, and prices "induced" a certain technological bias. The Green Revolution technologies, for instance, mostly biological and yield-increasing technologies, would "emerge" in order to increase output per land unit when land is scarce or labor is cheap.

Relative factor prices are essentially market incentives used as benchmarks for identifying the expected interests and/or behaviors toward technologies among individual producers. Although market mechanisms are found to give rise to expected behaviors among some producers, not all producers have been found to follow suit, as shown by the disproportionate mechanization of large farms in Brazil and the uneven diffusion of the Green Revolution throughout Latin America.[38] Differences in technological interests among producers are likely to occur when the "factor inputs" are of different kinds, as with wage labor vs. domestic labor or other forms of nonwage labor. Labor input in the form of wage labor typically appears in capitalist production and implies altogether different problems of labor recruitment, supply, and control than when labor takes a "domestic" or "precapitalist" form.[39]

Despite clear structural barriers (e.g., credit mechanisms and land tenure arrangements), the biological technologies of the Green Revolution can be appropriate to small farmers, and they do encourage inequalities within the farm sector at a slower pace than do mechanical technologies. Very often, however, small farmers are peasants with insufficient agricultural resources and a growing reliance on off-farm wage earnings. They may capture the benefits of the new technologies or may lose those benefits to their landlord in higher rents or to their agricultural employer in lower wages.[40] The structure of production helps determine the consequences of technological diffusion. The major point, however, is that production structure (or, rather, the social organization of production) helps determine producers' interest in specific forms of technologies. It also has important influences on the research institutions. For example, agribusiness interests and large farmers' control over agricultural resources (including cash or credit for inputs) have spurred the development of a rice variety with higher fertilizer needs and decided the location of Green Revolution development projects in India and Mexico.[41]

Political institutions ranging in scale from international decision-making bodies to nation-states to local community structures have influenced the research process, and their future decisions and policies are expected to weigh heavily on continued support for Green Revolution technologies. The decision in 1959 to establish the International Rice Research Institute, a mainspring of the Green Revolution, was encouraged by favorable economic conditions (e.g., low fertilizer prices), but it also occurred within a larger political context that included an emerging United States interest— politically and economically motivated—in South and Southeast Asia.[42] In another case, the resounding success of agricultural development in Taiwan from 1951 to 1965 owed much to the United States decision to allocate aid that provided 58.7 percent of all investment in Taiwan's agriculture in that period.[43]

High food prices threaten social stability and high wages render export commodities noncompetitive. Consequently, nation-states are under constant pressures to pursue policies to minimize food costs. A common strategy has been to subsidize Green Revolution technologies to increase domestic production of staple foods. Green Revolution research, however, has sought improvements in production of high-yielding cereal grains, often at the expense of production of more nutritious staples (e.g., peas, lentils, and beans) eaten by the poor.[44] Moreover, William L. Flinn and Frederick H. Buttel point out that political-economic circumstances (e.g., high energy costs and a growing international debt) are now making it less expensive for developing countries to "import staple foods than to produce them domestically through subsidized inputs."[45]

Further constraints on nation-states' support of Green Revolution technologies are likely to come from the capital-intensive "plantation" farmers who, since the 1960s, have gained economic and political power as the major producers of agricultural exports. These large-scale farmers are organizing to influence the priorities of agricultural research institutions.[46] In the past, nation-states have also indirectly created a need for technologies favorable to relatively few (but politically powerful) producers.[47] For example, the subsidization of mechanization in Brazil distorted market mechanisms by bringing new frontier lands into production rather than intensifying production on "old" lands and/or emphasizing new Green Revolution varieties.[48] The politically generated inducement of mechanical innovations tended to subvert producers' interest in Green Revolution technologies.

In a study of a Colombian village, A. Eugene Havens and William Flinn demonstrate that community structures cannot be ignored as a political factor determining the success of Green Revolution technologies.[49] They argue that when control is centralized the local elite will have little concern for issues of public welfare. In such cases, community programs that offer Green Revolution technologies (new coffee varieties in this case) to needy farmers are likely to be intercepted by local elites and used to their own economic advantage.

Little research attention has been directed at the institutional and organizational character of research institutions (for exceptions, see Busch and Lacy; Busch and Sachs), and little is known of their impact on the success of Green Revolution technologies.[50] In the context of existing socioeconomic structures and current pressures on nation-states, we suggest two dimensions within which to study the organizational character of research centers: international vs. national institutions, and reductionist vs. systems models of research.

With developing countries experiencing fiscal crises and responding to the increased political power of agricultural producers in their export sectors, privately funded research and even state-funded research is less and less likely to be sensitive to the broader social and economic concerns that initially inspired the Green Revolution. Because of restricted budgets in the public sector and the extremely high capital requirements for conducting biotechnical research, a significant proportion of these efforts is conducted in the private sector, which can control the flow of knowledge about genetic innovations. Private efforts may be profit-motivated ones that show relatively little concern for the small farmers who lack the cash or credit to buy and use these expensive technologies, however desirable small farm production might be from a social viewpoint (especially for domestic food crops). This possibility may well give international researchers and research institutions an added responsibility and importance in the coming years.

The environmentally specific requirements of the Green Revolution's biological technologies inherently limit the operations of international research institutions. Local harvest of the fruits of the Green Revolution, therefore, critically depends on the development of agricultural research institutions sensitive to a variety of regionally specific environmental and social factors. A "systems approach" to research is the organizational strategy that some believe will secure the development of environmentally and socially "appropriate" technologies.[51]

"Reductionism" and "systems" refer to two organizational research forms. Reductionist research is characterized by the pursuit of highly specialized problems with no systematic attempt to coordinate and integrate the various research results. The reductionist orientation stems from a narrow and optimistic view of technology as external to society and inherently beneficial. The systems approach, on the other hand, implies a conscious organization of the research process for maximum coordination and integration. It is inspired by a broader view of technology in society, one that is sensitive to the social consequences.[52]

We have argued in this paper, however, that past preoccupation with social consequences to the exclusion of social determination has concealed many types of sociopolitical influences on the research process itself. Systems research that is strictly and exclusively motivated by the "ecological" consequences of technologies, without knowledge of a variety of constraints and influences on the research process itself, is in danger of reproducing many of the same mistakes found in the Green Revolution.

The problem posed in this paper is one of viewing research and the Green Revolution as essentially sociopolitical processes. Although it is important to study the social consequences of the Green Revolution, the "appropriate" technologies were in many cases known beforehand and the social consequences were accurately anticipated. Why were these problems not attacked and proper technologies developed? We suggest that sociopolitical forces decisively intervened in the research process through a variety of means under the general categories of socioeconomic structures, nation-states, and the character of research organizations. Researchers and administrators of research institutions must be aware of the many social influences— sometimes obvious, sometimes subtle—in their research. They must work to create organizational strategies that anticipate sociopolitical influences and protect the research from undesirable interventions.

Future Challenges to Green Revolution Technologies

The intention of a focus on sociopolitical forces is not to present a "fatalistic" view of the research process but rather to attempt a realistic picture of the prospects for Green Revolution technologies in the coming years. The preceding discussion suggests two basic challenges: the development and sustained support of research organizations sensitive to the basic need for food in developing societies; and the creation of fully coordinated research organizations capable of successfully integrating research results from natural and social sciences.

We have noted a variety of sociopolitical circumstances which, if left unattended, will direct public institutions away from basic food production and undercut related research supported by these public institutions. Recent advances in biotechnology threaten to concentrate control of research and technology among a small but economically advanced and politically powerful segment of society where profit motives may run counter to social needs or consumer preferences. A notable example is the race to breed a "super-tomato."[53] With most of the technological applications of recent biogenetic discoveries several years away, time remains for international research centers and other organizations to join in seeking highly productive technologies and channeling them toward broader societal needs.[54] Capturing some control from proprietary interests over high technologies, however, is costly, and current public funding for international research centers is insufficient.[55] The possibility also exists that, in the long run, the costs of biotechnologies may be too high for the private sector and that they may, like some other industries, seek relief in public funding.[56]

There is much yet to be discovered about what types of organizational structures and administrative strategies give rise to effective coordination and integration of research from diverse scientific disciplines. Knowledge of the education, values, and behavior of local people must also become an integral component of the research process.[57] The same is true of the goals and values of the researchers themselves. John Bayley contends that academics seek ideas and cultivate theories because these are the "authorized" goals and strategies of the profession. The worlds of science and economics and their structure and terminology, he says, are invented by brilliant scientists dedicated to advancement in their profession: "Freud did not make discoveries. He was determined to invent things in order to impose his will on his colleagues and gain a reputation."[58] This organizational problem of the discipline must be solved if a truly interdisciplinary systems approach to research is to succeed. Long-term research projects and regionally specific designs for new technologies also imply added costs for research institutes.[59] Besides the need to attract financial resources, an equally important challenge is for researchers and administrators to design "systems strategies" within a broader view of technology that protect against sociopolitical constraints on the research process.

Notes

1. We gratefully acknowledge María de Fátima Guerra de Sousa and Linda K. Wright-Romero for their comments on an earlier draft and John Bielefeldt for editorial assistance.

2. Mary Alice Caliendo, *Nutrition and the World Food Crisis* (New York: Macmillan, 1979), p. 111.

3. "Sticky Potato Is Being Bred to Trap Pests," *New York Times,* March 13, 1983, p. 22.

4. Kenneth A. Dahlberg, *Beyond the Green Revolution: The Ecology and Politics of Global Agricultural Development* (New York: Plenum Press, 1979); Francine R. Frankel, *India's Green Revolution: Economic Gains and Political Costs* (Princeton, N.J.: Princeton University Press, 1971); Keith Griffin, *The Political Economy of Agrarian Change: An Essay on the Green Revolution* (Cambridge: Harvard University Press, 1974).

5. Andrew Pearse, *Seeds of Plenty, Seeds of Want: Social and Economic Implications of the Green Revolution* (Oxford: Clarendon Press, 1980).

6. Lawrence Busch and William B. Lacy, "Sources of Influence on Problem Choice in the Agricultural Sciences: The New Atlantis Revisited," in *Science and Agricultural Development*, ed. Lawrence Busch (Totowa, N.J.: Allanheld, Osmun, 1981), pp. 113–28; William H. Friedland, Amy E. Barton, and Robert J. Thomas, *Manufacturing Green Gold: Capital, Labor, and Technology in the Lettuce Industry* (Cambridge: Cambridge University Press, 1981).

7. Walter Goldschmidt, *As You Sow: Three Studies in the Social Consequences of Agribusiness* (Montclair, N.J.: Allanheld, Osmun, 1978).

8. Kevin F. Goss, "Consequences of Diffusion of Innovations," *Rural Sociology* 44, no. 4 (1979): 754–72.

9. C. W. Taylor, ed., *The Third (1959) University of Utah Research Conference on the Identification of Creative Scientific Talent* (Salt Lake City: University of Utah Press, 1959); *The 1957 University of Utah Research Conference on the Identification of Creative Scientific Talent* (Salt Lake City: University of Utah Press, 1958); *The 1955 University of Utah Research Conference on the Identification of Creative Scientific Talent* (Salt Lake City: University of Utah Press, 1956).

10. A. Eugene Havens, "Diffusion of New Seed Varieties and Its Consequences: A Colombian Case," in *Problems in Rural Development: Case Studies and Multidisciplinary Perspectives*, eds. Raymond Dumett and Laurence Brainard (Leiden, Holland: E. J. Brill Press, 1974), pp. 314–26; Carl R. Rogers, "Toward a Theory of Creativity," in *The Creative Encounter*, comps. Rosemary Holsinger, Camille Jordan, and Leon Levenson (Glenview, Ill.: Scott, Foresman, 1971), pp. 2–11.

11. Robert E. Evenson, "Economic Aspects of the Organization of Agricultural Research," in *Resource Allocation in Agricultural Research*, ed. Walter L. Fishel (Minneapolis: University of Minnesota Press, 1971), pp. 163–82.

12. For studies on inventions see: Yujiro Hayami and Vernon W. Ruttan, *Agricultural Development: An International Perspective* (Baltimore: Johns Hopkins University Press, 1971); J. R. Hicks, *The Theory of Wages* (London: Macmillan, 1932); Richard R. Nelson, "The Simple Economics of Basic Scientific Research," *Journal of Political Economy* 67 (1959): 297–306; Richard R. Nelson, Merton J. Peck, and Edward D. Kalachek, *Technology, Economic Growth and Public Policy* (Washington, D.C.: Brookings Institution, 1967); Abbott Payson Usher, *A History of Mechanical Inventions*, rev. ed. (Cambridge: Harvard University Press, 1954).

For studies on resource allocation and the rate of return on agricultural research investments see: Harry W. Ayer, "The Costs, Returns and Effects of Agricultural

Research in a Developing Country: The Case of Cotton Seed Research in São Paulo, Brazil" (Ph.D. diss., Dept. of Agricultural Economics, Purdue University, 1970); James K. Boyce and Robert E. Evenson, *National and International Agricultural Research and Extension Programs* (New York: Agricultural Development Council, 1975); Robert E. Evenson and Yoav Kislev, *Agricultural Research and Productivity* (New Haven: Yale University Press, 1975); Zvi Griliches, "Hybrid Corn: An Exploration in the Economics of Technological Change," *Econometrica* 25 (1957): 501–522; Zvi Griliches, "Research Costs and Social Returns: Hybrid Corn and Related Innovations," *Journal of Political Economy* 66 (1958): 419–31; Richard R. Nelson and Edmund S. Phelps, "Investment in Humans, Technological Diffusion, and Economic Growth," *American Economic Review* 56, no. 2 (1966): 69–75; Willis L. Peterson, "Return to Poultry Research in the United States," *Journal of Farm Economics* 49 (1967): 656–69.

13. Dale W. Jorgenson, "The Development of a Dual Economy," *Economic Journal* 71 (June 1961): 309–334; Arthur W. Lewis, "Economic Development with Unlimited Supplies of Labour," *Manchester School of Economics and Social Studies* 22 (May 1954): 139–91; Gustav Ranis and John C. H. Fei, "A Theory of Economic Development," *American Economic Review* 51 (Sept. 1961): 533–65.

14. Hayami and Ruttan, *Agricultural Development;* Hicks, *Theory of Wages;* Joseph A. Schumpeter, *The Theory of Economic Development,* trans. Redvers Opie (Cambridge: Harvard University Press, 1934).

15. Hayami and Ruttan, *Agricultural Development;* Robert E. Evenson, *Science and the World Food Problem,* Bulletin 758 (New Haven: Connecticut Agricultural Experiment Station, 1974); Vernon W. Ruttan, "Usher and Schumpeter on Invention, Innovation, and Technological Change," *Quarterly Journal of Economics* 73, no. 4 (1959): 596–606.

16. Joseph A. Schumpeter, *Business Cycles: A Theoretical, Historical, and Statistical Analysis of the Capitalist Process,* vol. 1 (New York: McGraw-Hill, 1939); Schumpeter, *Theory of Economic Development.*

17. Hicks, *Theory of Wages.*

18. Ibid., p. 125.

19. Hayami and Ruttan, *Agricultural Development.*

20. Ibid., pp. 53–61.

21. Edmund Oasa and Bruce Koppel, "The Ideology of Induced Innovation Theory and Its Application to Agricultural Development" (Paper delivered at the annual meetings of the Rural Sociological Society, San Francisco, Sept. 1–4, 1982); Ivan Sergio Freire de Sousa, "Accumulation of Capital and Agricultural Research Technology: A Brazilian Case Study" (Ph.D. diss., Dept. of Sociology, Ohio State University, 1980), pp. 39–41; Ivan Sergio Freire de Sousa, Edward G. Singer, and William L. Flinn, "Agricultural Research Technology and Social Reality: A Theoretical Appraisal" (Paper delivered at the annual meeting of the Rural Sociological Society at Cornell University, Ithaca, N.Y., August 1980).

22. Theodore W. Schultz, *Economic Growth and Agriculture* (New York:

McGraw-Hill, 1968); H. G. Johnson, *Economic Policies toward Less Developed Countries* (Washington, D.C.: Brookings Institution, 1967).

23. Homer Garner Barnett, *Innovation: The Basis of Cultural Change* (New York: McGraw-Hill, 1953); S. C. Gilfillan, *Inventing the Ship* (Chicago: Follet, 1935); S. C. Gilfillan, *The Sociology of Invention* (Chicago: Follet, 1935); A. L. Kroeber, *Configurations of Culture Growth* (Berkeley and Los Angeles: University of California Press, 1944); William Fielding Ogburn, *Social Change with Respect to Culture and Original Nature* (New York: Viking Press, 1922); William F. Ogburn and Meyer F. Nimkoff, *Sociology* (Cambridge, Mass.: Riverside Press, 1940); William F. Ogburn and Dorothy Thomas, "Are Inventions Inevitable?" *Political Science Quarterly* 37 (1922): 38–98.

24. Jacob Schmookler, *Invention and Economic Growth* (Cambridge: Harvard University Press, 1966).

25. Norman W. Storer, *The Social System of Science* (New York: Holt, Rinehart and Winston, 1966).

26. Mark Abrahamson, "The Integration of Industrial Scientists," *Administrative Science Quarterly* 9, no. 2 (1964): 208–218; Joseph Ben-David, "Scientific Productivity and Academic Organization in Nineteenth Century Medicine," *American Sociological Review* 25 (1960): 828–43; Frank Clemente, "Early Career Determinants of Research Productivity," *American Journal of Sociology* 79 (1973): 409–419; Jerry Gaston, "The Reward System in British Science," *American Sociological Review* 35 (1970): 718–32; Warren O. Hagstrom, "Inputs, Outputs, and the Prestige of University Science Departments," *Sociology of Education* 44 (1971): 375–97; William Kornhauser, *Scientists in Industry: Conflict and Accommodation* (Berkeley: University of California Press, 1962); Simon Marcson, *The Scientist in American Industry* (Princeton: Industrial Relations Section, Dept. of Economics, Princeton University, 1960); Robert K. Merton, *Social Theory and Social Structure* (Glencoe, Ill: Free Press, 1949); G. M. Swatez, "The Social Organization of a University Laboratory," *Minerva* 8, no. 1 (1970): 293–305; Harriet Zuckerman, "Nobel Laureates in Science: Patterns of Productivity, Collaboration and Authorship," *American Sociological Review* 32 (1967): 391–403; Leslie Sklair, *Organized Knowledge* (London: Paladin, 1973), p. 61.

27. Stanley Aronowitz, "Marx, Braverman, and the Logic of Capital," *Insurgent Sociologist* 8, nos. 2, 3 (Fall 1978): 126–46; J. D. Bernal, *The Social Function of Science* (London: Routledge and Sons, 1939); Harry Braverman, *Labor and Monopoly Capital* (New York: Monthly Review Press, 1974); N. I. Bukharin, "Theory and Practice from the Standpoint of Dialectical Materialism," in *Science at the Cross Roads* (London: Frank Cass, 1971), pp. 11–40; Edward Coleman, "The Present Crisis in the Mathematical Sciences and General Outline for Their Reconstruction," in *Science at the Cross Roads* (London: Frank Cass, 1971): pp. 215–29; Frederick Engels, *Anti-Duehring: Herr Eugen Duehring's Revolution in Science* (Moscow: Foreign Languages Pub. House, 1954); B. Hessen, "The Social and Economic Roots of Newton's 'Principia,' " *Science at the Cross Roads* (London: Frank Cass, 1971), pp. 151–212; Luke Hodgkin, "Politics and Physical Sciences," *Radical Science Journal* 4 (1976): 29–60; David F.

Noble, "Social Choice in Machine Design: The Case of Automatically Controlled Machine Tools, and a Challenge for Labor," *Politics and Society* 8, nos. 3, 4 (1978): 313–47; David F. Noble, *America by Design* (New York: Alfred A. Knopf, 1977); and Alfred Sohn-Rethel, "Science as Alienated Consciousness," *Radical Science Journal* 2, no. 3 (1975): 65–101.

28. Hodgkin, "Politics and Physical Sciences."

29. Ibid., p. 43.

30. G. A. Cohen, *Karl Marx's Theory of History: A Defense* (Princeton, N.J.: Princeton University Press, 1978); Michael Burawoy, "Toward a Marxist Theory of the Labor Process: Braverman and Beyond," *Politics and Society* 8, nos. 3,4 (1978): 247–312.

31. For relations among scientists see: Diana Crane, "Social Structure in a Group of Scientists: A Test of the 'Invisible College' Hypothesis," *American Sociological Review* 34 (1969): 345–52; Diana Crane, *Invisible Colleges: Diffusion of Knowledge in Scientific Communities* (Chicago: University of Chicago Press, 1972); Warren O. Hagstrom, *The Scientific Community* (New York: Basic Books, 1965); for relations among organizations see: Howard E. Aldrich, "The Environment as a Network of Organizations: Theoretical and Methodological Implications" (Paper delivered at meetings of the International Studies Association, Toronto, 1974); J. Kenneth Benson, "The Interorganizational Network as a Political Economy," *American Sociological Quarterly* 20 (1975): 229–49; Rue Bucher and Joan Stelling, "Characteristics of Professional Organizations," *Journal of Health and Social Behavior* 10 (1969): 3–15; Lucién Karpik, "Organizations, Institutions and History," in *Organization and Environment: Theory, Issues and Reality,* ed. Lucién Karpik (London: Sage Publications, 1978), pp. 15–68; for impact of organizations on scientists' work see: Lawrence Busch, "The Organizational Context of United States Public Agricultural Research" (Paper delivered at the Rural Sociological Society meetings, San Francisco, Aug. 1982); Donald C. Pelz and Frank M. Andrews, *Scientists in Organizations* (New York: Wiley, 1966).

32. Robert K. Merton, *The Sociology of Science* (Chicago: University of Chicago Press, 1973); Zuckerman, "Nobel Laureates in Science."

33. For problem choice in the research establishment see: Busch and Lacy, "Sources of Influence"; William B. Lacy, "Profile of U.S. Agricultural Scientists in the Public Sector: Analysis of Their Origins and Nature of Their Work," *Rural Sociologist* 2, no. 2 (1982): 85–94; for agricultural labor supply and control see Friedland et al., *Manufacturing;* for the role of the state see: Christopher Dale, "Agricultural Research and State Intervention," in *Science and Agricultural Development,* ed. Lawrence Busch (Totowa, N.J.: Allanheld, Osmun, 1981), pp. 69–82; Isao Fujimoto and Emmett Fiske, "What Research Gets Done at a Land Grant College: Internal Factors at Work" (Davis: University of California, Department of Applied Behavioral Science, 1975, Mimeographed); I. Fujimoto and William Kopper, "Outside Influences on What Research Gets Done at a Land Grant School: Impact of Marketing Orders" (Paper delivered at the Rural Sociological Society meetings, San Francisco, 1975); Sousa, "Accumula-

tion of Capital"; for structural determinations see: Lawrence Busch, "Structure and Negotiation in the Agricultural Sciences," *Rural Sociology* 45, no. 1 (1980): 26–48; Richard Lewontin, "Agricultural Research and the Penetration of Capital," *Science for the People* (Jan./Feb. 1982): 12–17; Sousa, "Accumulation of Capital."

34. Martin Kenney, Frederick H. Buttel, J. Tadlock Cowan, and Jack Kloppenburg, Jr., *Genetic Engineering and Agriculture: Exploring the Impacts of Biotechnology on Industrial Structure, Industry-University Relationships, and the Social Organization of U.S. Agriculture,* Cornell University Bulletin 125 (Ithaca, N.Y., July 1982); Kenneth O. Rachie and Judith Lyman, eds., *Genetic Engineering for Crop Improvement* (New York: Rockefeller Foundation, 1981).

35. Philip H. Abelson, "Biotechnology: An Overview," *Science* 219, no. 4585 (Feb. 1983): pp. 611–13; Norman E. Borlaug, "Contributions of Conventional Plant Breeding to Food Production," *Science* 219, no. 4585 (Feb. 1983), pp. 689–93; R. S. Chaleff, "Isolation of Agronomically Useful Mutants from Plant Cell Cultures," *Science* 219, no. 4585 (Feb. 1983): 676–82; Peter Farnum, Roger Timmis, and J. Laurence Kulp, "Biotechnology of Forest Yield," *Science* 219, no. 4585 (Feb. 1983): 694–702; Kevin M. Ulmer, "Protein Engineering," *Science* 219, no. 4585 (1983): 666–71.

36. Colin Norman, *The God That Limps* (Toronto: Worldwatch Institute, and New York: W. W. Norton, 1981).

37. Dahlberg, *Beyond the Green Revolution,* chap. 4; Caliendo, *Nutrition and the World Food Crisis.*

38. John H. Sanders and Vernon W. Ruttan, "Biased Choice of Technology in Brazilian Agriculture," in *Induced Innovation: Technology, Institutions, and Development* by Hans P. Binswanger and Vernon W. Ruttan et al. (Baltimore: Johns Hopkins University Press, 1978), pp. 276–96; Wallace Cloud, "After the Green Revolution," *The Sciences* 13, no. 8 (Oct. 1973): 6–12.

39. Amartya Sen, *Employment, Technology and Development* (Oxford: Clarendon Press, 1975).

40. M. Taussig, "Peasant Economics and the Development of Capitalist Agriculture in the Cauca Valley, Colombia," *Latin American Perspectives* 5, no. 3 (Summer 1978): 62–91.

41. Oasa and Koppel, "The Ideology"; Frankel, *India's Green Revolution;* Caliendo, *Nutrition and the World Food Crisis.*

42. Oasa and Koppel, "The Ideology."

43. Donald J. Puchala and Jane Staveley, "The Political Economy of Taiwanese Agricultural Development," in *Food, Politics, and Agricultural Development: Case Studies in the Public Policy of Rural Modernization,* eds. Richard F. Hopkins, Donald J. Puchala, and Robert B. Talbot (Boulder, Colo.: Westview Press, 1979), pp. 107–132.

44. Alan Berg, *The Nutrition Factor* (Washington, D.C.: Brookings Institution, 1973).

45. William L. Flinn and Frederick H. Buttel, "Socioeconomic Constraints on the Transfer and Adoption of Agricultural Technologies in Low-Income Countries," in *Economic and Social Perspectives on the Transfer of Food Technology to Developing*

Nations, ed. Joseph Milnar and Howard Clouts (Boulder, Colo.: Westview Press, 1983).

46. Alain de Janvry, The Agrarian Question and Reformism in Latin America (Baltimore: Johns Hopkins University Press, 1981).

47. Harry W. Ayer and G. Edward Schuh, "Social Rates of Return and Other Aspects of Agricultural Research: The Case of Cotton Research in São Paulo, Brazil," American Journal of Agricultural Economics 5, no. 4 (1972): 557–69.

48. Sanders and Ruttan, "Biased Choice of Technology."

49. A. Eugene Havens and William Flinn, "Green Revolution Technology and Community Development: The Limits of Action Programs," Economic Development and Cultural Change 23 (April 1975): 469–81.

50. Busch and Lacy, "Sources of Influence"; Lawrence Busch and Carolyn Sachs, "The Agricultural Sciences and the Modern World System," in Science and Agricultural Development, ed. Lawrence Busch (Totowa, N.J.: Allanheld, Osmun, 1981), pp. 131–56.

51. Kenneth A. Dahlberg, "An Evaluation of Research Strategies for Developing Appropriate Agricultural Systems and Technologies" (Paper delivered at meetings of the International Studies Association, Washington, D.C., 1978).

52. Ibid.

53. "Breeding a 'Supertomato,'" Business Week, Jan. 10, 1983, p. 33.

54. Abelson, "Biotechnology"; Borlaug, "Contributions of Conventional Plant Breeding."

55. Flinn and Buttel, "Socioeconomic Constraints."

56. "The Birth of Silicon Statesmanship: The High Tech Companies That Once Shunned Washington Now Seek Its Help," New York Times, March 6, 1983, sec. 3:1.

57. Caliendo, Nutrition and the World Food Crisis, p. 118.

58. John Bayley, "Professional Strategies," New York Times Book Review, Feb. 17, 1983.

59. Philip H. Birnbaum, "Assessment of Alternative Management Forms in Academic Interdisciplinary Research Projects," Management Science 24, no. 3 (1977): 272–84.

The Contributors

Roland W. Bergman, who received his Ph.D. from the University of Wisconsin, teaches geography and anthropology at Shepherd College in West Virginia. He is the author of *Amazon Economics*, a quantitative study of the efficiency of Indian food procurement in the rainforest. In 1984 he received a Fulbright-Hays Award for research in the Peruvian Andes.

William L. Flinn, professor of rural sociology and sociology at the Ohio State University, is a former president of the Rural Sociology Society. He has conducted research and published extensively on various Latin American countries and has taught in the Faculty of Sociology at National University in Bogotá, Colombia.

Nancy Forster is a doctoral candidate in the Development Studies Program of the University of Wisconsin–Madison and has contributed articles on Cuban agriculture and rural change to the American Universities Field Staff and *Cuban Studies*. She is currently conducting research on peasant production strategies and household economies in Ecuador under grants from the Social Science Research Council, Inter-American Foundation, and Fulbright-Hays.

Ivan Sergio Freire de Sousa, rural sociologist, received his Ph.D. from the Ohio State University. He is presently coordinator of research for the Diffusion of Technology Department of the Brazilian State Corporation for Agricultural Research, Brasilia. His work has been published in *Rural Sociology*.

Lana Hall received her Ph.D. from the University of California, Berkeley, in 1978. She is currently an assistant professor of agricultural economics at Cornell University and a fellow of the Institute of Current World Affairs, studying agriculture in socialist economies. Her publications include articles in the *American Journal of Agricultural Economics*, the *Canadian Journal of Agricultural Economics*, *Food Policy*, and *Economica*.

Howard Handelman, professor of political science at the University of Wisconsin–Milwaukee, is the author of *Struggle in the Andes: Peasant Political Mobilization in Peru*. He has edited *The Politics of Agrarian Change in Asia and Latin America*, co-edited *Military Government and the Transition to Democracy in South America*, and contributed articles to the *Latin American Research Review, Journal of Inter-American Studies, Cuban Studies,* and other journals.

Manual Moreno-Ibáñez, a Chilean sociologist, is completing a Ph.D. dissertation on regional approaches to food production and food policy in Latin America at UCLA. He is a member of the UCLA Latin American Center Statistical and Computer Support Committee. He has studied political violence, depletion of natural resources, housing supply, comparative regional planning, and theories of alienation; several of his articles have been published in the *Statistical Abstract of Latin America.*

Vincent C. Peloso, a University of Arizona Ph.D., is associate professor of history at Howard University. He is conducting research on social change in plantation society in turn-of-the-century Peru. His work has appeared in *The Americas, Peasant Studies,* and other journals, and he currently serves on the editorial boards of *The Americas* and the *Handbook of Latin American Studies.*

Edward G. Singer obtained his Ph.D. in rural sociology from the Ohio State University in 1982. He is currently under contract with the Inter-American Institute of Cooperation in the Agricultural Sciences to study the public agricultural research process in Brazil. He has published on agrarianism and agricultural development in *Rural Sociology* and *Sociologia Ruralis.*

Rose J. Spalding is associate professor of political science at DePaul University. She received her Ph.D. from the University of North Carolina at Chapel Hill in 1978. Her work, which focuses on agricultural and economic policy in Nicaragua and Mexico, has been published in *Comparative Politics, Comparative Political Studies,* and the *Latin American Research Review.*

John C. Super, a Ph.D. from UCLA, is associate professor of history at West Virginia University. His primary research interests have been in the early history of Mexico and Ecuador and the history of food in colonial Latin America. He is the author of *La vida en Querétaro durante la colonia* (1983) and articles in the *Hispanic American Historical Review, Journal of Latin American Studies, Historia Mexicana, Medicina Española,* and other journals.

James W. Wilkie is professor of history at UCLA. The author and editor of many books on diverse areas and aspects of Latin America, he received the Bolton Prize in 1968 for *The Mexican Revolution: Federal Expenditure and Social Change since 1910.* Professor Wilkie currently edits the *Statistical Abstract of Latin America* and serves as president of the Consortium of United States Research Programs for Mexico.

Eleanor Witte Wright received her Ph.D. in government and politics from the University of Maryland in 1982. Presently a fellow at the Center for International Development at Maryland, she is conducting research on various facets of the politics of nutrition and has published in the *Consumer Nutrition Institute Quarterly.*

Thomas C. Wright received his Ph.D. from the University of California, Berkeley, in 1971. He is currently professor of history at the University of Nevada, Las Vegas. His publications include *Landowners and Reform in Chile: The Sociedad Nacional de Agricultura, 1919-1940* and articles in the *Hispanic American Historical Review, Journal of Latin American Studies,* and *Journal of Church and State.*

Index